Sociology of Displacement

Sociology of Displacement

Policies and Practice

Editors

Sakarama Somayaji
Susmita Dasgupta

RAWAT PUBLICATIONS

Jaipur • New Delhi • Bangalore • Hyderabad • Guwahati

ISBN 978-81-316-0597-4

Published by
Prem Rawat for **Rawat Publications**
Satyam Apts, Sector 3, Jawahar Nagar, Jaipur 302 004 (India)
Phone: 0141 265 1748 / 7006 Fax: 0141 265 1748
E-mail: info@rawatbooks.com
Website: www.rawatbooks.com

New Delhi Office
4858/24, Ansari Road, Daryaganj, New Delhi 110 002
Phone: 011 2326 3290

Also at *Bangalore, Hyderabad* and *Guwahati*

Typeset by Rawat Computers, Jaipur
Printed at Chaman Enterprises, New Delhi

Contents

Preface

The present volume, a set of edited papers written by eminent activists, administrators and scholars on various cases of displacement of indigenous people from their lands and livelihoods due to development projects, purports to draw out a scheme towards the study of displacement as a sociological phenomenon. Displacement is studied while a community or a set of people from within the community are in the active stage of being uprooted and removed from the land they occupy and the habitat of their existence. Unfortunately, people from displaced communities are then disbanded and disappear into the vast ocean of the world's largest population of the poor, that is, India. Among the beggars at the traffic lights of Delhi, the migrant workers at construction sites, the rickshaw pullers in towns and the shanty tea stall owner are all essentially displaced people. Among those children who do not attend schools, the undernourished adult, and the mother dying of childbirth are overwhelmingly constituted of people who have been at one point of time or other displaced. The present book does not delve into the aftermath of displacement, though that would have been more suited for the title of the book. Instead, the present volume treats the papers as case studies to understand the discourses of economic development, social opportunities, political rights and moral obligations of the State, ethics of institutions those which emanate out of the kind of society we are and the kind of society we see ourselves as creating. The sociology that the present volume draws upon is not how the various social groups respond to displacement but how the Indian society as a whole seems eager to use a developmentalist paradigm despite being fully aware of the inequalities and marginalizations that such paradigms create.

The book uses a Bordieuxian framework to understand the economics of development from a sociological perspective. The editors explore, through the papers presented, the kind of society we are pursuing, the kind of engagements we wish to enter into with our history where sections of our population need to be cast aside to make way for the rest of us. The book explores the legitimacy that the developmentalist ideology holds for the Indians today; why the Indian has little scorn for unequal powers of the rich, how the Indian finds consumerism a value today and how Indians are shaping the social and political life around discourses of greed, accumulation and ostentation. The policy of neo-liberalism that gives a free reign to limitless accumulation and creates poverty, unemployment, inflation is appreciated as a winner while critics of such mindless capitalism are looked upon as being losers. The proposed book attempts to find answers to these apparent paradoxes where a nation so proud of its democracy and freedom makes choices that curb such freedoms through its unabashed displacements in the name of development. The book underlines not merely the fact that economic growth has a poor face to show in terms of the increasing impoverishment, but it seems to be rather proud of being a strong and a decisive state in forcing displacement upon its own citizens in the name of economic logic. What are the reasons for a nation, the world's largest democracy is finding so much of fulfilment in economically marginalizing its own people, and why in such a vibrant democracy does displacement not find a political voice? Could displacement been avoided? Why do industries choose locations where population density is high, are there no arid land areas in India where industries can be set up? Why India is so indifferent to its growing poverty and what makes Indians indifferent to not being able to devise economic models those are more inclusive? These are the various questions that the editors of the volume attempt to answer using the papers as case studies.

The papers in this volume are detailed and exhaustive in covering the macro as well as the micro perspectives of displacement understanding it through contemporary developmental practices and also situating the question historically in the idea of decolonization and the nation state. It could serve as a ready guide for activists, scholars, lawyers, corporate houses, development consultants and policy makers. The proposed book tries to present material for developing sociology of economics which addresses the sociological roots of marginalization and the consequent displacement of sections of population in the name of pursuing the greater good of development.

Displacement, the contributors argue has three distinct but interrelated levels; firstly, there is a clear abrogation of the land acquisition norms set forth by the already existing policy and a disregard for the provisions for resettlement and rehabilitation. Secondly, there is an inadequacy in the very theoretical formulation of the notion of displacement and resettlement and rehabilitation precisely because there is very little understanding of economic activities and the long winded value chains that make prosperity at the top of the heap possible. Displacement would never have taken this callous dimension had economists and policy makers understood the worth and the value of how much the poor and the marginalized contribute towards the overall economy through their apparently 'useless' occupations. Thirdly, the organization of academic sciences, the preponderance of the entrenched middle class, the search for elegant economic models have created theories that cannot make sense of the so called subsistence level economic activities. The contributors also engage with the contemporary theories of the development to observe that the fact of economic development in the mainstream itself leads to joblessness and inequalities making it difficult to include a wider section of the population and hence is displacing.

The papers are roughly divided into three sections cutting across the above themes, viz., policy perspectives, displacement as a built-in phenomenon in centralized planning for economic growth and the idea of the nation state; and specific cases of displacement induced by specific projects like river dams and hydel power projects. The papers are located in the aftermath of the Narmada Bachao Andolan and hence the various issues and the voices that were articulated in the course of the Narmada movement find a more concrete political expression in the cases cited. Displacement, a phenomenon that existed since Independence suddenly finds a greater awareness in the aftermath of economic liberalization because of a higher frequency in its occurrence as India sets on the path of high development. The papers in the volume argue that as long as development creates displacement as its natural paradox, one cannot hope for a better society. Displacement creates poverty which then needs more resources to fight than the resources the projects for which displacement happens can generate. The contributors argue for new ways to track and account for displacement and suggest new methods of information management of displacement.

Contributors

Bhaskar Majumder is at present a Professor in Economics in G.B. Pant Social Science Institute, Allahabad, India. He is a visiting faculty in Central University of Bihar, Patna. He taught in Calcutta colleges and Calcutta University for long years. He has published several articles and books on various social issues. At present, he is engaged in research in Internal Migration and Internal Displacement.

Deepa Joshi is currently Assistant Professor, Wageningen University, The Netherlands. She is interested in the political representations of water conflicts and the gendered impacts of dynamic mega-water transitions on poverty and livelihoods security. She has worked in South and South East, Africa and Latin America – managing programmes, conducting policy research and leading local research capacity building. She is interested in analysing the drivers and processes of reforms, understanding how policies evolve within different institutional cultures and structures and the knowledge and power hierarchies in these institutional spaces which re-shapes practice.

Ganesha Somayaji has been teaching sociology for more than two decades at various levels ranging from undergraduate to postgraduate students. Currently, he is Professor and Head of the Department of Sociology at Goa University, India. Enterprise in Food and Sociology of Development are Dr Somayaji's current research interests. He has so far co-edited three volumes on Sociological Perspectives on Globalization, Environmental Sociology and

Tribal Communities and has published several research articles in professional journals.

Joanna P. Coelho obtained PhD degree from the Goa University for her thesis on the issues pertaining to language use in the public sphere. Since 2007 Dr Coelho has been working as Assistant Professor of Sociology in Goa University. Sociology of Language and Environmental Sociology are Dr Coelho's current research interests.

K.B. Saxena, former Secretary to Government of India and, presently, Professor, Social Justice and Governance in the Council for Social Development, New Delhi. He has written extensively on the subject of land acquisition, displacement, rehabilitation and resettlement. His areas of interest include the tribal studies, health, forest and environment.

M. Gopinath Reddy is a Professor with the Centre for Economic and Social Studies (CESS) in Hyderabad, India. A Political Science and Public Administration specialist, he has been working on the areas of Decentralized and Community Forest Management issues for two decades and published a number of academic papers in national and international journals and books. He recently brought out a book (co-authoring with Professor V. Ratna Reddy and Professor John Soussan) on 'Political Economy of Watershed Management: Policies, Institutions, Implementation and Livelihoods' by Rawat Publications.

Nagaraju Chikkala, a Research Associate (Anthropologist), working in the Research Unit for Livelihoods and Natural Resources (RULNR) at the Centre for Economic and Social Studies (CESS), Hyderabad. He has two publications and is co-author for few CESS Working Papers.

Narendra K. Behera obtained his PhD from Sambalpur University, Odisha. Currently teaching in Larambha College, an affiliated Degree College in District Bargarh, of Sambalpur University, Odisha. He has published a book titled *Displacement, Resettlement and Rehabilitation.* He has also contributed a number of research articles to reputed journals and edited books. Presently, he is engaged in a UGC supported major research project: Land Acquisition, Resettlement and Rehabilitation in West Odisha.

Patrik Oskarsson is an Assistant Professor at Azim Premji University in Bangalore. His work relates to the political economy of industrialization and economic development in India. His areas of interests are the various ways in which poor and marginalized groups in rural India are affected in terms of livelihoods, environmental quality and natural resources, international human rights legislation and policies for corporate social responsibility.

Prajna Paramita Mishra is Assistant Professor at the Department of Economics of University of Hyderabad in India. She has a doctoral degree from the University of Hyderabad in Economics. Her main research interest is in the area of mining and livelihoods and economic valuation of environmental impacts. Prior to joining University of Hyderabad, she worked as an Assistant Professor in the Research Unit for Livelihoods and Natural Resources (RULNR) of Centre for Economic and Social Studies (CESS), Hyderabad.

Ramesh S. Mangalekar is Associate Professor and Head, Department of Sociology, Government First Grade College, Belgaum, Karnataka. Ramesh received PhD from Goa University, Goa. His areas of interest include Development, Displacement and Rehabilitation, Social Ecology and Environment, Life Skills, Higher Education. He is the author of *Development, Displacement and Rehabilitation*. He has completed one UGC sponsored Major Research Project (2008–11). He has presented papers in the national and international seminars and conferences and published research articles in the reputed journals and books.

Sakarama Somayaji, a trained development sociologist from Jawaharlal Nehru University, New Delhi, is currently working as a Social Development Advisor for the Sirsa Lok Sabha Constituency of Haryana. He started his career with the National Dairy Development Board (NDDB), Anand; worked as Senior Fellow with the Council for Social Development (CSD), New Delhi and as Fellow and Area Convenor, Social Transformation Division, in the Relocation and Rehabilitation group at the Energy and Resources Institute (TERI), New Delhi. He has worked extensively on issues pertaining to the rehabilitation of project-displaced people in the states of Odisha, Madhya Pradesh and Jharkhand. He also designed and conducted training workshops on rehabilitation planning for development practitioners, senior bureaucrats, representatives of NGOs, as well as corporate audiences.

Somayaji is the co-editor of *Environment, Development, and Social Change in the Himalayan Region, Development-induced Displacement, Rehabilitation and Resettlement in India: Current Issues and Challenges, Environmental Concerns and Sustainable Development: Some Perspectives from India,* and *Sociology of Globalisation: Perspectives from India.* He is a regular resource person to the UGC Academic College, JNU, Forest Research Institute, Dehradun, and TERI University.

Satya Prakash Dash, PhD and LLB, is working as a Lecturer in Political Science in the PG Department of Social Science, Fakir Mohan University, Balasore, Odisha. Earlier, he was a Fellow in the Council for Social Development, New Delhi, and conducted a project on 'Aspirations and Perception of People on Displacement in Odisha'. He visited China in 2010 under the ICSSR-CASS Fellowship programme. He is also associated with Research and Analysis of Public Policy Institute, Cuttack, Odisha.

Susmita Dasgupta is a Masters in Economics from Jadavpur University and a PhD in Sociology from Jawaharlal Nehru University. She is employed for the past 25 years as a policy economist with the Joint Plant Committee, Ministry of Steel. She has published various articles in books. Her doctoral thesis on Amitabh Bachchan the filmstar is published as a book from Penguin. She is a regular resource person in JNU's Academic Staff College.

Vimal Khawas is Assistant Professor at the School of Policy Planning and Studies, Sikkim University. He is trained in Geography, Development Planning and Environmental Studies. His interests and expertise include Applications of Traditional Knowledge in Disaster Risk Reduction, Socio-Economic Aspects of Climate Change Impacts, Regional Planning and Development Studies with particular emphasis on the Eastern Himalayas.

Walter Fernandes, a former Director of Indian Social Institute, New Delhi and Editor of *Social Action*. He moved to Assam in late 1999 to found North Eastern Social Research Centre, Guwahati and direct it till early 2012. He has worked extensively on tribal issues, gender issues and land displacement, resettlement and rehabilitation, particularly development-induced displacement. He has guided groups in ten states to conduct study on 'Development-Induced Displacement 1947–2010'. He has more than 30 books, over 150 professional articles and around 90 newspaper articles to his credit.

Introduction

SAKARAMA SOMAYAJI AND SUSMITA DASGUPTA

It is an act of serendipity that today all over the world, displacement has come to be regarded as the obvious and non-detachable other side of the development coin. Amy Chua writes in her work, *World on Fire* that the neo-liberal capital is the reincarnation of colonialism, where a global capital displaces local people, misappropriates local assets and livelihood, marginalizes local capital and reduces the vast chunk of humanity into proletariats working hours together to earn respectable lives as consumers. It is a world where real development in terms of ecological sustainability, quality of intellectual and emotional life, leisure activities, social bondings, family ties does not happen. It is also a world where an individual's agency as a social and political participant reduces and life seems to be slipping away from his/her command. There are far fewer things that individuals can control about themselves than they could in the past century and this is despite the fact that humans can consume many more things today that they could ever dream of. Our human culture today faces a schism: whether we would like to be consumers and place ourselves at the will of a very thin space of capital to earn our salaries in order to be able to spend, or would we like to be entrepreneurs setting up our livelihoods and remain independent of others for employment. The individual as an agent is in conflict with the individual as a consumer; yet this is a truth which media, advertisement and even cinema try to efface. We are told by the powers that the real merit lies in us being able to buy that posh flat, have that plush office, and drive fast cars on Formula One racing tracks. These are myths that are being created and fed into us so that we do not notice our daily displacement in face of a supposed economic development.

What we claim in the above paragraph is perhaps only a repetition of the Marxist doctrine of how capital, which naturally faces a falling rate of profits, expands into monopoly power in order to secure its profits and in this way snatches away every other source of production which lay with the community and proletariarizes the people. So we have a super capital on the one hand and a sea of vagabonds moving about displaced and disbanded, on the other. Displacement, in the Marxian scheme, is therefore an obvious and inevitable fallout of development. Over the past two centuries, societies, states, politics and intellectuals have all opposed this thesis and insisted on the various ways in which such a disaster can be avoided. Trade unions were invented against the unopposed will of capital, while the welfare state, civil rights, and ideas of citizenship helped provide buffers against an increasingly tenuous social security under the market systems. Then, in the aftermath of the World War II and especially with the development of Fordism, flourish neo-classicism with its centeredness around the economics of the firm and henceforth the dominance of ideas of efficiencies, productivity and profit margins. The idea of the market and the resurgence of the famous invisible hand as proposed by Adam Smith firmly established a regime of capital led by greed and selfishness casting aside any and every claim that challenged its profit margins. While colonialism fought on the might of the superiority of the European civilization, neo-liberal capital sets the world on fire upon a logical and technological rationality of promoting economic development and growth. Capitalists are supposed to be saviours and heroes who slay Gorgons of poverty and fight the Minotaurs of mediocracy. The insistence that profits are the motives for investments and investments alone lead to growth through the instrument of the income multiplier has not been universally valid. India is a case in the point where years of development and efforts at development leave it with the world's largest number of poor – even more than sub-Saharan Africa. The stories of displacement around projects that threaten to assume vital political dimensions in India are actually processes of impoverishment.

When we look at the profile of India's development, we observe that there have been two very distinct periods. The first is the era between independence in 1947 and just the year before economic liberalization in 1991, a stretch of 42 years, and thereafter the era of liberalized India from 1991 to the present. In the first period, displacement was an unintended consequence of development, whereas in the latter period it is the sole intention of development. In the first instance, displacement was due to a misunderstanding of the kinds of economic relations and the economic milieu in which goods and services were produced and exchanged among local communities. In those days, development emanated out of a centralized source of planning from the metropolitan through English-educated elite in institutions modelled around the American universities. Curriculum was designed around the American courses, and theories that emerged from the Western contexts were mindlessly applied to India. In such a blind driving behind the West, Indian intellectuals implemented models developed and tested elsewhere to Indian situations. The propounders of these models had no idea of village and tribal people, imagining that progress meant a unidirectional journey from agriculture to industry a la Rostow's stages of development. What these people had assumed that agriculture had to ultimately decline and industry had to rise almost as metaphysical preordainment. Not only this, such people had no idea of how structural transformations from an agrarian economy to an industrialized one could take place when farmers used surpluses from land to invest into manufacturing. In India, the lion's share of farming lies with the subsistence farmers who use agriculture as food security while manufacturing offers avenues for industrial employment. The thousands of workers employed in our factories have farmlands in villages back home which help them meet their ends. A possible reason why India never had a massive labour uprising was perhaps because the worker was well ensconced in his family farm upon which he could fall back upon. In India, farming and attachment to land are sort of social security measures provided by the family,and not by the state. Displacement where land is taken away amounts to the same thing as a welfare state retracting from providing social security measures. This is the reason why displacement cannot be brushed away as something that affects only a handful of the poor while benefiting many.

During the period between 1947 and 1991, we pursued a growth founded upon heavy industries notwithstanding concessions to the medium, small, tiny and cottage industries. The state sector often was the largest employer and the displaced people often found employment in the very public sector units that displaced them;

besides, the displaced people, as our stories from Kalinganagar show, always seemed to have found other spaces in which to settle in. The idea of development was to set up heavy industries, produce raw materials from mineral sources and lay roads and rail tracks and electricity transmission lines. In those days, India was considered to be a developing economy and neither the scale of industry nor the size of the economy was anything as vibrant as it is today. Presently, not only is India a superpower and the scale of the economy has increased manifold and all of a sudden but today's development is directed towards displacement because the final aim of capitalist profit is to be able to control natural and land resources whose supply is limited by nature. It is the control over resources that cannot be produced out of human effort that seems to be final aim of capitalist development in today's age. The world's greatest assets today are oil, coal, iron ore, gold, copper, silver, lead, chrome and water. This is why we observe that companies are rushing towards control of minerals and irrigated lands, forests and aquifers. The ownership and patenting of plant species, gene pools and other natural products is the key to super wealth.

The problem with the existence of super wealth is that it sets a race towards even higher targets and enhances the worth of every asset. For a subsistence farmer it means that his land which hardly had any use for anyone now suddenly assumes a great value. This has no meaning for the farmer because he cannot sell it and despite an increase in the absolute value, in relative terms he continues to remain at the bottom of the heap. But, the very same asset helps a person in the social class just above the subsistence farmer to buy off the land and become richer. This does not explain why the subsistence farmer sells his/her land. The reason for this lies elsewhere.

The present kind of development has varied features. On the one hand, the predominance of the market converts everything into its tradeable value like the land, drinking water, public toilets and garbage, and on the other hand, it reduces social security for workers, ending the idea of lifetime employment, and reduced outlay on public education and public healthcare. In other words, while some kinds of goods which were non-traded like subsistence farming land, wastelands, forests and swamps have acquired exchange value, some other kinds of non-traded sectors like education, health and public goods are now relegated to the family sphere. This means that the people have to pay more for food, water, shelter and clothes; they also have to spend more and more on the enabling public goods like education. The cost of earning wages has been pushed up and the need for cash to even seek employment makes many farming families sell off their lands. Proceeds from land sales go into funding professional courses for children where private institutions are a rip off, to pay for rents in cities, to help children buy homes as accommodation, and pay for their mobiles, internet and laptops. The sale of land to meet costs of employment even if it is only as wage labour is the story throughout India of willing displacements. The ever-growing body of migrant labour that are absorbed in petty professions and tenous employment under exploitative contractors is the living showcase of the wide-scale displacements that are taking place in India. Such displacements are willing and rational decisions perhaps not forced by armed goons of business houses but indeed imposed upon the relevant decision-makers by the expanding market.

The global capitalist insists upon expanding and widening the market precisely because he has more accumulated wealth to command the resources whose increasing future value provides him his profits. No wonder, land and natural resources have emerged as such valued properties only because of the promise of future price escalations. For the person who is relatively weaker, sale of an existent asset becomes important for him to tide over current investments for earning an income. Hence displacements happen when assets of the weak are dissolved to be able to meet income earning costs. These income earning costs, such as education, communication, accommodation, are those sectors which due to the expansion of markets assumed exchange value setting their prices into an upward spiral. The weak surrenders the future value of assets to pay for the current expenses which must be incurred while looking for employment. This is the crux of displacement. Therefore, displacement is actually a displacement of a person from his/her own future; this is why resettlement and rehabilitation programmes for displaced people are so out of context.

In case of project displacements, especially where such displacements are often met by resistance from the people, there is something else which is at stake and this is the social and the cultural capital of the community. The social and cultural capital of communities helps produce future worth for the members of a community; integrated communities produce thinkers, intellectuals, skilled people, and so on. Jobless growth where the asset price to wages favours the worth of assets disturbs the community bonds and social ties. Social alienation is tied to the disparity between asset value and wages. This makes it so important for nations, states and societies to involve people in its growth story so that this disparity between assets and incomes is not aggravated. The experience of partition of India helps us understand this process very well. In case of East Bengal, the partition of the land as East Pakistan saw a number of people migrating back into West Bengal. Among them most were Hindus but there was also a significant number of Muslims. For either community, members had to leave behind their homes and farms, shops and warehouses, factories and businesses. There was an immediate collapse of Bengalis as a people in terms of intellectual output: they lost businesses, there was unrest, unemployment, rise in crime and in general Bengal fell in terms of opportunities. The decay took place monotonically and has not been reversed even after sixty years. The migration of workers from Bengal has been an avalanche; it is possible to travel across Faridabad, Gurgaon, Noida, Navi Mumbai, Jaipur, Ahmedabad and Pune talking freely in Bengali.

When cultures and community ties vanish beyond recovery, the people of the community suffer in terms of emotional security, cultural input and historical continuity. Not only this, lying like a severed part of a larger whole, humans in such alienation rot intellectually too. Such societies have no myths to bind them, no shared stories to hold them together, no song to root them and persons live as atoms, with failed cognition, without purpose and in the darkness of directionlessness. And then follows poverty, without a semblance of social cohesion, people cannot act as economic agents. When Adam Smith wrote about the market and the market solving people's problems of what to produce, how much to produce, for whom to produce, what he did not notice was England's and Europe's very tight village society, held together by the Church and though progressively secularizing through modernity and a tight gemeinschaft despite evolving towards an associative gesellschaft based upon contracts. Ferguson, de Soto, and many others never tire of saying that capitalism developed in Europe because of its excellent implementation of contracts; one never mentions however that contracts could be honoured in Europe because of a high level of trust which in turn was possible because of tightly woven social fabric. One associates Europe with individualism and selfishness but the pursuit of the individual autonomy and agency and the pursuit of self-interest has been possible because of strong roots in culture, philosophy and religion. In short, modernity is not possible without deep roots of tradition, nor is progress possible without being grounded into a coherent society and continuous memories of that social life. Displacement not only takes away the web of life but also snaps its continuity and thus renders people ineffectual with coherent personalities and consistent character.

When displacement was an unintended consequence of development during the phase, prior to the arrival of neo-liberalism in the country, it was thought that economic growth could be achieved only through a top-down industrialization and industries constituted a 'public purpose' under which the state could acquire land. Displacement was recognized as necessary if greatest good for the greatest number had to be pursued. The displaced persons too accepted their fate and took their displacement as misfortune. Neither was displacement purposely planned nor did the displaced people show the level of consciousness as now. Further, displacement did not find a voice in our democratic politics.

Democratic politics, says Professor Amartya Sen, is the most certain panacea against famines and democracy is the sole reason why India has been relatively free of famines while China has fallen to famines and often harboured chronic food insecurity. But the very same democracy that saved India from acute food shortages in the 1960s and the 1970s seems helpless in the face of displacement of populations that everyday grow in numbers, of which the tribals form a definite majority. Development therefore goes against tribals the most, who live in isolated and self-contained economies and find it difficult to organize the same self-sustenance when their ecologies are taken away. With political parties wooing minorities, one wonders why politics of displacement has not yet been a part of the mainstream political discourse.

Were displacement to become a part of politics, then such politics would challenge the very foundation of development and when that happens, the foundations of the system upon which our democratic politics rests are invariably shaken. What is the foundation of democracy in India? It is neither cultural pluralism, nor multilingual universalism, nor a unity that absorbs and transcends diversities; but it is capitalism which creates and sustains a middle class in such a manner that the rest of the society races to occupy this narrow space. India's democracy is successful because all of us agree to participate in the same race. All our diversities assume significance and live of their own only because of a strong unity in all our purpose, which is to occupy this narrow band of lifestyle called the middle class. Before economic liberalization the Indian state was by and large capitalist as not only through the public sector and the bureaucracy it was the largest employer, but it also decimated smaller capitalists by taking over units and allowing only those units to thrive as were required to serve its cause as ancillaries.

The Indian state created a middle class based upon competition as the aspirants were always larger in number than the incumbents. The *game* was well defined and universally accepted and everyone knew that there was one *game*, modern education, competitive examinations, and salaried employment to grab that refrigerator, dining table, sofa set, and later the television and the Maruti car. The well-known sociologist, Professor T.K. Oommen termed this phenomenon as the 'Marutization of the Indian nation'. The Marutization tells us of a certain one-dimensionality that manifested because of a universally accepted model of competition through which one acceded to the middle class and remained there. The universality of the rules of the game to attain the universally accepted modes of existence is the real reason why we have a model of economic development which cannot tolerate any other modes of economic production and hence displacement. Thus, while we are tolerant of cultural multitudes and linguistic diversities, we are absolutely intolerant of economic diversities.

The competitive model belonging to the middle class makes all of us not only pursue the same goals and play the same game but also accept the singular source of that game, namely, the model of economic development with fewer winners and more losers. This game destroys the middle class – a class from where ideas of freedom and liberty, discourses of rights and duties and philosophies of citizenship and governance emanate.

The displacement, which is taking place in the aftermath of economic liberalization, is an end in itself. Corporates must have water, land, swamps, bio species, minerals and vacant land just for real estate. They target well-irrigated tracts, farm lands, fishing ponds, marine shelves to grab all that is there to natural resources. When displacement is a fallout of development, one feels compassionate towards the poor but not really alarmed, but when displacement is the mode of development, one can see in it not an exception but the very rule of economic development. Corporates aim at claiming monopoly over food production, food processing, retail chain, supermarket, drinking water, municipal services, real estates and every other conceivable aspect of human needs. In the early days of capitalism, capitalist expansion grew on the merit of technological superiority; today, they target lower levels of technology but with greater control over volumes and hence they strive to make potato chips and ready-to-cook noodles instead of sophisticated steel for building ships or aeroplanes. This makes things dangerous for us for our lives will soon be commanded centrally by companies and displacement is the mere start of this hopeless end for us.

During the last couple of decades India made news nationally as well as internationally for its fastest economic growth. However, as a consequence of this double-digit growth, there was a series of involuntary land acquisitions and the compulsory displacement of communities across the country. The recent decades of consistently high economic growth rates in the country have seen contested notions of 'development', 'public purpose' and 'greatest common good' being played out in the national media, but nowhere with as much intensity as is the case with the increasingly scarce resource – land. Violent social conflicts over compulsory land acquisitions have brought to sharper focus the tension inherent in these two roles, and attendant media coverage has served to widen the impact of these discourses among the larger public. Land, a resource limited by nature, seems to be now the most contested arena over which the rich are trying to displace people relatively poorer to them. Development suddenly has taken on a desire to own those land and other natural resources, whose supply cannot be increased through the act of human agency. Land acquisition expectedly displaces those persons who depend on the acquired land for livelihoods. When displacement of people occurs from the land to which they are tied to for purposes of livelihood, there are not only economic losses, but also losses in culture, community ties, family systems, and the entire plethora of what is known as social capital. Those who acquire land emerge as powerful owners of the asset and since the number expropriated of land is larger than the ones who own it, such acquisitions lead to a rise in inequality. Land acquisition and rising inequality of wealth go hand in hand in liberalized India.

Some of the fundamental challenges faced in the process of land acquisition, displacement, rehabilitation and resettlement in India are old and archaic. Land Acquisition Act, scarcity of land, lack of proper land records in many parts of the country, lack of a scientific mechanism to determine the real value/price of land, lack of trained manpower to handle the process of land acquisition and rehabilitation and resettlement, and undue delay in settling the dues of the oustees. Numerous puzzles inform the entire process of land acquisition. India not only has an inadequate and fuzzy data on land titles, it has also no national map showing occupation groups, commons used by tribes, forest areas and hydrological and ecological sensitive areas. One wonders that a country known as the world's largest democracy, has an elaborate system of census and voting, and is trying to introduce unique identity card, should be so insensitive to matters of land records and maps.

While development projects are intended to reduce poverty, in practice, involuntary resettlement has often created new pockets of poverty. There is growing public concern in India over the long-term consequences for project-affected people, which is resulting in greater public scrutiny of the rehabilitation and resettlement process, particularly for large development projects. There is growing public recognition for the fact that the purported public benefits of large-scale development projects need to accrue to the local community that is directly affected by the project's establishment as well. There is hardly any successful model or story of a smooth land acquisition, rehabilitation and resettlement project in the country, particularly when it comes to the livelihood restoration/compensation. Hundreds of thousands of displaced people of the past projects are still roaming around without a proper alternative livelihood/employment scheme. The displacement of people from land and the greed to appropriate natural resources and common property is an expression of neo-liberalism in which capital seeks neither to extend its manufacturing base nor to expand markets but to accumulate land resources, or resources which are renewable/infinite and yield profits on future speculation. Land acquisition is not intrinsic to industrialization but essential to the particular path of economic development which encourages a rush towards acquisition of those properties whose supply is finite. The development that proceeds through displacement follows an economic model based upon speculation rather than of creation of value. This is why we observe that this model of development not only destroys value in the sense of economic production of so many people, but also kills so many occupations and value chains because it survives better by keeping more and more people out of its ambit so that asset ownership is most concentrated.

Some of this public sentiment has filtered up to the state and is reflected in a recent spate of policy actions both at the central and state levels in India. Recent policy guidelines that have been issued including the latest draft Bill on Land Acquisition, Resettlement and Rehabilitation (2011) and state-specific guidance in a number of jurisdictions – for example, Resettlement and Rehabilitation Policy, Odisha (2006), Jharkhand (2008), Arunachal Pradesh (2008), Haryana (2010), etc. These new normative frameworks crafted by these policy statements seek to regulate more sensitively and sustainably rehabilitation of project-displaced people. While these documents wholly recognize the pathetic plight of the displaced and also acknowledge their right to be rehabilitated into conditions as close to possible to the state before displacement, such policy instruments never seem to question the very premise, namely, is displacement necessary?

It is pertinent to note however that these policy promulgations do not fundamentally alter the principles underpinning the Land Acquisition Act, 1894 which is the central piece of legislation that is applicable to the compulsory acquisition of land in India. Central among these principles is the notion of 'eminent domain' that is robustly applied in several common law jurisdictions. The notion describes the inherent power of the state to seize a citizen's private property or to seize a citizen's rights in property with due monetary compensation, but without the owner's consent. The property is taken either for government use (therefore, a larger 'public purpose'), or may by delegation be used by third parties who are to devote it to public or civic use. The nation's economic development, broadly speaking, is deemed to fall within this notion of 'public purpose'. The appropriation therefore is neither of markets, nor of economic value, nor of value producing capital but of property, whose value is created because of its appropriation. This makes displacement not a mere fallout or a by-product of development but central to its thesis and intrinsic to its logic.

The vast literature generated over recent decades on resettlement and rehabilitation issues in the country has largely focused on recording the detrimental social, cultural and economic consequences development projects have had on the lives of local project-affected families. Analysts have pointed to the inadequacy of the current normative and legal policy framework, in particular of the pivotal notion of 'eminent domain' underpinning the Land Acquisition Act, 1894. This literature has been useful to identifying systemic problems that underlie resettlement and rehabilitation in India, in particular, the intractable power relations that nullify efforts to sustainably assist project-affected families. In every case of failed rehabilitation there seems to be purposeful negligence which emanates from the fatalistic approach that development under neo-liberalism is a race towards acquisition of as much as property as is possible. The acquisition of property sets about a competition of everyone with everyone else and such race for grabbing property lay at the base of the subprime crisis in the US, the Greek tragedy and Euro zone crisis. Development is crisis; and displacement is a manifestation of such a crisis.

Development projects, such as hydroelectric and irrigation dams, highways, airports, industrial estates and new urban settlements, increasingly entail acquisition of private lands, often in populated areas. This increase in the development agenda of the state is coinciding with a marked decrease in the quantity of land that is easily available for these projects. It is increasingly difficult to locate land over which there is no other competing – land that is available in contiguous tracts, and land that is of a large enough size to facilitate the mega-development projects that have become attractive to planners today. While the state was able to acquire land with impunity in the decades immediately following the country's independence, land acquisition proceedings are increasingly contested, not just through strident visible protests by displaced communities across the country, but also by the engaged analysis and involvement of civil society organizations as well as a wider public. Maximal efforts need to be made to reduce the quantity of land that is forcibly acquired to the absolute minimum required, so as to minimize the necessity of displacing people without their consent. In every case of displacement this consent is easily sidestepped, the reason being that displacement is not an option, instead, it is the very thing that creates value for development. Development must proceed by acquiring speculative value and once land is forcefully taken can its value rise as a desirable property.

In a democratic country, there is little justification for legislation that confiscates private property while restricting scope for challenge to minor secondary issues such as the methodology and quantum of compensation allowed. While there is little political will in the country currently to fundamentally challenge the state's powers of 'eminent domain', there is however scope to ensure greater democratic dialogue over what is in the 'public interest' before land acquisition proceedings are initiated. A more robust public whetting of projects that actively involved directly affected communities would ensure development that was more truly consonant with a 'public purpose'. The process of public dialogue would also have the practical benefit of ensuring that only the minimum quantity of land required was acquired. The idea of 'public purpose' gets obliterated under neo-liberalism because of large-scale privatization where private parties invest in and carry out the functions earlier reserved for the state. As far as the generation of 'public goods' is concerned, it is now the private party which produces the same and hence public interest is coterminous with the interests of the private monopoly capital. The larger the private capital is, the greater the public interest it purports to serve and hence the 'eminent domain' of the state is now in the hands of the large private capital.

Thus, there is urgent need for the proposed Bill to incorporate language that more strongly protected the livelihoods of displaced people or which ensured a process by which alternate livelihoods were established prior to displacement over a long enough time span to test their viability. Traditionally, rehabilitation planners in the country have focused on the actual physical displacement of project-affected families, addressing issues pertaining to the loss of shelter and the actual process of relocation. What is required is to place greater focus on the fact that project-affected families tend to permanently lose access to productive assets as well as income sources as a result of involuntary land acquisitions. Restoring incomes permanently lost due to displacement has proven to be the toughest of several sustainable development challenges associated with rehabilitation and resettlement. The idea of restoration of livelihood can take shape only through employment. Wages keep falling relative to profits and as property prices keep rising, expropriation of land assets becomes even more pronounced. Were the families of the poor to hold on to the assets, they could have hoped to improve their position in comparison to the rest of the society, but pushing them into wage income means to push them down to relatively lower rungs of the society. Loss of land can never be compensated by gains in wage employment; this is not to say that wage employment requires very different kinds of skills than those the displaced communities possess.

Part of the reason why it has proven so difficult to recreate these incomes and create viable alternative livelihoods is because the compensation that is sought to be given to displaced families under the existing normative framework is extremely narrow in its understanding of what the displaced families have lost. In particular, there is no scope under the existing (and proposed) framework for compensating a loss of access to common property resources, including common land. Therefore, displaced families are not compensated for the loss of access to public lands, lands owned by the panchayat and forest lands. Communities dwelling in close proximity to forest area may obtain a great deal of their everyday requirements from this, through usufruct rights that may or may not be formally recognized by the state. It is pertinent in this regard to mention that the rights of members of Scheduled Tribes and other traditional forest dwellers in respect of forest land have received a degree of statutory protection under the Scheduled Tribes and Other Traditional Forest Dwellers (Recognition of Forest Rights) Act, 2006. It would be prudent to ensure adequate linkages between the proposed Bill and the rights specified under this Act, so that the right to compensation for the enforced loss of access to this common property resource is statutorily protected.

The history of resettlement and rehabilitation in India has not been a happy one. However, the new Bill offers the possibility for the introduction of a new normative framework to regulate rehabilitation and resettlement and to address some of the known negative consequences of involuntary displacement even if the fundamental power of 'eminent domain' is left untouched. Analytical work in this field has recently started to stress the potential that exists to use rehabilitation norms and compensation to assist local communities to meaningfully rebuild and improve their lives, using the best analytical and planning tools available to development practitioners. If these norms and planning tools are to be of any practical benefit to displaced communities, it is only by sustaining an active public engagement with the development choices that are made on our behalf, to problematize actions taken ostensibly for the 'public purpose', and to ensure that these actions do not go unscrutinized. At stake is nothing less dramatic than the democratic future of this country, of whether it can deliver on a constitutional promise of a better future that was given to the most marginalized communities across the land.

In the cases of economic development, one may observe that the path India has chosen is a suicidal one. As the world's largest democracy and the only democracy in the world to have granted universal adult franchise as early as 1947, the fact that its political economy encourages to discard its own citizens into utter destitution shows that India is either keen to compromise on its democracy and become a non-democracy like Bangladesh and Pakistan, but it is also not averse to using democracy to serve the interests of the monopoly capital. The Indian society that is gradually legitimizing aggressive competition where only one is a winner and the rest are losers is promoting an economy where chances of survival for everyone except the large single monopolist become an impossibility. India is a society where politically, administratively, judicially and academically people have accepted this mindless competition and where one can only grow by throwing the other out of existence. What kind of a society this would be? What kind of a world are we bringing about where everyone is out to kill the other, where every human is an enemy and where all but one must die? Accepting displacement as justified for development, we are not only taking the poor people, especially the tribals, for granted but we are also setting forth a process by which appropriation of property is the rule. Once industries have grabbed the poor person's land, they will extend their hand towards the middle class as the land acquisition in Singur, West Bengal has shown.

There is a new found respect in India towards the rich and the powerful. Fondness for celebrities, exclusive dining, exotic holidays and highly priced apartment living are now the quintessentially sought. The rich and the powerful are the role models of today. There are no considerations that these rich and the powerful depress our wages, sack us at will only to maximize profits, much in the same way that they never seem to pay for the poor's rehabilitation. The rich have a new legitimacy in the eyes of our society and hence whatever they do in order to become even richer appears to be fine with the people. Displacement of the poor is only a small part of a much larger story where capital in the mindless pursuit of endless wealth will impoverish everyone of us.

Organization of this Volume

The first article in Part I by *K.B. Saxena* discusses the newly proposed Land Acquisition Bill of 2011 and observes that while compensation packages have been improved, resettlement plans made more sensitive, yet the idea of increasing the worth of land as property, the legitimacy of pursuit of profits as 'public purpose', the lack of data on livelihoods and local economies, the poor system of disposal of objections, the non-updation of land records remain very much at the core of the Bill. Until these issues are corrected and settled, land acquisition will remain a terror for the people who are displaced by the same.

Bhaskar Majumder analyses the Acquisition Bill of 2007 and says that while it speaks of better compensation packages for the displaced persons, it does not challenge the fact of displacement. The Bill seems to continue speaking about the 'higher purpose' of development through imposition of heavy capital.

The second part has six articles. *Walter Fernandes* estimates that between 1947 and 2000, some 60 million persons have been displaced due to large projects like mineral industries and power generation. Of the displaced persons an overwhelming proportion are India's indigenous population, namely the tribals. Displacement means that the land upon which people depended for livelihood is taken away from them, leaving such disappropriated people not only landless but socially disbanded and culturally dissolved. Members of communities become vagabonds, helplessly dependent upon the mainstream society where they have no entitlement to participate and benefit from. The loss of means of livelihood leads to loss of dignity, cultural and social capital leaving the displaced utterly deprived. The problem of displacement is even more acute in the north east where the tribal population forms a majority; this is because tribals do not have a mainstream society to go to when they are displaced from their moorings.

Ramesh S. Mangalekar observes that the Indian Government's defence project, namely, the Sea Bird in Uttar Kannada, a district in northern Karnataka. The project acquired agricultural lands where locals who depended on land for livelihood were displaced out of agriculture. But the project in the area created huge demand for services like vendors, shopkeepers, repair units and thus created more employment than what existed before the project. The author investigates that there was an active intervention of the State machinery in creating these opportunities for the displaced people.

Narendra K. Behera argues that displacement is a logical fallout of the kind of development that we follow. In this mode of development where we try to place the so-called infrastructure for a larger society in the name of a greater good and in the pursuit of the unchallenged ideal of GDP growth, we tend to displace local population. Such displacement not merely hurts the displaced that today forms 1.45 per cent of the population but we set forth a process whereby an imposition of capital from above destroys the wider base of our economy. This process which allows only the very large capital to survive and excluded the rest brings forth dangers for our society. To challenge displacement is to challenge development.

Vimal Khawas and *Deepa Joshi* draws our attention to the hydel power generation projects in Sikkim in particular and the Himalayas in general and conclude that there has been no systematic hydrological, geological, ecological and seismic study of the Himalayas especially in the context of setting up of power projects. The lack of any systematic study and monitoring and evaluation has led to ecological fragility, deforestation, loss of livelihood for the people due to loss of forest cover. Besides, the migration of people from outside the area to work as labourers in the projects has increased an ethnic mixing and brings with it social conflict.

Patrick Oskarsson in his article observes that only the fertile lands are acquired because of the water resources in these fertile lands. He observes that direct negotiations between the private buyers and the farmers are worse for the poorer compensation, use of violence and threats and crimes against the villagers.

M. Gopinath Reddy et al. talk of the bauxite mining projects of the public sector unit NALCO in southern Odisha and mentions that while care has been taken to resettle the displaced population and provide them with jobs, yet the people are worse off as wage employees. The emissions from the project has contaminated their surroundings, reduced access to safe drinking water and subjected to toxic wastes mixed with water. The colonies are far off from the site of work and hours are spent in commuting creating trouble for the children and the elderly who are deprived of care. The ecological problems are mounting and poor environment management is creating enormous hardship for the people both local residents as well as the resettled people.

The last part of this volume has three contributions. *K.B. Saxena* tries to give a comprehensive picture of displacement, resettlement and rehabilitation situation in India. Saxena argues that the model of development pursued by the Indian state since independence has never come up for such sharp scrutiny as, lately, in the context of the magnitude of displacement it has produced and the trauma and impoverishment it has caused to the displaced persons due to the apathy towards their rehabilitation and resettlement. This explains why the iniquities in development and resettlement of persons displaced by it have acquired a degree of centrality in public and policy discourses never witnessed before. Further he suggests that the challenges faced in the process require strong determination, sustained commitment, dedication, resources and capacity over a period of time.

Ganesha Somayaji and *Joanna P. Coelho* have argued that there is a need to re-examine the Rehabilitation and Resettlement (R&R) policy that is presently being discussed in India. The policy takes displacement as a given, as a necessary corollary to the implementation of the ideologies of progress and development. Displacement needs to be looked at from a pluralistic socio-culturally sensitive perspective. Such a perspective calls for a broadening of the category displacement. Such an understanding which takes into account the heterogeneity of the experiences of displacement will ensure a more people oriented and therefore humane R&R policy.

Satya Prakash Dash studies the provisions for resettlement and rehabilitation packages in China in the context of the Three Gorges Dam. The compensation varies inversely according to the level of development of the resettlement area and directly to the level of activities in the land from which people are displaced. China's records are impeccable owing to its very ancient practice of the family registration system but such record keeping has its flip side as well because locals resist the resettlement of outsiders leading to political conflicts and village violence.

We would like to record our sincere thanks to all the authors for their valuable contributions. Our thanks are also for numerous friends in the field who supported our venture of understanding the phenomenon of rehabilitation and resettlement process. Finally, we are thankful to the Rawat Publications for their timely and beautiful publication of the book.

Part I

Policy Issues

1

People's Concerns in Land Acquisition and Resettlement

Does the New Bill Address Them?

K.B. SAXENA

Displacement constitutes a major human problem in India. It dislocates people from their home, land and environment and has traumatic consequences for their lives. Displacement can be caused by natural calamities such as flood, cyclone, tsunami, earthquake and manmade factors such as political conflict, wars and social strife. Development process, also man-made, has been added to the third source. While the first two causes have been a recurring phenomenon in the evolution of civilization, the third cause has emerged from the efforts of governments to modernize traditional societies. Of the three, the first two categories of displacement are unplanned and usually unanticipated. The third category of displacement, however, is the result of prior and conscious planning and is therefore anticipated. Of the two categories of unplanned displacement, the one that is due to natural calamities is usually of a shorter duration while the rather arising out of war, political conflict, and social strife may have a little longer duration and, in some situations, even of a permanent nature if the issues giving rise to it do not set satisfactorily resolved. But displacement from development projects is invariably permanent. This is because modern development is associated with big projects requiring huge areas of land, such as dams, airports, extraction of minerals, industrial plants, housing, provision of social service, etc. Since huge chunks of vacant land at a particular location are available in rural areas only, though already under productive use by and large, it is the people in rural areas subsisting on these lands who bear the brunt of acquisition for them. As a result of this acquisition, the persons affected by it are shifted to alternative location. The acquisition of land is carried out in a specified manner under a law which empowers the state to do so even without the consent of affected persons in public interest though a limited opportunity is given to them to raise any objection and the acquisition authority is required to compensate the land losers for this loss. Altogether, this exercise is heavily tilted in favour of the state which has overriding powers to take over the desired land, if necessary, by using force. Thus, the land acquisition is increasingly becoming a coercive operation lacking in sensitivity to human consequences involved in trail of devastation and trauma it leaves behind.

There are several laws, central and state, under which land is acquired. While most other laws confine the acquisition for a specified sector of 'public purpose' such as coal mines, atomic energy, post and telegraph, highways, town planning, bulk of the acquisition takes place under the Land Acquisition Act, 1894 which applies to acquisition for any 'public purpose' and also provides the general structural framework for it. The law was enacted by the colonial government along with the Indian Forest Act, 1865 to have control over natural resources of the country for their commercial exploitation. The acquisition law has continued to be used by the government after Independence for diverse development activities. This has led to the displacement of a large number of persons from their land, habitat and livelihood. The changes made in the Act in 1984 extended its use to acquisition of land for companies, public and private including registered societies and cooperatives, as well which added to the scope of acquisition. The shift to a neo-liberal economy and its integration with the global economic order has widened the scale of acquisition of land and accelerated its pace. The enactment of Special Economic Zone (SEZ) Act, 2005 has brought a new dimension to the demand for acquisition of land in terms of area, location, size and geographical spread. The resistance to such acquisition has been spontaneous and widespread. The government has responded with use of force to suppress this opposition.

In the discourse on the political economy of land acquisition, the existing Act has come in for a very sharp attack on grounds of its conflict with democratic ethos and considerations of equity and social justice. The economic rationality, environmental compatibility and moral propriety of large scale acquisition of land have also been questioned. There has been a long pending demand for drastic changes in the law and even for its abrogation and several suggestions have been made on the nature of changes required to be incorporated in the formulation of new proposals. These pressures were, however, resisted till recently. But faced with widespread discontent in the affected peasantry on account of ever increasing land acquisition and consequent delay in execution of the projects, the government first introduced the Land Acquisition (Amendment) Bill, 2007 in the Lok Sabha (MoRD, 2007[a]). The Bill was referred to the Parliamentary Standing Committee of the Ministry of Rural Development which submitted its report in 2008 (Lok Sabha Secretariat, 2008[a]). Based on the recommendations of this committee, some changes were made in the Bill, 2007 and the revised Land Acquisition (Amendment) Bill, 2009 was introduced in the Lok Sabha (MoRD, 2009[a]). This Bill was passed in the lower house but before it could be taken up in the upper house, the parliament was dissolved on account of general election. The Bill, 2009 therefore lapsed. Meanwhile, the affected people's resistance to acquisition continued as the revised Bill, 2009 too did not address their core concerns. The civil society too continued to oppose the Bill, 2009 for the same reasons and placed before the government several proposals of amendments for facilitating enactment of a more humane law on the subject. After getting reelected, while the government was contemplating to reintroduce the Bill, 2009 which the preceding Parliament could not approve, there was some difference in the ruling UPA about some of its provisions which required to be sorted out before the revised law could be reintroduced in the parliament. Meanwhile, the National Advisory Council of the UPA sent its detailed recommendations to the government on the subject suggesting radical changes to be inserted in the Bill, 2009 before its reintroduction in the parliament. Also, some landmark judgements of High/Supreme Courts were delivered during this period which quashed the land acquisition proceedings under challenge and made critical observations on the unresponsiveness of the government to the problems of the affected persons. The Ministry of Rural Development, the nodal ministry for this subject, also had a new minister who unlike his predecessor was more inclined to reopen the Bill, 2009 and incorporate some further changes to accommodate the recommendations of the NAC. These factors were responsible for an altogether new draft law on land acquisition replacing not only the existing Land Acquisition Act, 1894 but also going beyond the changes made in it in the Bills, 2007 and 2009. The government also abandoned the idea of having separate laws, one for land acquisition and the other for rehabilitation and resettlement and instead integrated the two in the proposed new Bill on Land Acquisition, 2011. The Draft National Land Acquisition and Resettlement and Rehabilitation Bill, 2011 (MoRD, 2011[a]) was first placed on the website for eliciting feedback of the civil society. The views of the state governments was also sought. Based on the feedback, the Land Acquisition and Rehabilitation and Resettlement Bill, 2011 was introduced in the Lok Sabha (MoRD, 2011[b]). The Bill, 2011 was sent to the Parliamentary Standing Committee. After the report of the committee is received, the Bill would take a final shape for consideration by the Parliament.

The public discourse on land acquisition has thrown up a rich material on how the architecture of the existing Act and its contents hurt the affected people. Several issues have been raised in this discourse ranging from conceptual to operational, structural and those relating to governance. The subject brings centre stage an old issue of political theory – state's relationship with its citizens. The existing law is built on the construction of this relationship as viewed from the interests of a colonial government whose only concern was to have total control over natural resources of a colony which were hitherto under use of the communities as per their customary practices to facilitate their exploitation for serving the interests of the mother country. Being an undemocratic state, it did not bother how the law it enacted would impact the people affected by it. With this sole objective, it enacted two major legal instruments. The one appropriated the forest converting it into state property and extinguishing/curtailing customary entitlements of the local communities to access its resources. It also took over its management depriving local communities of any say in the matter. The second brought on the statute book a law to take over privately occupied land thereby depriving its users of livelihood, displacing them from their habitat, environment and social networks, limiting their choices in life and forcing them to accepting consequences that were highly detrimental to their dignified existence. The only conditionality that the law imposed in the exercise of this power was that a larger public good should guide this action and land losers should receive financial compensation. This change was achieved by decimating community and its control and management of resources, radically altering the contours of individual entitlements and tilting the balance of relationship overwhelmingly in favour of the state. The new relationship that crafted was by the law and continued, rather reinforced, by the postcolonial state is not only anti-thetical to democracy but also the negation of humanism and social justice. The expanded ambit of land acquisition law and the enormity of its application in independent India further tilted the relationship against citizens, without being checkmated by constitutional provisions, participatory institutions, vibrant judiciary and the prescriptions contained in international conventions and instruments.

What are the critical dimensions of this law which confer the absolute power to the state to acquire peoples land and reduce citizens as silent sufferers of its traumatic consequences on their lives and which the people are persistently challenging? The following major features have been highlighted in the discourse:

Iniquitous and Inhumane Law

The following characteristic features of this law make it an instrument of injustice:

(a) Juristic rationality embedded in the notion of 'eminent domain' which permits forcible acquisition of private property by the state without the consent of user/occupier/owner as an unchallengeable right flowing from its sovereignty.

(b) Ethical packaging of use of this power conveyed through the utilitarian expression of 'public purpose'.

(c) Unjust nature of this power which ignores its devastating consequences on the affected citizens and fails to mitigate them by appropriate set of alternatives, limiting its responsibility only to payment of mere financial compensation.

(d) Enactment of multiplicity of laws with divergent procedures and entitlements which further disempower people to resist application of their provisions.

(e) Compensating mechanism governed by market fundamentalism.

(f) Bureaucracy-centric procedures of law enforcement with no element of participation of the affected persons.
(g) Privileging land acquisition law over other laws, thereby creating a double whammy for tribal communities.

Absolute Power to take over Private Land

The laws of acquisition of land empower the state to compulsorily acquire private property. The authority is rooted in the juristic notion of 'eminent domain' which justifies sovereign prerogative to exercise control over natural resources in its territory. The rights and interests of individuals or groups exist only with its authority. This implies that the citizen holds property subject always to the right of the state to take it for a socially desirable purpose. As a consequence, the right of a person or a community to resist state action for compulsory acquisition of land is obliterated. This legal rationality of 'eminent domain' makes state immune to any challenge to its action in the courts. This skewed balance between state power and individual/community rights is considered untenable in a democracy as its consequences are patently unjust and, therefore, unacceptable to citizens. There has therefore been a strong demand to abandon 'eminent domain' and to acquire land only with the consent of its holder.

Arbitrariness in Defining 'Public Purpose'

The moral imperative in acquisition of land for a 'public purpose' implies that the acquisition is justified only when the prospective use of land serves the interest of larger society and not of an individual or a group or an entity. As the law itself does not spell out the definition of 'public purpose' it has been left to the executive to decide which activity would justify this label for exercise of this power. The courts have upheld the judgement of the government in this regard. This flexibility has permitted the government to enlarge the scope of acquisition without facing any judicial scrutiny and has enormously increased the quantum of an acquisition of land, life-supporting assets of people with no consideration for its deleterious consequences on their dignified survival. A drastic limit to the use of 'public purpose' through a tighter and precise definition has been sought along with the right of the affected persons to challenge the propriety in the court of law.

Rehabilitation of Displaced Persons

The most glaring tilt in favour of the state lies in the law failing to cast any responsibility on it to provide a satisfactory rehabilitation of those displaced by it as its integral feature. The moral responsibility of the state towards these persons is not discharged by mere payment of compensation since acquisition of land causes their impoverishment and inmiserization. The state practice and judicial oversight have also failed to respond to this imperative thereby making law as an instrument of destitution. This has highlighted the need for a legal entitlement to a strong and comprehensive rehabilitation and resettlement of displaced persons as a precondition to acquisition of land.

Multiplicity of Laws

There is a virtual jungle of laws with as many as 16 central laws and equal number of state laws dealing with land acquisition. These laws are not uniform in processes and entitlements they provide. These laws cater to different sectoral activities for which land is acquired. As a result, different laws may operate in the same area affecting the same people depending on the situation. This diversity of laws completely disempowers people and emasculates their ability to respond to their processes. Their operation only serves to extinguish any possible right of the affected people to raise objections to the acquisition of land and put up their claims of compensation, and smoothen the process of acquisition using force where they resist them. Government has not even tried to harmonize them so as make the beneficial provisions applicable to all, not even by an executive order. The result is virtual expropriation of people's land. A single law to accommodate all purposes and contingencies is considered adequate.

Centrality of Bureaucracy

The entire processual frame of land acquisition gives a pivotal role to the bureaucracy. Two levels of bureaucracy are involved in it. The collector in the district and the land revenue department in the secretariat. It is the satisfaction of the state exercised through its agent in the district, i.e., the collector, which triggers the process leading to unhindered acquisition of land and thereafter the resettlement of displaced persons. The process as collector centric at every stage of acquisition process. The second level is the state secretariat which sanctions the proposal for land acquisition, and approves the compensation award formulated by the collector. The government at this level also decides the contours of the resettlement policy.

Given this centrality of bureaucracy, the orientation of officials involved in decision-making is important. This orientation is tilted in favour of the project backed by government and disregards the views and interest of those adversely affected by it. It provides no space for participation in this decision-making to make the outcome less traumatic and painful. This explains the demand for a participatory made of acquisition to democratize the process of acquisition and humanizes its outcome.

Privileging Land Acquisition Law over other Laws

The law of land acquisition is only one of the laws impinging on the transfer of land. The Constitution of India contains special provisions for protection of tribal communities, one of which relates to restrictions on transfer of land from tribal land holders to non-tribal persons. The 'Samatha judgement' of the Supreme Court has laid down a framework of restrictions from transferring tribal land to industry or mining or for any other alternative use in Scheduled Areas. The Central Government has also enacted the Panchayats (Extension to Scheduled Areas) Act, 1996 which mandates consultation of the concerned Gram Sabha on the proposal relating to acquisition and transfer of land in schedule V area. Similar provision exist in respect of Schedule VI area. Recently, the government has enacted Scheduled Tribes and Other Traditional Forest Dwellers (Recognition of Rights) Act, 2006. These laws are ignored while processing land acquisition proposals. The government thus becomes instrumental in violation of these laws by privileging land acquisition law over them thereby contributing to the disintegration and destitution of the tribal communities. The need for eliminating this conflict by making land acquisition law consistent with protective laws relating to the tribes has been asserted.

Market Fundamentalism of Compensation Assessment?

In the matter of award of compensation, the law is centred on 'market assessment' as the fair and adequate parameter of the value of land. But the market is a thoroughly inadequate instrument of determination of value of land. It is not neutral to the parties involved in transaction and is manipulated by powerful economic entities and social pressures. The purchase and sale transactions are also distorted by undervaluation of land to avoid tax liability or to conceal unearned income. In the case of tribal land, the legal restrictions on its transfer results in absence of market transactions and/or, where transactions exist, highly undervalued amount in them. The market also cannot assess the 'value' of land for individuals and social groups with unequal socio-economic status and vastly different and even conflicting cultural values. Also, land being an asset used for livelihood has a different value than other commodities exchanged in the market. Besides, vesting power of valuation in the government which is an interested party in the acquisition process makes the outcome unfair to the affected persons. A more acceptable formulation which accommodates different strands of thought and does justice to the different interests of those affected has been sought.

Undemocratic Practice

Besides the provisions of law, the undemocratic practice in enforcement of the law compounds the misery of the affected persons. Some of the features of this practice are discussed below:

Control over Information

The Land Acquisition Act, 1894 does provide for mandatory consultation of affected persons in the acquisition proceedings at two stages. The first stage is when a preliminary notification is issued about intention to acquire land. The second stage is when affected persons are asked to file compensation claims. The first consultation is undertaken by issue of notice in two newspapers circulating in the locally, its publication in the official gazette and placing the substance of it in convenient places. But the information contained in the preliminary notification is too meagre and sketchy to permit interested persons to have a clear knowledge about the project, its present and future, its rationale for selecting the site, the magnitude of displacement it would cause and specific area in villages which would be affected. There is an undercurrent of information squeeze and control, and urgency to rush through the process of acquisition. There has therefore been insistence on acquisition of land only with informed consent of the affected persons.

Taking Possession of Land

The law has failed to require that the physical possession of land should be taken only after compensation has been paid and resettlement arrangements have been completed. As a result, the acquisition authority takes formal possession of land after the conclusion of the acquisition process, and hands it over to the project authority without always making payment of the entire compensation amount and completing the resettlement requirements. This leaves the people without livelihood, financial means to subsist and even a dignified habitat. This inadequacy is sought to be corrected by making delivery of possession by affected persons conditional to fulfillment of all entitlements of compensation and resettlement.

Multiple Displacements

The law does not take into account the phenomenon of multiple displacements and therefore provides no relief for it. The callousness in effecting multiple displacements of the same persons is caused by failure to anticipate further development of the area and undertake permanent resettlement of the displaced persons at a safe site after the first displacement. The alternatives to avoid it are also not seriously explored.

Property-Centric View of Compensation

The connotation of compensation in the law has a limited meaning. It is equated with the value such land would fetch in terms of money when sold or the notional value of land in the market. Additionally, an amount of thirty per cent of that compensation as solatium is paid to reduce injustice caused by the vagaries of the market. The compensation amount so paid does not make up for the whole range of losses, social, cultural and economic, resulting from forced eviction. Social and cultural losses relate to, among others, social disruption loss of community networks and emotional trauma suffered by the affected people. No value is attached to these losses in the computation of compensation. Economic loss resulting from acquisition of land is conceived in terms of income derived from its cultivation and does not include in it the loss of access to common property resources the benefits of which cover a sizeable part of the income of the poor.

Disregards Community Rights

The law is narrowly fixated on the individual title holders of the land as its valid claimants. It does not recognize the existence of a collective entity called the 'community' which is more than the sum total of individuals with interests of its members. The law excludes from its purview loss of rights collectively enjoyed by the affected persons as a community and, in the process, repudiates the social environment and tradition built over centuries.

Change of 'Public Purpose'

Land is acquired for a 'public purpose'. The nature of 'public purpose' is usually declared in the preliminary notification issued for acquisition. But after the land has been acquired, quite often, the project/government utilize the land for some other 'public purpose' which is a violation of the law. But the courts have not found fault with this change of use. There is no provision in the law that such a change would require reprocessing the case of acquisition and declaration of a fresh award. This deficiency shows that the declaration of 'public purpose' was arbitrary and deprives the affected persons of the opportunity to raise objections and seek a fresh award on the basis of prevailing 'market value' of the land. The insertion of a provision for reprocessing the proposal of acquisition and declaration of a fresh award would put a check on indiscriminate use of 'public purpose' for acquisition of land.

Extending the Ambit of Acquisition

The proposals for land acquisition have almost invariably been opposed by persons adversely affected, particularly the poorer among them. This resistance is growing as the scale of acquisition has increased. The government far from restricting the scope of such acquisition so as to minimize the displacement has expanded its ambit over a period of time. It added acquisition of land for the companies, public and private, by an amendment made in the Act in 1984 and further extended its application to SEZ projects by separately enacting the SEZ Act. This reflects the insensitivity of the government to the affected persons. Various proposals for a drastic reduction in scope and scale of acquisition have therefore been suggested to the government by the civil society to lessen the hostility of the people to deprivation of their land through this mode.

Unutilized Land

In most cases, the considerable portion of acquired land remains unutilized for years as the land acquired was far in excess to the present and future need of the project. This highlights the utter casualness in accurately estimating the land required for the project leading to waste of public resources as well as unnecessary suffering to the affected persons. In most instances, unutilized land remains unprotected and is encroached upon by squatters or land grabbers. There is no provision in law for setting a time limit for utilization of land and, failing which, for return of the land to the government and, thereafter, to the land losers. This deficiency needs to meet by a suitable legal provision.

Absence of Participation

The only safeguard provided in the law against arbitrary action acquisition of land is the frame of rule of law and the quasi-judicial nature of its proceedings. The acquisition process provides a modicum of participation to persons likely to be affected. The participation is, however, limited to raising objections/contesting the proposal of acquisition and, later, to submission of views on the quantum of compensation sought. This participation carries no value as the acquisition authority is tilted in favour of the project and is guided by the views of the government. It brushes aside affected people's opposition to acquisition. Courts have also declined to undertake a judicial review of this issue. There is also absence of participation in defining and establishing rights and determining the design of compensation. The provisions of participation are also outdated as the panchayats are not involved in dissemination of information and seeking views of the people affected out. Thus, the majority of those affected by acquisition have neither access to information required nor have the capacity and resources to 'participate' in the proceedings. Besides, formal records of acquisition proceedings contain very limited information on decisions taken and factors influencing the process of making these decisions. There is minimal effort to ensure reach of information to the affected persons and create an enabling environment for them to express their views much less to have a re-look at the proposal for acquisition in the light of concerns expressed by them. Effective and institutionalized participation affected persons with adequate information at all stages of land acquisition and rehabilitation has therefore been sought.

Bias Against People

The operation of law as reflected in the practice of officials handling acquisition and relocation arrangements carries an unmistakable bias against the affected persons resisting acquisition of their land. They are clearly committed to expedition's acquisition of land and any opposition to it is perceived as anti development activity which warrants no empathy. Some instances of this bias can be observed from this following.

Lack of Concern for Rehabilitation of Displaced Persons

In the absence of an obligation in law for the state to rehabilitate and resettle affected person, the concerned governments have resorted to most minimum amenities required for shifting the displaced persons after evicting them from the land acquired. Even the limited ad-hoc assurances given to the displaced about rehabilitation to neutralize their opposition to the project have been diluted or reversed in the course of implementation. Government feels that payment of compensation, a provision of a small house and a minimum of infrastructure at the resettlement site is sufficient to discharge its obligation. This has left behind a trail of devastation. The affected persons are left to face an uncertain and bleak future. This deficiency is responsible for increasing hostility of the affected persons to acquisition proposals. A legally enforceable commitment to provide comprehensive rehabilitation and resettlement to all the displaced persons who should include, besides financial assistance for subsistence during the transition period, alternative land, employment, residential house, skill development, infrastructure facilities and social amenities has been sought to prevent this catastrophic consequence.

Cost-Benefit Assessment

The project authorities deliberately underestimate the 'cost' of acquisition by ignoring social cost (adverse effects on people and environment) and overestimate the benefits (gains of employment and improved living conditions) in order to present a favourable picture of the cost-benefit analysis necessary for clearance of the project. Neither the government nor the land acquisition authority evaluates the correctness of information and assumptions made from it in this analysis and go along with the project calculations. The number of people likely to be displaced is underestimated and the social and cultural consequences of displacement and the damage to environment are not even assessed let alone taken into account by the project authority so as to deflate the cost. This approach makes the task of restoration of environment impossible and resettlement of displaced persons unachievable.

Coercion to Force People to Agree to Acquisition

Officials are, as a rule, hostile to any expression of resistance against proposals of acquisition. They try to suppress this opposition in various ways. They connive at the manipulative tactics used by the requiring agencies to coerce resisting villagers into agreeing to the land acquisition proposal. Mine owners, for example, obtain mining lease on the government land adjacent to the private land of people who are unwilling to its acquisition and then frighten them by continuous blasting operations on it. Project agencies dealing with the construction of dams use the threat of submergence to hasten their eviction. There have been cases when officials of industrial projects have polluted drinking water sources on which people of the village depended to break their resistance to acquisition. At times they use divisive tactics by favouring a few displaced persons with extra benefits to weaken the united opposition to the project. The project officials are known to employ intermediaries and muscle men to threaten, assault leaders/local participants and involve them in criminal cases to intimidate opponents of project. The district officials are known to keep opponents of the project out of public hearing so as to present a manufactured consent in its favour. The victims get no help from the government agencies in these situations. Adequate safeguards are needed to check such practices.

Property-Centric View of Entitlement

The law requires 'person interested' to make their compensation claim for the acquired land to the acquisition authority. The officials through their interpretation of the term 'person interested' have restricted the eligibility for this entitlement to land owners only. The numerous persons who do not own land but lose livelihood on account of acquisition of land are not considered for compensation. This has been a sore point with the affected persons who want all those whose livelihood is lost such as tenants, sharecroppers, agricultural labourers, fisher folk, etc., to get compensation and other benefits which the land owners get.

Deprivation of Enhanced Compensation

The officials force the unwilling land losers to accept whatever compensation is offered. Later this acceptance is used to prevent them from making a reference to the court for enhanced compensation. The acquisition authority is also disinterested in reaching enhanced compensation to all eligible persons where a reference court has revised the amount declared in the award. The land acquisition officials make no effort to convey the necessary information in time the affected persons and to assist them in filing their claim. This results in deprivation of enhanced compensation to them.

Tilt in Favour of Project

The officials dealing with acquisition of land are primarily interested in observance of legal provisions only to the extent that acquisition proceedings do not face any hurdle from the courts which may delay the project, and therefore make them liable for financial loss resulting from it. They are also interested in completing the acquisition process most expeditiously and at least cost so as to avoid delay in execution and cost and time overrun. They also protect the interests of the government in respect of compensation payment by restricting compensation claim to only title holders whose names are entered in land records. The rights of tenants and other interests who are not reflected in land records due to pressure of land owners are ignored. The concerns of poor displaced persons therefore do not receive comparable attention. Even the semblance of neutrality between the project and the people so as to do justice to the interests of both is not maintained. Only legally embedded rights of affected persons can prevent such a tilt in official behaviour.

Disposal of Objections

The law provides an opportunity to the affected persons to raise objections to acquisition proposal. The acquisition authority is required to consider them and communicate its views to the government for a decision. It has been observed that objections from the affected persons to acquisition of land are routinely rejected. There is no effort to undertake physical verification of the site and to talk to the people before forming this view. The judicial review of acquisition has also failed to look into this dimension and confined itself to the fairness of compensation only. Hence, the need for a legal right to challenge acquisition and a clear provision for the acquisition authority to look into the objections rose seriously in a transparent manner and record the reasons for the decision taken.

Failure to Discharge Responsibility

The authorities dealing with acquisition of land and rehabilitation of displaced persons do much graver injustice to the affected persons than what the law has done by failing to discharge their elementary duties towards preparatory action and responsive implementation. The following would give some idea of the deficit in governance:

Quantum of Land

No parameters have been laid down in the law nor a scrutiny by experts envisaged on the quantum of land required for a given project. Consequently, the assessment made by the requiring agency for the proposed acquisition is accepted as valid. The acquisition authority has also no expertise to verify the rationality of demand. This has resulted in such distortions as widely varying quantum of land acquired for a similar project in two different locations and land acquired much in excess of the need, current as well as in the foreseeable future. As a result, a substantial part of acquired land remains unutilized, encroached upon, injudiciously used or is transferred for a purpose other than the one acquired for. A rigorous scrutiny of the land requirement for the project and return of the unutilized land to the erstwhile land holders have therefore been advocated.

Environmental and Social Impact Assessment

A radical change of land use after acquisition has serious environmental implications which are never taken into account while taking a decision on the project, resulting in environmental degradation, and loss of biodiversity. Similarly, projects entail large scale displacement of people leading to social destabilization, impoverishment and emotionally disturbed conditions.

Neither the government nor the acquisition authority direct the project agency to get environmental and social impact assessment carried out so as to realistically assess negatives of the project in the absence of an express provision to this effect in the law. This underlines the demand for such an assessment by an independent agency as a pre-condition to initiation of land acquisition proceedings so that information based on it could form the basis for a decision on whether the project should be cleared the scale and contours of and rehabilitation of people and restoration of environment, that would be needed if the project is cleared.

Outdated Land Records

The acquisition process proceeds on the basis of land records which contain the details of land and persons who have interests in land. The land acquisition proceedings can suffer from serious errors and can cause grave injustice if land records are not up to date. The land records across the country are outdated. They do not reflect the transfer of land, changes in land use and those emerging from court cases, mutual settlements, encroachments, alienation of land and tenancies. These results in deprivation of entitlements to those who in the absence of updated land records on this account fail to get compensation or other benefits. The mandatory updating of land records has therefore been advocated before initiating land acquisition proceedings.

Manipulative Transfers

As soon as it becomes public knowledge that land in a specified area may be acquired for a project, those with resources and power exert pressure on the poorer landholders to transfer their land to them cheaply by spreading disinformation and creating a fear psychosis that their land may be taken by government without any compensation. Many persons among the poor particularly tribals became easy prey to this manipulation. The transferees report to this fraud, to claim enhanced compensation as also benefits of resettlement. There is no provision for freezing such transfers before initiation of acquisition proceedings. Insertion of such a requirement has therefore been sought.

Failure to Reach Compensation

State machinery quite often resorts to eviction of people from their land and houses without payment of full compensation by the acquisition authority. The officials also fail to ensure that payment of compensation is reached to the affected persons are forced after eviction. In the absence of employment and means of subsistence, the displaced persons are forced to leave the area in search of work. There is no effort to trace the whereabouts of such persons. There are cases, where people displaced in the 1950s and 1960s have not received their compensation till date. As per official rules, undisbursed amounts are deposited in the treasury the withdrawal of which involves a lot of harassment and is riddled with corrupt practices. Full payment of compensation and other financial entitlements before land is taken possession of is the best safeguard against such a situation.

Shoddy Relocation

The acquisition authority takes a great deal of interest in acquiring land for the project most expeditiously but the same interest is not shown in developing the resettlement colony to which the displaced persons are hurriedly shifted. The result is a shoddy relocation which compounds the misery of people who have already lost livelihood and are going through a traumatic transition. The relocation sites lack even elementary amenities forcing people either to spend their meagre compensation amount on improving their living conditions or to migrate. They also face hostility of the host communities in accessing resources if they are shifted to an existing village. This explains insistence on benchmarking the minimum conditions of infrastructure and facilities in the resettlement colony before displaced persons are shifted to it.

Lack of Transparency and Accountability

The secretative manner in which the officials carry out their tasks is well known. This is intended to escape any questioning of their action. They are particularly hostile to any challenge to their authority from an agency external to the government. They achieve it by the following ways:

Accountability

The acquisition authority escapes any accountability for their deficient or biased action resulting in adverse consequences which people suffer in the matter of recognition of their rights, inadequate compensation, and absence of rehabilitation or some other entitlement. On the other hand, it protects the interests of the government and the project as also their own to avoid any financial loss to the government, delay in project execution and personal responsibility for any lapses on this account. It is prepared to sacrifice the interests of the people such an approach may entail. It even resorts to extra-legal and coercive methods to push acquisition of land. There is no forum where the adversely affected persons can hold the authority accountable. Hence the demand for institutional arrangements for grievance redressal and enforcement of accountability of officials involved.

Lack of Transparency

The practice of acquisition reflects a glaring lack of transparency and sharing of information regarding acquisition proceedings with the affected persons. The land acquisition records are processed in a secretive manner. The records themselves are brief and contain the barest minimum information required by law. They are not open to public scrutiny except where an interested party insists on their perusal. There is no attempt at all to voluntarily and willingly convey all necessary information to the affected people and make records available for display to the interested persons or organizations representing them. The records also do not usually reveal the considerations which have gone into taking of crucial decisions. This affects the ability of people to participate. The transparency of the process and the mechanism to ensure it need to be enshrined in the law.

Access to Records

Existing law does not bind the acquisition authority to allow interested person to access records concerning land acquisition proceedings. By virtue of being quasi judicial in nature, it is presumed that these proceedings fulfil the requirement of transparency and access to records would not be denied when insisted upon by the lawyer of an interested party. But interested persons fail to get access to even routine information. The law therefore needs to cast an obligation on the acquisition authority to facilitate easy access to records.

Acquisition in the case of urgency: Where the 'public purpose' is of an urgent nature. The land can be acquired simply by issuing a notice and giving fifteen days for taking its possession skipping the process of seeking the views of the affected persons and declaration of award. In the case of a building, possession can be taken after 48 hours of the issue of notice. In all cases of urgent acquisition, 80 per cent of compensation is to be paid to the land loser. This provision does not define parameters of urgency which leads to its misuse. Many cases of acquisition under urgency have been struck down by the higher courts on account of arbitrary application of this provision. Further, no distinction has been made between temporary acquisition and permanent acquisition. There is no obligation to arrange for alternative accommodation where the occupation is temporary and no provision for immediate resettlement where the acquisition is permanent. The return of land in the case of temporary acquisition is also not envisaged. No consideration is given to the subsistence needs of the land loser in wake of sudden acquisition of his land which leaves him/her little time to seek alternative livelihood. These dimensions need to be accommodated in the law.

No Oversight Mechanism

The law does not provide for an institutional mechanism to check the arbitrary and unjust use of power by the acquisition authority. There is a limited provision of a reference to a court in case where redetermination of compensation is sought. The government has been given the power to call for records of the acquisition proceedings before the award is made to satisfy itself as to the legality or propriety of any finding. But this power is rarely exercised and, in any case, the government does not look into the validity of the proposal for acquisition land since government has itself sponsored it. The courts have also not questioned the judgement of the government in acquisition of land or rehabilitation arrangement. This leaves aggrieved people without any space to question governmental action and place their grievances for redressal. An independent authority to provide such an oversight has been sought to meet this deficiency.

The LARER Bill, 2011

The current Bill, the Land Acquisition and Rehabilitation and Resettlement Bill, 2011 (MoRD, 2011) (henceforth the Bill, 2011)) is an advance on the earlier two Bills, 2007 and 2009. Both the earlier Bills had conceded the obligation of the state to rehabilitate and resettle people displaced from projects for which land is acquired. To that extent the balance of power between the state and the citizens in the existing Act, 1894 which is heavily loaded in favour of the former was made considerably even by the responsibility cast on the state to go beyond the payment of financial compensation and to undertake rehabilitation and resettlement of displaced persons. Since the responsibility would be embedded in law, the affected citizens, hopefully, would be in position to get it enforced by courts if the executive action fails them. The Bill, 2011 places this responsibility on a footing equal to that of land acquisition by incorporating the provisions of rehabilitation and resettlement in the body of the same law which deals with acquisition of land. In the earlier two Bills, 2007 and 2009, the rehabilitation and resettlement was dealt with in a separate law but simultaneously introduced in the parliament. This meets a long pending demand from civil society organizations for a single law on land acquisition which covers rehabilitation and resettlement as well so that the land acquisition authority is directly responsible for the latter and pay equal attention to it. A single law also conveys the clear intent that rehabilitation and resettlement is an integral part of the land acquisition process.

Not only this, the ambit of responsibility for mandatory rehabilitation and resettlement of displaced persons is now proposed to be extended to the private acquisition carried out through the market route. The Bill, 2011 provides that where the quantum of such acquisition involves more than 100 acres of land in the rural and 50 acres in the urban areas, or where a private agency requests that part of acquisition of its requirement for a 'public purpose' should be carried out by the government, the persons displaced by such acquisition including that part which the company has carried out through market transactions shall be rehabilitated and resettled by the concerned agency. This removes the injustice done to the persons affected by private acquisition that were deprived of the benefits of rehabilitation and resettlement which is available to those affected by government acquisition. The government has in the Bill, 2011 also removed the provision inserted in the Bills, 2007 and 2009 that 70 per cent of acquisition of land should be undertaken out by the private agency through the market route before the request is made to the government to acquire the remaining 30 per cent of land through the compulsory route. It has been left to private agency to decide how much of its land requirement would be met by direct transactions with the owners of land before requesting the government to chip in.

The glaring omission in the earlier two Bills, 2007 and 2009 on the unresolved disharmony between the laws relating to protection of tribal land and the Land Acquisition Act, 1894 has also been taken note of. The Bill, 2011 for the first time mandates that no land shall be transferred by way of acquisition in contravention of the laws in the scheduled areas. Similarly, the mandatory requirement of PESA, 1996 regarding consultation with Gram Sabha in this matter has also been dovetailed. The Bill provides the consultation with the Gram Sabha before the issue of preliminary notification. Thus, the violation by government itself of the constitutional protection available to the Scheduled Tribes with regard to their land by privileging land acquisition laws over tribal land protection laws would, hopefully, be avoided.

The major concession made in the Bill, 2011 is by way of dilution of the exercise of 'eminent domain' in the matter of acquisition of land. The acquisition of land for 'public purpose' is now divided into two categories – the one where the land is acquired by government for armed forces, national security, defence, state police, safety of people, specified development activities and infrastructure projects for use by the government or public sector companies and the other, where such acquisition is for use by the government for projects not covering the above activities the benefits of which largely accrue to the public, or public–private partnership projects for production of public goods and services or for private companies for production of public goods and services. In the former category of acquisitions, the absolute power of state to acquire land without the consent of the affected persons would continue to operate and the rigour of 'eminent domain' would apply as before. In the latter category of acquisitions, the consent of at least 80 per cent of the project-affected people obtained through a prior informed process would be necessary. Thus, in sharp departure from the existing provision in the Land Acquisition Act, 1894, as also those in the Bills, 2007 and 2009, the use of land for a public purpose which earlier applied to cover all acquisition by government irrespective of the category of purposes has been differentiated. Only the acquisition of land required by the government directly or for a public sector agency implying that the projects for which this acquisition has been done would be executed by them and the land would not be transforced to a private agency would qualify for undiluted exercise of power under 'eminent domain'. Where a private agency in partnership with government or independently uses the land even if it is for production of public goods and services, the acquisition shall have to follow the consensual route. The other significant dimension of this proposal is that this consent shall be obtained from at least 80 per cent of the affected persons and not merely the land owners who are usually outnumbered by non-owner residents using land in some capacity or the other. This implies that those who lose livelihood as a result of acquisition of land owned by others shall also have an equal say in the process of decision-making and the prescribed percentage of eighty would ensure that the views of a large majority of affected persons including owners and non-owners would influence the decision. A small section of land owners (usually absentee or having large holdings) or elite of the affected area would not be in a position to override the interests of the landless and powerless sections of the village. The conditionalties to be fulfilled and prescribed procedure to be observed for obtaining the consent of the affected persons have also been specified. This involves giving in advance necessary information about the project and the nature of acquisition to such persons to enable them to make up their mind before the process of obtaining their consent begins. This requirement would, hopefully, ensure that the process of obtaining consent is not hustled through, or manipulated as happens at present in the matter of consultation with the Gram Sabha in respect of land acquisition in Schedule V areas.

The indiscriminate acquisition of land including irrigated and multi-cropped land has all along been sharply critiqued by those concerned with food security of the country. Still this concern did not attract attention of the government and the Bill, 2007 ignored it while formulating its amendment proposal. However, it was taken note of by the Parliamentary Standing Committee which examined the Bill. The Committee recommended a number of pre-conditions for acquisition of such land to ensure that irrigated and multi-cropped land were acquired as a last resort and that too after observing the requirements laid down so as to limit the damage. These conditionalties were incorporated in Bill, 2009 but still left the scope for continued acquisition of such land albeit with difficulty. The Bill, 2011 has tightened these restrictions by disallowing acquisition of such land as a rule but, where unavoidable, limiting it to 5 per cent of the total area of the district, and, where no irrigated multi-cropped land is involved in acquisition, placing the ceiling of such acquisition to10 per cent of the total net sown area of that district where the net sown area is less than 50 per cent. In the latter case, where the net sown area of the district exceeds 50 per cent, the implication is that there would be no restriction on acquisition of latter category of land.

The definition the term of 'person interested' has been further enlarged to include any person whose primary source of livelihood is likely to be adversely affected which was missing in the Bills, 2007 and 2009. This is a significant addition. The plain reading of this provision seems to entitle non-land owners affected by land acquisition also to claim compensation and benefits of rehabilitation and resettlement. If this understanding is correct, it is another major concession which removes the property centric approach in the implementation of the Act. Similarly, the considerably enlarged definition of the term 'affected family' so as to cover livelihood losers and *patta* holders from the version contained in the Bills, 2007 and 2009 makes it comprehensive and ensures that no genuine displacee is left out of the ambit of rehabilitation and resettlement. It also removes gender discrimination by including an adult of either gender with or without spouse or children or dependents as a separate family. The cost of acquisition added to the long list of Definitions for the first time in the Bills, 2007 and 2009 so as to cover fully the expenditure to be incurred on rehabilitation and resettlement has been further elaborated in the Bill, 2011 to specify its each and every component. This would leave no ambiguity for the 'requiring agency' to escape the responsibility of making adequate financial provision for it before placing its acquisition proposal before the government. This in turn would ensure that rehabilitation and resettlement work does not suffer for lack of resources. The term 'infrastructure project' also introduced for the first time in the Bills, 2007 and 2009 has been expanded in the Bill, 2011 by adding social development and production relating activities to its large ambit. This further widens the definition of 'public purpose' for compulsory acquisition of land and has therefore implications for the scale of displacement. The definition of 'land owner' in the Bill, 2011 is more progressive than its version in the Bills, 2007 and 2009 as it includes not only the *patta* grantees under any law but also those entitled to grant *patta* rights as also those who have been so declared by an order of a court or authority. This removes a cause of resentment and injustice to those who on account of inaction of the revenue machinery to grant *pattas* and update land records were deprived of the benefits of the law relating to participation in the proceedings, laying claim for compensation and seeking entitlement to rehabilitation and resettlement.

The definition of 'public purpose' has been enlarged by adding to its scope social development activities which had been omitted in the earlier Bills, 2007 and 2009 though included in the existing Land Acquisition Act, 1894. This omission was sharply critiqued for its corporate orientation and anti-poor bias. But the definition has added to its ambit production of public goods and public services undertaken by private companies either in partnership with the government or entirely on their own. When this is read with the definition of 'infrastructure' the ambit of acquisition is considerably widened rather than reduced and therefore defeats the purpose of seeking a change in the existing definition. The definition now explicitly includes acquisition for private companies which the Bill, 2007 sought to dilute by externalizing the process of acquisition to direct transactions between the agencies and the land owners to the extent 70 per cent of their requirement leaving only the remaining 30 per cent to the government to acquire. The only conditionality for such acquisition is that it would have to be for production of public goods and rendering public services. The two terms not having been defined, the scope of their application to corporate requirement of land would be flexible so as not affect current corporate led economic growth.

Also regressive in the Bill, 2011 is the omission of requirement that 70 per cent of its need for land should be acquired by the private agency through market transactions before a request is made to the government to acquire the remaining 30 per cent of land by compulsory acquisition. This change virtually reverts to the existing position in the Land Acquisition Act, 1894. The obligation to carry out rehabilitation and resettlement of affected persons even in respect of private acquisition through the market route if the area involved is 100 acres or more would induce the companies to seek compulsory acquisition for their entire land requirement. The quantum of acquisition therefore is not likely to reduce which was main purpose for advocating that 'public purpose' should be defined precisely.

The need for pre-acquisition study of the proposal of the requiring body with regard to its social impact had been accepted in the Bills, 2007 and 2009. But its provisions were considered inadequate and did not include an enquiry into whether the activities of the project would constitute a 'public purpose' and the rationale for its quantum. The Bill, 2011 has elaborated the dimensions of social Impact Assessment including the rationale for charactering the proposed project activity as a 'public purpose' and sequential structuring of this exercise. This has been done by prescribing a three step structure for this purpose. The first step consists of a study of social Impact Assessment to be carried out at habitation level in the affected area in consultation with the Gram Sabha within the prescribed time limit. The report of this study would be subjected to a public hearing in the affected area after giving adequate publicity to ascertain the views of the affected families and would also be published after revision on this basis, if necessary. The second step is evaluation of this report by an Independent Multidisciplinary Expert Group which would examine the rationale of the project, its 'public purpose' and its costs and benefits. The third step is High Level Committee at the government level to take a decision on whether to acquire land on the basis of the two reports above as also the report of the Collector. This Committee would ensure that the proposal involves a bonafide 'public purpose', only minimum land has been proposed for acquisition, irrigated land has been included as a last resort and the option of utilizing barren, waste, degraded land has been explored with a view to minimizing displacement and disturbance that may be caused to infrastructure and ecology. These provisions are an advance over the contents of Social Impact Assessment contained in the earlier Bills, 2007 and 2009.

Insufficiency of arrangements to reach the vital information to the affected persons about the intention of the government to acquire their land had been improved upon in the Bills, 2007 and 2009 by placing the notification on the website of the government and making it available at the office of collector, tehsil and Gram Panchayat/local body. The Bill, 2011 makes it mandatory that Gram Sabha at the village level, municipality in the urban areas and Autonomous Councils in the Sixth Schedule areas should be consulted before issue of preliminary notification. This incorporates the requirement laid down in PESA, 1996. The contents to be included in the notification have also been specified so as to enable informed participation of the affected persons in the consultation process and placement of their objections in response to the notification. The sale and purchase of any land covered by the notification was already barred in the earlier Bills, 2007 and 2009 and has been continued in the Bill, 2011. Similarly, the requirement that land records should be updated before the final decision on acquisition of land is taken was also incorporated in the earlier Bills, 2007 and 2009 and has been carried in the Bill, 2011.

With regard to compensation, the issue of entitlement has already been addressed by expanding the definition of 'person interested' so as to entitle livelihood losers the benefit of compensation besides rehabilitation and resettlement though this does not appear to be the case as has been argued later. On the mode of determination of 'market value of the land', the earlier Bills, 2007 and 2009 had laid down the criteria for this exercise. This includes areas where there are restrictions on sale/purchase of land. These provisions do not undergo any change. The Bill, 2011 only enhances the amount of compensation over the norms laid down in the earlier Bills, 2007 and 2009 by requiring that the compensation payable shall be the assessed market value multiplied by a factor of two in the case of rural areas and a factor of one in the urban areas. The solatium payable likewise would be 100 per cent of the market value assessed multiplied a factor of two in the case of rural areas and a factor of one in the urban areas. In short, the assesse would be entitled to four times the assessed market value as the final award. The hallmark of the Bill, 2011 is the substantially improved compensation package. Besides, the Bill, 2011 introduces individual award of compensation in respect of each affected person. A separate award has also been introduced for rehabilitation and resettlement which includes rehabilitation grant, house sites, subsistence allowance and other entitlements. This would enable the awardee to contest the grounds of assessment of compensation and its adequacy as also the entitlements relating to rehabilitation and resettlement in the court of Land Acquisition, Rehabilitation and Resettlement Authority.

The Bill, 2011 also removes ambiguity on the timing of the possession of acquired land. It mandates that land shall be taken possession of only after all entitlements are delivered within the prescribed time limit, i.e., cash award of compensation within a period of three months, monetary portion of the rehabilitation and resettlement award within a period of six months and infrastructural facilities in the resettlement colony within a period of eighteen months from the date of award. This would prevent use of force for taking possession of land and relocation of displaced persons without paying entire compensation, and rehabilitation of grants and delivering infrastructural entitlements. The prescription of time limit for each entitlement would exert pressure on the Land Acquisition Authority to complete its homework expeditiously and enable the awardee to approach the Land Acquisition, Rehabilitation and Resettlement Authority where this has not been complied with.

The provisions relating to acquisition of land under urgency were already restricted to a minimum area required for defence, national security or emergency arising out of natural calamities. The affected households were entitled to additional 75 per cent of the market value of the property as assessed. There is no change or further improvement in the provisions.

The Bill, 2011 empowers the government to withdraw from acquisition any land of which possession has not been taken subject to the payment of compensation for the damage suffered by the owner together with cost if any incurred by him in the prosecution of the land acquisition proceedings. This implies that once possession is taken, the process cannot be reversed irrespective of whether the land is utilized or not. The Bill also bars any change from the purpose or related purposes for which land was originally acquired. It also disallows change in ownership of land without permission of the government. The provisions are a continuation of the similar provisions in the Bills, 2007 and 2009. But the Bill, 2011 has made the provisions regarding unutilized land regressive from those made in the Bills, 2007 and 2009. The earlier Bills had mandated that the land remaining unutilized for a period of five years shall revert to the government. This period has been increased to 10 years. Also, the reverted land would be included in the pool of vacant land called the 'land bank' implying thereby that government would utilize it for some other purpose. Despite the strong advocacy of the civil society group that such land should revert to the original owners or their heirs, this has not been conceded. Similarly regressive is the provision that where land acquired is transferred to any other agency on a consideration, 20 per cent of the appreciated value shall be shared amongst the erstwhile land owners. The Bills, 2007 and 2009 had provided that 80 per cent of the amount minus the cost of acquisition would be given to the erstwhile owners.

The Bills, 2007 and 2009 had replaced the reference court, a judicial body to settle cases relating to compensation claims, with a quasi-judicial compensation Settlement Authority with more than one member. Its membership had a combination of judicial and non-judicial persons. The provisions were sharply criticized as an attempt to dilute the independence of judicial process and influence decision-making. The Bill, 2011 has substantially changed the provisions and proposed a composite Land Acquisition, Rehabilitation and Resettlement Authority for speedy disposal of disputes relating to land acquisition, rehabilitation and resettlement. It would be a single member body which would be head by a serving or a retired Judge of a High Court or a person who has been a District Judge for at least five years. The Bill has also laid down the procedure for disposal of reference cases and the grounds on which compensations to be awarded shall be determined.

With regard to rehabilitation and resettlement, the Bill, 2011 is an advance over the Bills, 2007 and 2009 (MoRD, 2007[c]) and (MoRD, 2009[b]). This is particularly so in respect to allotment of land and provision of employment or cash in lieu thereof or annuity. In the case of irrigation projects, land losers or others who as a result of acquisition of land are reduced to the status of a marginal farmer, the provision of a minimum of one acre of land in the command area has been made. This provision existed in the earlier Bills too. The new addition is that in every project, land losers belonging to the Scheduled Castes (SCs)/Scheduled Tribes (STs) would be provided land equivalent to land acquired or two and a half acres whichever is lower. This provision meets the strongly advocated demand that the members of these groups, particularly the STs, are extremely vulnerable and, without land, their dignified survival would be threatened. The second new provision is that in urban areas, 20 per cent of acquired land which has been developed would be earmarked for distribution to the land owning affected families in proportion to the area of their land acquired at a price equal to the cost of acquisition of land and its development. This amount would be deducted from the compensation package payable to the land owner. In other words, the affected land owning families can have a choice of having a small share of the developed land but only at a price. It is not an additional benefit but a part substitute of compensation. It, however, has the attraction that land can be utilized for income generating activity. The second additional feature is that the affected families have been given three options from which they can choose. These options consist of (a) job at a remuneration not lower than the minimum wages under the law to at least one member of the family, (b) onetime payment of five lakh rupees per affected family, (c) annuity policy that shall pay not less than ₹ 2,000 per month per family for 20 years with appropriate indexation to Consumer Price Index for agricultural labourers. The other cash entitlements regarding subsistence, resettlement, transportation allowances, cattle shed/shop, one time grant to artisans and traders, fishing rights, etc., continue to be the same as they were in the Bills, 2007 and 2009. Similarly, infrastructural entitlements are also a replication of the earlier Bills.

The Bill, 2011, like the Bills, 2007 and 2009, provides for an informed and participatory land acquisition, resettlement and rehabilitation arrangement. This participation is intended to take place through the provision of a public hearing on the report of Social Impact Assessment and consultation with the Gram Sabha before initiation of acquisition proceeding are initiated. Also, the draft of the Rehabilitation and Resettlement Scheme is required to be subjected to a public hearing preceded by adequate publicity. There is also a provision for publication of the revised scheme in the official Gazette, after taking into account objections raised in public hearing making it available in the affected area and its placement on the website. The review of the revised scheme by the Collector with the Rehabilitation and Resettlement Committee at the project level also provides modicum of participation. The structures for monitoring include a Rehabilitation and Resettlement Committee at the project level with three non-officials along with officials, local MPs and Panchayat heads, and a National Monitoring Committee consisting of officials and experts at the national level. These provisions have been diluted when compared to the Bills, 2007 and 2009 (MoRD, 2007[c]) (MoRD, 2009[b]) which had provided for a three tier participatory structure, an Ombudsman and a National Commission. In the current Bill, 2011 there is no structure of monitoring above the level of the project other than the National Monitoring Committee. Neither of the two structures have representation from the displaced persons.

Notwithstanding certain improvements made in the Bill which address some concerns of the affected displaced persons, it is unlikely that the Bill, even if passed without any regressive amendments, would neutralize the widespread discontent arising out of land acquisition for development projects which involve large scale dispossession of people from their land, livelihood, habitat and environment. What people desire (barring a small section of rich/absentee land owners and those near the metropolitan centres) is a stop to the destabilization of their lives resulting from ever increasing threat of displacement. The Bill provides no assurance that the scale of acquisition would get drastically reduced not to speak of a halt to the acquisition spree currently in process and forthcoming. The proposed pre-acquisition scrutiny of land acquisition to minimize displacement of people and the area of acquisition of land is far from reassuring as the exercise is to be carried out by a committee dominated by officials and is hardly likely to inspire any confidence in its deliberations. This committee which would take final decision on the subject has no representation from the affected households. Given the aggressive commitment of the government in favour of fast economic growth which is overwhelmingly centred around extraction and exploitation of natural resources and the nexus between officials and corporates so crudely visible in governance at all levels, the decision of the committee in favour of acquisition proposals is a foregone conclusion. For similar reasons, the composition of expert group which would examine the Social Impact Assessment report does not inspire much confidence because the selection of experts would be made by the government. It is also not without significance that in the composition of this committee too there is no representation of the affected people which could provide modicum of objectivity to its deliberations. It is difficult to miss the underlying inevitability of land acquisition for a project in this process of scrutiny since it does not envisage at any stage that the project may be rejected if there is strong opposition to it or if the cost taking into account social and environmental impact outweighs the benefits that are claimed to accrue. This makes the exercise of scrutiny a cosmetic effort.

Though some relief has been provided in the aggressive application of 'eminent domain' for land acquisition by mandating informed consent of 80 per cent of the affected families for certain categories of projects, where the land to be acquired would be used for production of public goods and provision of public services by the corporates either entirely on their own or in partnership with the government, this has to be related to the experience of the people in respect of the a similar provision in PESA, 1996 on consultation of Gram Sabha. The land acquisition agencies have been known to subvert this process and 'manufacture' consent of affected persons by forcibly driving out dissenters from or preventing their entry into the meeting venue of the Gram Sabha or even falsely recording 'consent' despite overwhelming opposition to the acquisition of land. Besides, there is no reason why the other category of acquisition where the government is the user of land either directly or by transfer to a public sector agency, the ambit of which is large, should be left out of this conditionality of consent and the route of compulsory acquisition should be used. Overall, the willing submission of the affected people to acquisition of their land is unlikely and use of force, specifically provided for in the current amendments, to take possession of the acquired land would continue to generate hostility and bitterness among them. The most regressive part of the current amendments is the backing off from the commitment made in the Bill, 2007 that no land would be acquired for private companies and accordingly the chapter VII of the existing Act which lays down the procedure and conditionalities for acquisition for companies was proposed to be deleted. Though this declaration turned out to be cosmetic as the private companies were brought from the back door in the definition of 'public purpose' and 'infrastructure', the Bill, 2011 does not hide its readiness to use state power to acquire land for them and virtually reverts back on this issue to the status in the Land Acquisition Act, 1894 and yet deletes the conditionalties in it to make the exercise easier and smoother.

The commitment incorporated for adherence to the laws prohibiting alienation of tribal land in the Scheduled Areas should ordinarily stop acquisition of land in most of the industrial and mining projects which are concentrated therein. But this does not seem to be the intention going by a general reading of the law as there is no let up in the acquisition of land for projects proposed for such areas. This implies that some way would be found out to subvert this provision to push their dream proposals. Much worse, some state governments are amending their protective laws for the Tribals and resorting to other subterfuges to facilitate acquisition of the tribal land in the scheduled area. In respect of persons displaced on account of private acquisition through the market transactions while imposition of an obligation on the company to rehabilitate and resettle them would prevent their inequitions treatment in future, the prescription that this benefit would be available only if acquisition of 100 acres in rural areas and 50 acres in urban areas is involved has no rationale. It is counterproductive. It would induce the companies to split the requirement of their acquisition to avoid this liability. The industry, in any case, is lobbying hard for deletion of this provision. On the food security front, the dilution of the ban on acquisition of irrigated and multi-cropped land shows that these prescriptions would be difficult to enforce when the government is so strongly committed to attracting FDI for sustaining its economic growth. It would manipulate data to facilitate such acquisition. The district agencies are known to misrepresent the nature of land (particularly when land records are not updated) to push acquisition proposals. As for the expansion of the definition of 'person interested', its enlargement to include tenants and share croppers would fail to make it inclusive as bulk of the tenants/share croppers are informal with no record of their oral contract. It would be difficult for them to establish their identity as tenants. Besides, the landowners whose land they are cultivating would deny their status as tenants on their land. Their exclusion from laying claim to compensation would therefore continue. Further, the inclusion of livelihood losers in this definition creates false hopes of breaking the property rights driven paradigm of compensation entitlement. The provisions relating to compensation continue to remain land ownership centric. The livelihood losers get no compensation. Their inclusion in the definition of 'person interested' would merely entitle them to a second grade rehabilitation and resettlement. The definition of 'public purpose' far from being restrictive, precise and tightly constructed so as to replace the existing one which expanded the ambit of acquisition enormously has now been made so wide and elaborate that virtually no 'purpose' is left out of its purview. What the redefinition has done is to include not only activities listed in the existing Act but also all types of corporate requirements explicitly what it did implicitly under the present Act. It conveys not even the remotest inclination to reduce the level of acquisition through the construction of this term which the affected persons were looking for.

The adequacy of increased compensation would have to be tested on the ability of a land loser to purchase equivalent land of the same productive capacity in the vicinity. The concept of 'replacement value' would have rendered greater justice and would have reduced intensity of resistance to acquisition. This is all the more necessary since the Bill, 2011 has backed off from the commitment in the National Rehabilitation and Resettlement Policy, 2007 (MoRD, 2007[b]) to base assessment of compensation on the appreciated, value of land rather than its value at the time of the issue of notification for acquisition. With project coming up in the area, land prices would shoot up enormously and even the increased cash compensation that the Bill, 2011 promises would not enable the land losers to replace their lost asset. As a result, the affected persons would inevitably become land less. But even in terms of cash entitlement offered, the proposal in the Bill, 2011 is regressive when compared to the 'six times increase in market value' that had been promised in the draft Bill (MoRD, 2011[a]) for circulation. Similarly regressive is the provision that the period of utilization of acquired land for attracting its reversion to the government has been increased from five years in the Bills, 2007 and 2009 to 10 years in the Bill, 2011. It is also disappointing that the recommendation of the National Advisory Council to distribute the unutilized land after its reversion to the government among the erstwhile land losers has been disregarded. Therefore, the purpose of inserting the provision has been defeated. The proposed reversion of unutilized land to the government for use as Land Bank would only benefit the government and the corporate but not the affected displaced persons.

As regards the acquisition practice, some changes in the Bill, 2011 have diluted the bureaucratic-centric land acquisition process for effecting participation. This is exemplified by a provision to consult the affected persons on the report of Social Impact Assessment of the proposed acquisition of land through a process of public hearing so to get their feedback before it is subjected to further scrutiny by experts. The constitution of an Expert Group to examine the Social Impact Assessment Report prepared in the light of the views expressed in public hearing though techno-centric in its composition would subject the report to a slightly more diversified scrutiny than the one provided for in the Bills, 2007 and 2009 where it had been proposed to be carried out by a body dominated entirely by officials. This, of course, pre-supposes that the experts are chosen in a manner that inspires confidence in their objectivity. Though the body carrying out this scrutiny does not have a representation from the affected population or the local political leaders, at least it has non-official social scientists and rehabilitation experts who are expected to bring to bear in its deliberation a view point different from that of the officials. Further, the provision for consultation with the Gram Sabha municipality/autonomous council in the Scheduled Areas before the issue of preliminary notification as required under PESA, 1996 in Scheduled V and concerned laws in Scheduled VI Area also dilutes the bureaucratic dominance in the acquisition process. These bodies have also to be consulted in respect of the Rehabilitation and Resettlement Scheme. This requirement facilitates a modicum of participation in the proceedings. The other participatory structure embedded in the Bill, 2011 is with regard to the constitution of Rehabilitation and Resettlement Committee at the project level. These provisions which are in addition to the space available already in the existing Act, however ineffectual, dilute to some extent the bureaucratic centrality in the process though the degree to which genuine participation would be encouraged, given the past experience, is difficult to guess at this stage. Similarly, some degree of transparency in the process has also been introduced through the provision of publication of SIA study and placing it in public domain, publication of summary of Rehabilitation and Resettlement Scheme, the requirement that the summary of entire proceedings of the land acquisition including compensation Award shall be kept open to the public and the collector shall display it on the website. This requirement would also apply to the decision of the Land Acquisition Committee which finally recommends the proposal of acquisition. The catch however is that the way documents are prepared for exposure to the public domain do not ever reflect how decisions have been arrived at. The minutes merely record the decision and not the considerations that formed its basis. They do not bring out the social dynamics of this process so as to permit public scrutiny and challenge, where necessary. The attitudinal factors, the pressures which are brought to bring on the land acquisition process, the undercurrent of bias in favour of the project, etc., would therefore continue to vitally influence the decision-making, which would have to be unravelled and challenged by the affected people through collective mobilization.

Also, disappointing is the change in the rehabilitation package, where the provision relating to the allotment of land to the ST land losers has been reduced from 5 acres in the draft Bill, 2011 to 2.5 acres in the current Bill, 2011. The latter is too low an area to restore lost livelihood and dignity. Even more insensitive is the deletion from the current Bill, 2011 the earlier proposal contained in the draft Bill, 2011 regarding allotment of at least 1 acre of land to the landless ST displacees. This proposal would have saved them from destitution and vulnerability to exploitation in the rapacious labour market. It would have also prevented disintegration of the tribal community and its attendant consequences for their survival. The provision of mandatory employment in the draft Bill, 2011 has also been diluted by substituting it for cash if no employment is given. Through this monetary equivalent, an escape route is provided for project agencies to fulfil their responsibility of giving payment of financial compensation in lien of employment. But, as money equivalent, the promised amount does not even precarious represent the capitalized value of the wage of an unskilled agricultural worker over a period of 20–25 years. The option of annuity in place of employment provides too low an amount to assure even precarious survival let alone a dignified one. The provision that in the acquisition of land relating to the STs, alienation of their land shall be treated as null and void and benefits of compensation and rehabilitation and resettlement would accrue to the original ST land owner would be unenforceable as alienation of land in most cases gets validated by revenue and judicial courts. The non-tribal alienators of tribal land would drag every such case to prolonged litigation. There is no provision to negate such a possibility. Besides, in the absence of similar provisions being inserted in the land alienation laws of the concerned states, this declaration in item 11 of the second schedule of the Bill, 2011 is cosmetic and would generate unrealizable hope. The provision of ST development plan in the rehabilitation and resettlement policy and included in the Bill, 2011 lacks conceptual clarity. It does not take into account diverse needs of different ST groups, their ecological situations, social and cultural traditions and the economy on which they subsist. The existing provision would fail to render any meaningful rehabilitation to them. This is specifically true of the Particularly Vulnerable Tribal Groups (earlier PTGs)-hunters, food gatherers, shifting cultivators who are neither socialized in agriculture nor in sedentary activities and therefore would be ill suited to the homogenized model of rehabilitation and resettlement envisaged in the Bill, 2011.

Overall, the Bill, 2011 does not provide any relief to the affected persons from the threat of displacement by reducing the scope of acquisition of land. What it offers is a little more cash, a more rigorous process of acquisition with some space for participation and accountability of those entrusted with the task of rehabilitation and resettlement. But the disrupted life resulting from displacement cannot be rebuilt without assured and dignified employment and access to productive asset for this purpose. Even with provision of these inputs, continued development support and affirmative action would be required over a long period of time. The Bill lacks the vision and inclination to provide such a support. The Bill is also totally silent on the backlog (75%) of rehabilitation from earlier displacement. These victims of development have become invisible in policy discourse and have again been left in the lurch in the current Bill. The Bill, 2011 also ignores plight of the victims of multiple displacement. It makes no effort to address the severity of their trauma caused entirely by the incompetence and insensitivity of officials. It has even declined to accept the recommendation of the Parliamentary Standing Committee for enhanced compensation for them (Lok Sabha Secretariat, 2008[a]). Besides, there are 16 other central laws through which land is acquired and there is equal number of state specific laws of acquisition. The limited beneficial provisions of this Bill, 2011 do not even apply to the acquisition under them unless the central government issues a specific notification to this effect with such modifications or exceptions as may be notified.

It is therefore evident that prospects of a resolution of conflict on account of land acquisition are bleak and greater social instability is on the horizon. There is no escape from a serious rethinking on the land acquisition policy which is rooted in the paradigm of economic growth and development and its attendant multidimensional inequities.

References

Lok Sabha Secretariat (2008[a]). The Land Acquisition (Amendment) Bill, 2007, Thirty-Ninth Report of the Standing Committee of the Ministry of Rural Development (2007–08), October 2008.

—— (2008[b]). The Rehabilitation and Resettlement Bill, 2007, Fortieth Report of the Standing Committee of the Ministry of Rural Development (2007–08), October 2008.

Ministry of Rural Development (MoRD) (2004). Report of the Expert Group on Prevention of Alienation of Tribal Land and its Restoration.

—— (2007[a]). The Land Acquisition (Amendment) Bill, 2007.

—— (2007[b]). The National Rehabilitation and Resettlement Policy, 2007.

—— (2007[c]). The Rehabilitation and Resettlement Bill, 2007, Bill No. 98 of 2007 as introduced in Lok Sabha on 6 December 2007.

—— (2009[a]). The Land Acquisition (Amendment) Bill, 2009, Bill No. 97–C of 2007 as passed by Lok Sabha on 25 February 2009.

—— (2009[b]). The Rehabilitation and Resettlement Bill, 2009, Bill No. 98–C of 2007 as introduced in Lok Sabha on 25 February 2009.

—— (2011[a]). The Draft National Land Acquisition and Resettlement and Rehabilitation Bill, 2011, August 2011.

—— (2011[b]). The Land Acquisition and Rehabilitation and Resettlement Bill, Bill No. 77 of 2011 as introduced in the Lok Sabha on 7 September 2011.

2

State-led Development-Induced Dispossession and Displacement

Some Recent Experiences in India

BHASKAR MAJUMDER

The accelerated economic development of a national economy is based on industrialization by setting up of industries having higher order technological capacity to transform natural resources into commodities and to enhance the capacity for further extending the frontiers of production. This path of development through industrialization was followed by all the developed countries of the world and is now being followed by the post-Second World War independent countries chasing the developed countries. The core of industrialization is the conscious application of advanced technologies to increasing human productivity, diminishing the limitations imposed by nature, and raising standards of living (Magill, 1997: 721). The origin of industrialization is located in pre-history but the fundamental changes associated with industrialization are usually derived from the industrial revolution in the United Kingdom (UK) that began in the late 18th century and subsequently spread to other countries and continents (Deane, 1984). Setting up of industries needed land which had multiple long-term impact on agriculture and housing in all the countries that followed the path of industrialization. It is recorded that between 1870 and 1914, more than 50 million people were displaced from the agricultural sector in Europe, who resettled in US, Canada, Australia, New Zealand, South Africa, Argentina and Brazil (Nayyar, 2002: 145). The displacement was driven by both the push factor of 'land scarce' Europe and the pull factor of 'land abundant' Americas in particular (ibid.). In Russia planned industrialization after the 1917 Revolution led to millions of peasants being evicted from land and shunted into urban industries, mining, hydroelectric projects, thousands of collective farms (*kolkhozy*), and state farms (*sovkhozy*). In Japan the path of industrialization based on the post-Meiji restorations in 1868 ended Japanese feudalism (Magill, 1997: 723–24). The percentage of population working on land gradually declined not only in the UK and the US but also in Japan and China, particularly since the days of the first industrial revolution in the UK. Around 1600 AD 2.76 per cent of the total land was enclosed and 50,000 persons out of a total population of around 4 million were evicted in the UK. In China, since the 1950s, around 10 million people have been displaced due to hydraulic and hydroelectric projects alone (Sarkar, 2007: 1436).

Despite the upheaval in the lives of common people that results from industrialization most of the countries that were decolonized post-Second World War including India have accepted industrialization as an inescapable route for development. The economic policy of the state in favour of industrialization shows not only technological advancement but also an emerging production relation weighted in favour of the controllers of capital and technology and against manual workers based on land and hence different from the agrarian economy that preceded it. Industrialization provides the space for the workers to get united as a working class to come out from the local economy based inertia and start realizing their own strength (Plum, 1977: 68). In a frame of Darwinism it breaks isolation and localization in favour of global division of labour. As opposed to limited flexibility in locating agricultural operations, industrialization has higher flexibility – by the availability of raw materials, market size-cum-access, transport and communication, availability of physical infrastructure, cluster of firms for externality advantages, inter-industry linkages, and hence, by location. In case of India modern industries were supposed to dissolve the hereditary divisions of labour based on the rigid caste system and hence remove the 'decisive impediments to Indian progress and Indian power'. Industrialization was seen as not only inescapable but also a step forward in breaking the 'self-sufficient inertia of the villages' (Marx, 2006).

However, any path of development carries with it unequal consequences for people located at different layers of the society.

With the urban boundaries extending to annex the rural areas that circumscribe cities, annihilation of agricultural land and displacement of people are natural corollaries. The immediate victims in this process are the people living at the bottom of the socio-economic ladder who are displaced by execution of state-led development projects. Development thus results in capital accumulation by A representing the privileged sections at the upper end of the socio-economic ladder, simultaneously with the dispossession of physical means of production of B. In India, B represents the people who continue to practice socially inherited caste-cum-gender division of labour that is characteristic of India with its caste based social structure. As a consequence of long-term stagnation at the bottommost level of the economy B has failed to develop the capacity to be a partner in the decision-making processes of development projects planned by A. This failure gets prolonged by the multiple boundaries erected against B like obstructive education, power language (English by colonial inheritance), caste, community, height-weight-colour, gender, and access to institutions and privileges. The additional factors that prolong the vulnerability of B are ignorance, immobility and tradition-custom-belief. B remains confined to a traditional society as fait accompli. As a corollary, B fails to foresee changes and in the same process often B symbolizes anti-development. What B fails to communicate is an unequal impact of development planning executed by the state that goes decidedly against it; it benefits the already privileged A by the power of the purse, education and free walk on the corridors of power, and goes against B who are rooted, tradition-bound, and localized sections. In other words, development (accumulation) of A and displacement (dispossession) of B go together.

Land acquisition by the state in India for development projects has emerged as a major issue in the country at present. From the recent experiences in a few places in India mainly in the state of West Bengal, it might lead to unwarranted socio-political consequences, critical enough to disrupt the pace of industrialization. The reason for this is that although at the macro-economic level land acquisition for development projects like roads, townships, bridges, airports is inescapable, but at the micro-economic level this phenomenon entails displacement and dispossession of a large population which includes mainly those at the bottommost layer of the social hierarchy who are still dependent on land and agriculture for their livelihood (Bhaduri, 2007: 1598–99). However, the growth of a strong civil society in India in conjunction with a vibrant mass media has facilitated the affected people to put up a strong resistance to the land acquisition and has increased the visibility of the resulting conflicts (Majumder, 2008: 1008–10).

This paper focuses on the displacement of people following acquisition of land by the state for industrialization and suggests safeguards that the state should adopt for the land acquisition. The rest of the paper is structured into the four sections. In the section that immediately follows we discuss the law on land acquisition in India and the role of the state. This is followed by some general observations on the industrialization-induced dispossession of people in India citing three examples. We then present a critique of the state and finally, propose safeguards in land acquisition for industrialization.

Laws on Land Acquisition in India: Role of the State

Land acquisition refers to the process by which the government acquires private property for 'public purpose' without the prior informed consent of the land owner, which is different from a market purchase of land. In India land acquisition is done by the Indian State under the Land Acquisition Act, 1894 which says that the government can acquire land 'whenever it appears to the (appropriate government) the land in any locality (is needed or) is likely to be needed for any "public purpose" (or for a company)'. 'Public purpose' includes land needed for village sites, town or rural planning, land for residential purposes for poor or displaced due to natural calamities, land for planned development (including education, housing, health and slum clearance), or land needed by a state corporation. The Act adds that the Collector 'shall serve notice to the same effect on the occupier (if any) of such land and ... pay the compensation which in his opinion should be allowed for the land'. If any person does not accept the award the matter may be referred by the Collector to the Court which will then settle the matter. In determining the amount of compensation to be awarded for land acquired under this Act, the Court shall take into consideration various criteria like the market-value of the land at the date of publication of the public notice, damage sustained by reason of taking the crops which may be on the land at the time of taking possession, the expenses likely to be incurred if the person is compelled to change his residence, and so on.

The Land Acquisition Act, 1894 was comprehensively amended in 1984, nearly after a century, by introducing some transitional provisions with regard to compensation paid to the population settled on the land which mainly includes poor tribals and lower castes. In 1996 the Draft National Policy for Rehabilitation of Persons of the Ministry of Rural Development, Government of India, acknowledged that cash compensation was not an acceptable proposition for most of the tribal people who inhabit the remote and backward regions full of mineral resources like coal, iron ore and manganese reserves (GoI, 1996: 1541). While tribal people constitute 8.08 per cent of India's population, they constitute more than 40 per cent of the project affected population (PAP); another 22 per cent of the PAPs are dalits (lower and marginalized castes), and the rest, including the above, are rural poor (Lobo and Kumar, 2009: 9). In 2003, the National Policy on Resettlement and Rehabilitation for Project Affected Families, was passed which was replaced by the National Policy on Rehabilitation and Resettlement, 2007 (Chakrabarti and Dhar, 2010: 4). On 30 November 2007 the Government of India introduced The Land Acquisition (Amendment) Bill, 2007 in the Lok Sabha (Lower House of Indian Parliament) to 'further amend the Land Acquisition Act, 1894' (Source: Bill No. 97 of 2007, Lok Sabha). The Bill is yet to be passed as an Act and once passed it will be called the Land Acquisition (Amendment) Act, 2007. The Bill changes 'public purpose' to allow land acquisition only for (a) strategic naval, military, or air force purposes, (b) public infrastructure projects, or (c) for any purpose useful to the general public where 70 per cent of the land has already been purchased from willing sellers through the free market. The Bill defines 'infrastructure' as any project relating to electricity, construction of roads, highways, bridges, airports, rail, mining activities, water supply, sanitation and sewerage, any other notified public facility. Currently, private land may be acquired on behalf of a company for a 'public purpose' project and prohibits land acquisition for companies unless they have already purchased 70 per cent of the land needed. The Land Acquisition Act, 1894 had defined 'person interested' to include those who are claiming land compensation and those interested in an easement (limited right of use of the land) on the land. The 2007 Bill proposes to expand the definition to include tribal and other traditional forest dwellers that have lost any traditional rights as well as individuals with tenancy rights under state law. If land acquisition results in the displacement of 400 families in the plains or 200 families in the hills or tribal areas, a social impact assessment study must be conducted that will include the effects of displacement, a Tribal Development Plan, and provisions for infrastructure development in resettlement areas.

For fixing the amount of compensation to be paid to the affected persons, while in the Land Acquisition Act, 1894 the Collector only needed to determine the current value of the land for compensation amounts, the 2007 Bill requires the Collector to take the highest value of (a) the minimum land value for the area as specified in the Indian Stamp Act, 1899; (b) the average sale price of at least of the higher priced sales of similar land in the village or vicinity; or (c) the average sale price of at least 50 per cent of the higher priced land purchased for the project. The value of trees, plants, or standing crops damaged must also be included. In the event that a price is not available or the land is in an area where land sales have been previously restricted, the state government shall set the floor price per unit of land. This price will be determined by the average prices of at least 50 per cent of the higher priced land in the vicinity. While determining compensation the Collector must also factor in the intended use of the land and the value of such land in the current market. The Bill also adds that the payment for acquired land must be made within one year from the date of declaration. The Collector can extend this time limit by six months with a penalty of 5 per cent per month. After the compensation amount is determined the Collector must ensure that payment occurs within 60 days. Possession of land shall not be taken unless full compensation is paid or tendered to the land owner. In addition, land owners whose property has been acquired under urgency shall be compensated an additional 75 per cent of the market value of the land. If the acquisition is for a company, shares or debentures of 20–50 per cent of the compensation amount must be offered through these options. The interested person may either accept this offer or opt for a full cash settlement.

The Bill 2007 pledges to make the process of land acquisition transparent through notification in the official gazette and in two daily newspapers circulating in that locality. The Bill says that the appropriate government shall, for the purpose of providing speedy disposal of disputes relating to land acquisition, set up, by notification in the official gazette, the Land Acquisition Compensation Disputes Settlement Authority. Thus, following the proposed Act 2007 the state (of India) owns the responsibility of land acquisition for which the catalyst is the District Collector and the Disputes Settlement body is the court. The role of the judiciary is limited by the guidelines provided by the proposed Act. By regulating market value of land for 'the compulsory nature of the acquisition', and by guiding the judiciary in determining compensation, the state aims to execute the development model that it perceives fit for the country.

In addition to the compensation offered by the Central Government for land acquisition, on 3 September 2010 the Chief Minister of the state of Uttar Pradesh (UP) in India declared a new system of rehabilitation of farmers at the time of land acquisition. The Chief Minister decided that an amount of ₹ 20,000 per acre per annum in addition to the compensation would be provided as annuity for a length of 33 years to the affected farmer whose land had been acquired. The amount would be increased by ₹ 600 every year and would be payable every July. If a farmer did not want to take the annuity then he would be paid a one-time amount of ₹ 2,40,000 per hectare as rehabilitation subsidy. If a company acquired the land then the farmer would have the option to hold 25 per cent share of the land acquired by the farmer. The Chief Minister also announced other benefits for farmers whose land would be acquired for land development projects.

The actual rehabilitation of the affected people is done under the National Policy on Resettlement and Rehabilitation for Project Affected Families, 2003, Ministry of Rural Development, Government of India, which pledges to minimize displacement and to identify non-displacing or least-displacing alternatives, to plan the resettlement and rehabilitation of project affected families (PAFs), including special needs of tribals and vulnerable sections, to provide better standards of living to PAFs, and to facilitate harmonious relationship between the requiring body and PAFs through mutual cooperation. In addition, each corporate body which acquires land through the state also has its own policy on resettlement and rehabilitation (R&R) which it implements for rehabilitating the PAFs. However, in the following section, we show that the ground reality is far from those pledged in the policies of the government and the corporations requiring land.

State-led Development-Induced Dispossession and Displacement of People in India: Some Observations

Late starting countries like India on the trajectory of industrialization relative to the countries called industrialized today face several economic problems due to the falling carrying capacity of land. The demographic condition in India in 1951 showed a size of population more than any other country in the world excepting China. During the post-independence 60 years, of the total population dependent on land the absolute number of population working on land has increased but the percentage of population has remained more or less unchanged. Its agriculture is characterized by a monotonically declining land-man ratio, low labour productivity and declining share of agriculture in national income over time. The declining land-man ratio in India follows the natural increase in population, service sector-led urbanization, and shift of agricultural land for non-agricultural purposes. Apart from the natural shift, there has also occurred a state-sponsored shift since the state of India, in the frame of state-centric development, has been executing a 'top-down' approach in development after independence by setting up industries and projects like mines, dams, ports, plants and expansion of road and rail network. For example, the state of Odisha used 40,000 hectares of land for industry between 1951 and 1995 while the state of West Bengal used 2 million hectares of land between 1947 and 2000 for industry. Apart from state-sponsored projects, private corporations like Reliance, ESSAR, Jaypee and also transnational corporations headquartered in different countries have been targeting mining land and hills in the states of Odisha, Jharkhand, and Chhattisgarh in India for both power generation and mining that inescapably displace people (Sharma and Singh, 2009: 62, 64–66). Mostly the mineral-rich, land-abundant, less industrialized states with large tribal populations like Odisha, Jharkhand, Chhatisgarh, are being targeted for acquisition of land, almost all of which lead to displacement of huge populations of tribals and cause large scale environmental degradation. For example, Posco, the world's fourth largest South Korean steel company, had signed a Memorandum of Understanding (MoU) with the Government of Orissa in 2005 to set up a plant near Paradip port in Odisha's Jagatsinghpur district that would produce 12 million tonnes of steel per annum. Vedanta Aluminium's proposal to mine bauxite in the Niyamgiri Hills in Odisha is destined to oust the local tribal community and also violates forest and environment laws, as reported by the National Advisory Council to the Government of India (*The Hindu*, India, 24 August 2010: 1). The Narmada Dam Project, which will feed drought-prone areas around the Narmada river that flows into the Arabian Sea after passing through the states of Madhya Pradesh, Gujarat and Maharashtra, is notoriously famous for the legal disputes because of the displacement of the people living in that region.

According to estimates during 1947–2000 around 60 million persons have been victims of displacement in India, 40 per cent of them are tribals and 20 per cent each dalits and backwards (Fernandes, 2007: 203). Of this, development projects like dams and canals displaced 70.9 per cent people up to 1989 while industrial set ups displaced 6.4 per cent. Overall only 25.5 per cent of the displaced people could be rehabilitated (Fernandes, Das and Rao, 1989). The government announced monetary compensation for the affected people in all the cases; for example, the Government of Odisha on 9 July 2010 announced a ₹ 70 crore rehabilitation package for a population of 3,000 to-be-displaced by land acquisition (*Hindustan Times*, Lucknow, India, 31 August 2010). However, payment of money as compensation does not make the displacement of the people voluntary. The reason is that the displaceable people living at the bottommost of the economic ladder do not understand the intricacies of industrialization and may fail to understand the long-term consequences of displacement (Lobo and Kumar, 2009: 14). They are neither made part of the decision-making processes ex-ante nor do they have the capacity to bargain vis-à-vis the controllers of capital. These people-to-be-displaced who were earlier thought of being the cause of underdevelopment are in reality the consequence of development. Land acquisition is in reality the acquisition of cultivable soil area plus trees and plants, water bodies, residential buildings, animal sheds and many other assets that 'land by area and volume' carry, which is a much greater loss to the displaced persons than mere land since more than being a means of production land is a base of livelihood that provides the space for self-employment and allied activities. Development following land acquisition thus has a tendency to displace the people living at the bottom of socio-economic ladder from the trajectory of development (Sharma, 2003: 909–10; Majumder, 2010: 84).

Land was never thought to be a factor of production in industry either because the supply of land was abundant relative to what was required or because the required land area was insignificant relative to the available land area of any particular economy. In India, however, there existed inequitable ownership of land with oppressive production relations in agriculture. This was a major cause of concern for the state and the statesmen, which was the reason behind the launching of the *Bhoodan* movement in India immediately after independence. The *Bhoodan* movement was basically a method of collecting land from land owners through land donation for distribution among the landless agricultural labourers that was launched in India post-independence. It was based on the Sarvodaya ideology of Mahatma Gandhi which is the removal of all kinds of inequalities in society by the formation of a Sarvodaya (equal) Samaj. The movement was launched by Acharya Vinoba Bhave, a staunch Gandhian, as a response to the non-legitimized 'land grab' by the landless labourers of the Telengana region of the state of Andhra Pradesh in India who had risen in open revolt against the landed interests under the influence of the Communist ideology (Nanekar and Khandewale, 1973: 5). However, this voluntary attempt towards land donation-cum-distribution did not go too far in absence of state intervention (Karve, 1961: 977).

The land selected for setting up or for extension of industries is either near the market-cum-urban areas or near mining areas, forests, and hills. The consequence of the displacement of both these sets of people, i.e., those living in the villages adjacent to the urban areas, and those living in the forests and hills remote from the urban areas, is similar. While landowners get compensation by the state for giving up their land, landless people are ineligible for compensation and are also deprived from the opportunity to work as wage workers hired by the land owners. In addition, the landless people are also deprived from their access to common property resources (CPRs) in the form of firewood and fruits from the forests, and so on, which too are taken away in the process of land acquisition. Access to CPRs for their sustenance is one of the major reasons why poor people in India remain rooted in rural regions. Since CPRs belong to no one, they are outside the purview of compensation of any type and so the individuals dependent on CPRs fail to be compensated for loss of access to CPRs following land acquisition. Because land acquisition results in loss of livelihoods of the affected people, the latter often put up resistance to land acquisition. While the acquisition results in the loss of agricultural land, along with loss of residential areas, CPRs, and so on, it also leads to an emotional loss incurred at leaving behind their native places, which cannot be recompensed by the money given to them as compensation with resettlement at new locations. Even if the people agree to the acquisition they usually face enormous problems both while claiming the compensation money and while settling down in their new habitats.

As a part of the stipulation of conducting social impact assessment studies for state-led land acquisition that will lead to the displacement of a large number of people, we were assigned the task of conducting a few such studies by the organizations for whom the state was acquiring land in the state of Uttar Pradesh (Majumder, 2007, 2009, 2011). We cite here three examples of actual and attempted land acquisition to illustrate the effect of the land acquisition on the affected people and their response to the land acquisition. All the three projects were for setting up thermal power plants for generating electricity and while two were for the National Thermal Power Corporation (NTPC) representing the public sector, one was for Reliance Energy Limited in the private sector. Of the three examples, one was a successful case of land acquisition, one aborted mid-way, and the rest trying its best to be a case of success.

Example I: Meja, District Allahabad, UP: A Case of Successful Acquisition

On 22 November 2007 the NTPC Limited and Uttar Pradesh Rajya Vidyut Nigam Limited signed a Memorandum of Understanding (MoU) to set up a thermal power plant of 1,320 MW under the name, Meja Urja Nigam Private Limited (MUNPL), at Kohrarghat of Meja block in Allahabad district of east UP. On behalf of NTPC the UP government acquired a total land area of 2,500 acres for setting up the plant covering seven villages partially, namely, Kohrar, Bhagdeva, Esauta, Mai Khurd, Salaiya Kala, Salaiya Khurd, and

Patai Dandi. This land acquisition affected 469 settled households, most of whom received compensation. However, many of the Project-affected persons (PAPs) faced severe hardships in the process of obtaining compensation. The major reasons for pending or delayed payment of compensation were court cases, 'speed money' asked by the officials of District Land Acquisition Office, outstanding bank loans of the displaced persons, errors in the name written on the bank cheque book, objections raised by the displaced persons against the compensation money offered, disputes between Treasury and Special Land Acquisition Officer (SLAO), official apathy, family disputes, and expiry of validity date shown on the bank cheque book.

In addition to the monetary compensation most of the project-affected households were rehabilitated at new settlements by caste-cluster type housing. For example, the Mallahs (fishermen community) along with a few Mushahars (pig-rearing community) have been rehabilitated at Nai Basti in Jhariyahi, while the Yadavs (cattle-rearing community) have been rehabilitated at Nai Basti, Yadav Nagar, Koyaltara. The process of rehabilitation was fraught with obstacles as the original inhabitants of the location of rehabilitation of Mallahs who were Thakurs (upper caste), initially expressed hostility to the entry of the displaced persons. However, following the intervention of police, harmony was restored. The resettled people also faced several adjustment problems at their new habitat chiefly because the women had to search for a proper public space for sanitation. Also, no provision had been made for rehabilitation of domestic animals in the new settlement for Mallahas as there is absence of both animal sheds and grazing land, resulting in loss of livelihood of the people. The approach road to the new location has also remained non-motorable because of a large dry canal between the village and the main road. The children, however, have access to the same elementary school as earlier because of the proximity to the school where they were enrolled before displacement.

Overall, the displacement immediately resulted in landlessness, and loss of non-land productive assets like wells, fruit trees and timber trees. Alongside the loss of CPR like common grazing land has led to loss of food, fuel and fodder. The worst-hit are the landless stone quarry workers who were ineligible for compensation because of landlessness and also suffered joblessness because of the demolition of the stone quarries to set up the plant. In spite of the problems faced by the PAPs the land acquisition was carried out. The households displaced by land acquisition are now hopeful to derive the benefits of urbanization. In addition, they also expect to be employed by the MUNPL after it starts functioning (Majumder, 2009).

Example II: Dadri, Ghaziabad District, UP: A Case of Aborted Acquisition

In 2004 the Government of UP acquired about 1,011 hectares of land in seven villages in Dadri region in Ghaziabad district of west UP for Reliance Energy Generation Limited (REGL) to set up a 3,500 MW gas-based power plant. On 13 July 2007 the Government of India gave environmental clearance to the project. The villages were Dehra, Jadopur, Bajhera Khurd, Kakrana, Nandlalpur and Baharmandpur and Dhaulana of which Nandlalpur and Baharmandpur were uninhabited. The major assets covered in land acquisition were canals, ponds and wells and would have led to displacement of a large number of settled families. The rate of compensation offered to the affected people at the time of the proposal was twelve times the annual output value calculated at the-then current market price and many of the affected people signed on the agreement letter and accepted the compensation money.

Subsequently, the farmers who were affected by the land acquisition started protesting against the acquisition claiming a much higher compensation than what was offered to them. The rate of compensation that was initially fixed was ₹ 150 per square yard, which was higher than the market rate prevailing there before the land acquisition. Immediately after the land acquisition the market rate rose to ₹ 300 per square yard at the minimum and ₹ 400 per square yard at the maximum. The farmers formed an association called Maharana Pratap Sangram Sangharsh Samiti and jointly claimed a compensation of ₹ 500 per square yard.

On 30 December 2006, Reliance Energy Limited decided to start the construction work by applying the 'Urgency Clause' of 1894 Act. The Maharana Pratap Sangram Sangharsh Samiti then launched a series of protests under the leadership of ex-Prime Minister of India, V.P. Singh. The farmers and V.P. Singh, later filed a writ petition in the Allahabad High Court against the low compensation claiming that the petitioners were forced to sign on documents and accept the meagre compensation offered by the Collector. Following continuous protests since 2004 against the low rate of compensation, and based on the magnitude of loss of fertile agricultural land, on 4 December 2009 the Allahabad High Court cancelled the acquisition, quashing of urgency powers to acquire land exercised by the-then Government. The Court said that the farmers had the option to refund the compensation received (Majumder, 2007).

Example III: Tanda, District Ambedkar Nagar, UP: A Case of People's Struggle

The thermal power plant at Tanda, District Ambedkar Nagar, UP with a capacity of 440 MW was set up in 1980–81 by the UP State Electricity Board (UPSEB) under the Government of UP. On 15 January 2000 the plant was transferred to NTPC under an agreement between the UP government and NTPC Limited. In 2009 NTPC decided to go for 'capacity expansion-cum-cost minimization' by acquiring land from nine adjoining villages, namely, Samariya, Husainpur Sudhana, Salarpur Rajpur, Keshopur Pachpokhra, Hasimpur, Sarifpur, Kakrahi, Ashopur and Ladanpur. The people who would be displaced by the land acquisition by NTPC had already been victims of repetitive displacement in different locations and were living in these villages since the last two decades. Initially, the small and marginal farmers who had no productive assets and those whose cultivable land was being adversely affected by the dumping of fly ash by the power plant circumscribing their land thereby creating negative externality, expressed their willingness to give up land in exchange of compensation. In addition, some of the households who had double settlement by housing and also some socially oppressed households expressed consent to give up their land. Later, following the agitation against land acquisition in the Agra-Mathura region in western UP for construction of an Expressway there was mass mobilization of affected people against land acquisition and in mid-2010 the potential victims became adamant not to give up their land. The affected persons in the targeted villages also formed an organization, namely, Kisan Mazdoor Sabha Samiti against the land acquisition. A virtual curfew was declared by the displaceable people in some of the targeted villages and the NTPC officials and the state authorities did not dare to enter them. At present, the state is in the process of negotiating the rate of compensation with the affected persons and has already applied its 'Urgency Clause' through a notification to acquire the land. The rate of compensation is expected to be fixed based on recent cases of land acquisition in affluent regions in the state of Uttar Pradesh (Majumder, 2011).

The land acquisition in Meja was successful because of the aspirations of the PAPs for the development of the region and consequently to have access to better physical infrastructure and alongside the possibility to get employment in the thermal plant and thus secure a better future. In the case of Dadri the PAPs initially failed to understand the gravity of the situation, and once understood took support from polity and subsequently the Judiciary to stop the land acquisition. In case of Tanda, the protest against land acquisition is still on.

A Critique of the State's Role

Since high growth via industrialization is urgent for operationalization of trickle down, the state first evicts people from land by its acquisition, makes them expendable and then catches them in the safety net. The objects caught in the net are never asked if they had the right to self-determination in the development map. The map is drawn and guarded by the state. It is arguable that the state historically followed similar measures for conversion of rural areas into urban areas in India and abroad. However, the extent of displacement is more acute today because of land scarcity relative to land area required for rehabilitation. In addition, in the 21st century the public response to the resulting dispossession and displacement is sharply different from earlier centuries chiefly because of the political democracy that empowers people to voice their dissent. This empowerment of the people is facilitated by the strong civil society and the vibrant mass media. The question of 'prior informed consent' that might have been not relevant earlier thus becomes relevant now. The state is now forced to take pre-emptive measures for those whom this very state took initiatives to throw out of the development trajectory by including them in the safety net of social welfare. The 2007 Land Acquisition Bill acknowledges that the acquisition of land leads to displacement of people, deprives them of their livelihood and shelter, restricts their access to their traditional resource base, and uproots them from their socio-cultural environment. Land acquisition would have traumatic, psychological and socio-cultural consequences for the affected population, which calls for protecting their rights, including those of the weaker sections of the society, particularly tribal people, and tenants. It is acknowledged that de facto, the 'persons interested' are the tribal people who generally do not possess any land records, the small and marginal farmers, the tenants and sharecroppers, the settled and migrant agricultural wage workers, and the women workers who collect food-fuel-fodder from the CPRs. However, none of these 'interested' persons are able to express their interest in the land because of their voicelessness and disempowerment. While the migrant agricultural workers living on the bottommost plank of the socio-economic hierarchy are disempowered by the new Bill by not being allowed to ask the District Collector for payment of any compensation when his employer's plot of land is taken away, the employer who is himself a small farmer is himself disempowered as his land is acquired. Alongside he has to wait in the queue for receiving compensation since the time period between acquisition and compensation is 60 days. The tribals and dalits (lower castes) who have lost their land are incapable of raising their voices for compensation equal to 30 per cent mark up of the prevailing market rate unless they are politically mobilized. Additionally, they are also evicted from access to CPRs, which has a major impact on their day to day living. The small and marginal farmers may feel shaky to move the Court and remain content with whatever cash compensation they are offered. Judiciary by its cobweb nature may itself be a trap for them. Fear factor works for the holders of petty property lest it is also lost in the process of bargaining and negotiating with the administrative authority. 'Public purpose' incorporated and interpreted by the state either gets camouflaged by 'silence of the displaced' or manifests itself in public response to land acquisition by protest. While 'silence' ensures easy implementation of the project by fixing the rate of money compensation from the player it is offered, protest is not prolonged in absence of political mobilization. The trade-off between the interests of the lightweight large public and the heavyweight few elite is weighted in favour of the latter.

Often the judiciary in India favours the development projects and the land acquisition and overrules the pleas of the affected persons as was observed in the case of Nand Kishore Gupta and Others vs. State of UP and Others (Writ Petition No. 31314 of 2009). In the judgment dated 30 November 2009 the court took the view that 'the scales of justice must tilt towards the right to development of the millions who will be benefited from the development of the area, as against the human rights of 35 petitioners therein, whose main complaint was that they were not heard before the declaration under Section 6 of the Act (Nand Kishore Gupta and Others vs. State of UP and Others, Civil Appeal No. 7468 of 2010). In the interest of development, hence, land acquisition from villages is an accepted proposition while living in villages and earning livelihood by cultivation is a losing proposition. The calculated trade off between development of the majority and human rights of the minority, in our understanding, is baffling. The baffle perhaps is solved by the observation that the concern of the state as the governing entity and the concern of the governed society are not necessarily synonymous. The state represents the ideology of the dominant political society and camouflages it by the declaration of a 'democratic republic'. State remains strong internally by imposition of laws it formulates for non-or-restricted access of the original settlers in forests and on land who are the initial insiders to the resources. State is strengthened as a protector of forests and land. On the other hand, state has a tendency to allow private capital to extract and convert natural resources, including land, into consumable goods for the mainstream. The sections that are considered not-in-the-mainstream at present constituted the original stream in the past. These constituents of the original stream were the tribal people and the dalits who distanced themselves from the institution of private property understood by 'excludability'. The sections are now evicted who protected these resources as the life-support system since pre-history not backed by any state laws. By acquisition of land, collective social ownership-cum-use is surrendered – what gets supreme is state authority.

Land carries dual meaning by uses by the people. Land essentially has precautionary value as opposed to immediate exchange value to its holders. For the state, land (including mining) is a resource for conversion into commodities for growth measured by gross domestic product. In view of the affected people, it is displacement and loss of livelihood. The ultimate decision-maker is the state that calculates the costs and benefits of land acquisition. Even if the outcome of the industrialization initiatives by the state is positive by accelerating growth, the time span between displacement and the final gross domestic product (GDP) outcome is long and displacement is often repetitive to lead to misery of many. Stagnation or decline of the village economy in India is also put forward as an argument for the dispossession of the village income-poor, which remains questionable (Bannerjee-Guha, 2010: 221). In an inter-generational frame, the successors of land may like to move out for a number of reasons like education-linked attractive urban life and living, opportunity to be engaged in higher wage earning occupations delinked from land, etc. This voluntary migration or mobility is different from displacement that is involuntary by nature.

The fact is that state is not the owner of natural resources. State can at best be the custodian of natural resources that belong to the people. State as an institution is itself accountable to the nation. State can show the guiding principles how the resources are to be conserved by optimal use and if needed preserved for future by non-use at present. In fact, land resources have not only use value and exchange value but also non-use value.

Safeguards in Land Acquisition for Industrialization: Some Suggestions

The state usually aims for vertical measures like constructing flyovers for surface transport, tunnels underground for metro rail and tube rail in cities so that buildings and other assets possessed by the urbane civil society, both public and private, are not affected. In the rural areas, however, the state goes for horizontal expansion by acquisition of private and collective cultivable land, which entails the eviction of people from their natural surroundings. The displacement that follows land acquisition destroys the inherited skills or indigenous knowledge of the people, destroys inter-generational social relations shaped over generations, imposes Social Darwinism by the state, empowers industrial capitalists by enhancing their unhindered access to natural resources, converts marginal and small landowners into manual labour-based wage workers, expands labour size in informal sector, and imposes forced migration to urban areas. In spite of these effects we accept that there is no alternative to industrialization for the long-run development of India and in order to ensure that the process does not result in misery for the project-affected persons we offer the following safeguards for state-led land acquisition. The proposed safeguards aim at minimizing the loss of livelihood that immediately follows the displacement by land acquisition:

- The 1894 Land Acquisition Act should be repealed because it was enacted in the interest of the colonial government.
- The farmers relying on self-production of food grains for family consumption should be exempted from giving up land under distress.
- The target for land acquisition by the state has to be the absentee landlords, the land owners with 'distress-free' double settlement and the big landowners. The land that remains idle as estate and in fictitious name should be acquired.
- The state has to select barren land far from human settlement for acquisition for industrialization. Accurate measurement of land by area for acquisition is needed to get rid of excess idle land post-acquisition.
- There has to be pre-project participation of people of the going-to-be affected zone as equal partners in the decision-making processes in 'public interest'.
- Land acquisition for industrial purposes has to minimize deforestation, diminishing water table, emission of gas and other health hazards.
- The real resources of a country are land, rivers, mines, forests, the coastal belt, and above all, the people. A national Resource Protection Policy has to be formulated by the state to preserve these resources.
- The people unsettled in the rural region by land acquisition have to be economically rehabilitated within a reasonable radius through employment programmes.
- CPRs lost have to be re-created at the site of rehabilitation.
- There has to be national land census on a regular basis. All land records have to be computerized and put on website.
- There has to be a land rights commission (LRC) to work as a vigilant over the activities of the government so far as land market is concerned.
- The corporate sector as the beneficiary of land acquisition has to shoulder corporate social responsibility (CSR) by adoption of one or a cluster of rehabilitation zones.

- The compensation has to cover land price post-acquisition plus the cost of surrendering domestic animals and other productive assets plus the cost for surrendered opportunity to have access to common space (CPRs) plus the cost for security loss.
- The technique for land acquisition has to be culturally conditioned, politically suited and economically feasible.

For those displaced by land acquisition, the government should in a time-bound manner

- ensure food security by provision of BPL (below poverty line) cards to the displaced families,
- ensure re-schooling of displaced children,
- open up vocational institutions at the resettlement site for the displaced, alternatively, arrange cost-free entry of eligible youth from the displaced families into nearby vocational institutions,
- develop physical infrastructure at the rehabilitation zone,
- develop cooperatives for the displaced potential entrepreneurs for credit with no property mortgage,
- provide low-cost rural housing along with animal shed to the displaced at the resettlement site, and
- ensure security, particularly of displaced women, in the new location.

Overall, in addition to a National Policy on Land Acquisition that incorporates an implementable R&R programme, there has to be regional planning within the national economy in advance for industrialization.

Acknowledgement

I thank M.G. Gupta, Tinku Paul, G.N. Jha, S. Jaiswal and A. Singh for the field work. The usual disclaimer applies.

References

Bannerjee-Guha, S. (2010). 'Revisiting Accumulation by Dispossession: Neoliberalizing Mumbai', in Bannerjee-Guha (ed.), *Accumulation by Dispossession*, New Delhi: Sage Publications.

Bhaduri, Amit (2007). 'Alternatives in Industrialization', *Economic and Political Weekly*, 5 May, pp. 1597–601.

Chakrabarti, A. and A. Dhar (2010). *Dislocation and Resettlement in Development: From Third World to the World of the Third*, London and New York: Routledge.

Deane, P. (1984). *The First Industrial Revolution*, Cambridge: Cambridge University Press.

Fernandes, W. (2007). 'Singur and the Displacement Scenario', *Economic and Political Weekly*, Vol. 42, No. 3, 20 January, pp. 203–06.

Fernandes, W., J.C. Das and S. Rao (1989). *Displacement and Rehabilitation: An Estimate of Extent and Prospects*, New Delhi: Indian Social Institute.

Government of India (GoI), Ministry of Rural Development (1996). 'Draft National Policy for Rehabilitation of Persons', *Economic and Political Weekly*, Vol. 31, No. 24, 15 June, pp. 1541–45.

Government of India (GoI), The Land Acquisition Act (1894). As amended up to 1985.

Karve, D.D. (1961). 'The Diversionists', *The Economic Weekly*, 1 July, pp. 977–78.

Kitay, M.G. (1985). *Land Acquisition in Developing Countries*, Boston: Lincoln Institute of Land Policy.

Lobo, L. and S. Kumar (2009). *Land Acquisition, Displacement and Resettlement in Gujarat, 1947–2004*, New Delhi: Sage Publications.

Lok Sabha (2007). The Land Acquisition (Amendment) Bill, 2007, Bill No. 97 of 2007.

Magill, F.N. (Ed.) (1997). *International Encyclopedia of Economics*, Vols I and II, London: Fitzroy Dearborn Publishers.

Majumder, Bhaskar (2007). *Development Hydra: Two Cases of Forced Industrialization in India*, Report submitted to G.B. Pant Social Science Institute, Allahabad, India (Mimeo).

—— (2008). 'Forced Industrialization and Workers' Struggle: Some Recent Evidences from India', *Indian Journal of Labour Economics*, Vol. 51, No. 4, October–December, pp. 1001–14.

—— (2009). *Socio-Economic Survey for Meja Urja Nigam Pvt. Ltd.*, Report submitted to Meja Urja Nigam Pvt. Ltd., Allahabad, December.

—— (2010). 'Social Justice in Economic Perspective: Displacement of People by Land Acquisition for Industrialization in India', *Journal of Social and Political Studies*, Vol. 1, No. 1, December, pp. 82–96.

—— (2011). *Socio-Economic Survey (SES) for NTPC-Tanda, Stage-II*, Report submitted to Tanda Thermal Power Project, Ambedkar Nagar, Uttar Pradesh, March.

Marx, K. (2006). 'The Future Results of the British Rule in India', in P. James and D. Phillip (eds), *Globalization and Violence*, Vol. 2, London: Sage Publications.

Nanekar, K.R. and S.V. Khandewale (1973). *Bhoodan and the Landless*, Bombay: Popular Prakashan.

Nayyar, D. (2002). 'Cross-border Movements of People', in Nayyar (ed.), *Governing Globalization: Issues and Institutions*, New Delhi: Oxford University Press.

Plum, W. (1977). *Industrialization and Mass Poverty: Points from Two Centuries of Debate* (Translated from German by Lux Furtmuller), Bonn, Federal Republic of Germany: Friedrich-Ebert-Stiftung.

Rangarajan, L.N. (1992). *The Arthashastra*, New Delhi: Penguin Books.

Sarkar, A. (2007). 'Development and Displacement: Land Acquisition in West Bengal', *Economic and Political Weekly*, 21 April, pp. 1435–42.

Sharma, R.N. (2003). 'Involuntary Displacement: A Few Encounters', *Economic and Political Weekly*, Vol. 38, No. 9, 1 March, pp. 907–12.

Sharma, R.N. and S.R. Singh (2009). 'Displacement in Singrauli Region: Entitlements and Rehabilitation', *Economic and Political Weekly*, Vol. 44, No. 51, pp. 62–69.

Supreme Court of India, Judgment (2010). Civil Appeal No. 7468 of 2010 (Nand Kishore Gupta and Others vs State of UP and Others).

Part II

Displacement under 'Eminent Domain'

3

Impact of Displacement on the Tribes

WALTER FERNANDES

India lacks a database on the number of persons displaced (DPs) or deprived of livelihood without physical relocation (PAPs) since 1947 in the name of national development and on their rehabilitation. One estimate puts the number of DP-PAPs at 60 million between 1947–2000 in India as a whole, around 40 per cent of them tribal who are a little over 8 per cent of the population. Its main reason is that they live in resource-rich regions. The argument given is that these riches should be used for the whole country. Even if one were to accept this stand one cannot accept their impoverishment and marginalization as intrinsic to national development. In reality that is a major consequence. It is caused mainly by the legal status of their land. The Land Acquisition Act, 1894 that allows displacement without rehabilitation recognizes only individual ownership while much of their land is common property resources (CPRs). The decision-makers who deprive them of their sustenance without their consent fail to understand their culture. The combination of these factors makes it difficult for them to begin life anew once they are alienated from their livelihood. These aspects are true of all the communities but are particularly so about the tribes and dalits, particularly women, because of their already disadvantaged state. Thus, the tribes are paying a high price of development but get very few of its benefits. This paper is an effort to study the impacts and search for possible solutions.

The Extent of Tribal Displacement

In the absence of an official database on displacement, rehabilitation and of land used for development projects, one has to depend on the studies that have been done till now. They show that the tribal proportion among the DP-PAPs is higher than their percentage in the population. It is even of states where their number is small. For example, in Kerala and Karnataka they are a little over 1 per cent of the population but they are a majority in major irrigation projects like Idukki (Murickan et al., 2003). Table 1 gives the number of DP-PAPs based on studies done till now in 13 out of India's 28 states. They have a total 20.42 million DP-PAPs but they do not include high displacement states of Madhya Pradesh, Maharashtra and Chhattisgarh. In Odisha, Andhra Pradesh, Assam, West Bengal and Tripura only around 80 per cent of the data could be accessed and in Mizoram, Jharkhand and Meghalaya it was around 60 per cent. Revenue commons were not available in Sikkim so their DP-PAPs are not included. Extrapolation based on updating these studies and on case studies from states where studies have not been done, brings one to 60 million DP-PAPs between 1947–2000 (Fernandes et al., 2012: 17).

What is said of India as a whole is doubly true of its North-East where four of the seven states have a tribal majority. Studies are yet to be completed in Arunachal Pradesh and Manipur. The remaining five tribal states DP-PAPs are 989,432 out of 2,468,674 (40.08%). But they are 63.04 per cent of the 1,569,534 DP-PAPs whose caste-tribe is known. There are indications that more than 50 per cent of the DP-PAPs whose caste-tribe is not known in Assam and Tripura are tribal. So their real proportion in the five states studied is more than 70 per cent. In the rest of India, 5,259,144 (29.34%) of the 17,891,960 DP-PAPs are tribal but they are 33.51 per cent of the 15,693,956 whose caste-tribe is known. There are indications that some 30 per cent of the DP-PAPs of West Bengal whose caste-tribe is not known are tribal. Tribe was not recorded in Kerala but one knows that its biggest projects like Idukki are in its tribal areas and have a tribal majority. So more than 10 per cent of Kerala's DP-PAPs are bound to be tribal. Probably a majority of the 2,198,004 DP-PAPs whose caste-tribe is not known are tribal. Moreover, Arunachal Pradesh, Chhattisgarh, Manipur, Madhya Pradesh, Maharashtra where studies have not been done, have a big tribal proportion. As stated above, even where studies

Table 1

Caste-Tribe of DP-PAPs from Some States with Tribal Percentage in 2001

State	*Tribal*	*per cent*	*Dalits*	*per cent*	*Others*	*per cent*	*NA*	*per cent*	*Total*	*Tribal %*
Andhra Pradesh	970654	30.19	628824	19.56	1467286	45.63	148856	04.63	3215620	6.6
Assam	424253	22.14	NA	NA	609509	31.81	882323	46.05	1916085	12.4
Goa	NA	NA	NA	NA	NA	NA	66820	100	66820	0
Gujarat	1821283	44.43	462626	11.29	1791142	43.70	23818	0.58	4098869	14.8
Jharkhand	620372	40.08	212892	13.75	676575	43.71	38178	02.47	1548017	26.3
Kerala	NA	NA	NA	NA	NA	NA	552233	100	552233	1.1
Meghalaya	110258	100	0	0	0	0	0	0	110258	85.9
Mizoram	200139	100	0	0	0	0	0	0	200139	94.5
Nagaland	62,675	100	0	0	0	0	0	0	62675	89.1
Odisha	616116	40.38	178442	11.64	671351	48.01	0	0	1465909	22.1
Sikkim	20178	36.14	1190	2.13	25720	40.79	8747	15.66	55835	22.0
Tripura	100195	56.66	20518	11.60	NA	NA	56082	31.72	176795	31.1
West Bengal	1330663	19.16	1689607	24.33	2566223	36.95	1357999	19.55	6944492	5.5
Total	6276786	30.75	3194099	15.65	7807806	38.25	3135056	15.36	20413747	8.2

Source: AP, Fernandes et al., 2001: 88; Assam, Fernandes and Bharali, 2011: 218; Goa, Fernandes and Naik, 2001: 57; Gujarat, Lobo and Kumar, 2009: 109; Jharkhand, Ekka and Asif, 2000: 87; Kerala, Muricken et al., 2003: 203; Odisha, Fernandes and Asif, 1997: 94; West Bengal, Fernandes et al., 2012: 237; Meghalaya, Mizoram and Tripura, Fernandes and Bharali, 2010: 90; Nagaland and Sikkim: Fernandes et al., 2011: 85 and 100.

were done, only 60 to 80 per cent of the data could be accessed. Once the studies are updated and all the DP-PAPs are counted, the tribal proportion is bound to reach 40 per cent of the estimated 60 million DP-PAPs in India as a whole (Fernandes, 2008: 93–94).

Tribal Land and Displacement

The abundance of resources in their habitats is basic to their high proportion among the DP-PAPs. The areas they inhabit account for some 70 per cent of coal, 45 per cent of iron ore, 80 per cent of bauxite, 100 per cent of mica and a high proportion of other minerals (Areeparampil, 1996: 6). That the Government of India is aware of it is seen in the opening statement of the second draft of the national rehabilitation policy. It says that with the new economic policy of 1991, i.e., liberalization, 'It is expected that there will be large scale investments, both on account of internal generation of capital and increased inflow of foreign investments, thereby creating an enhanced demand for land to be provided within a shorter time span in an increasingly competitive market ruled economic structure. Majority of our mineral resources are located in the remote and backward areas mostly inhabited by tribals' (MoRD, 1994: 1.1–2).

Equally important is the legal status of their land. Much of their sustenance is CPRs but the colonial land laws that continue to be in force even today recognizing only individual ownership. That also explains why most official figures are underestimates. For example, by official count Assam displaced 343,262 persons between 1947–2000 from 159,017.37 hectares (390,302 acres) used for development projects. In reality the state had not less than 19.1 lakh DP-PAPs from 14.1 lakh acres but it had counted only private land acquired through gazette notifications (Fernandes and Bharali, 2011: 107). Individual projects too show this difference. For example, by official count the Hirakud dam in Odisha displaced 110,000 persons in the 1950s (Government of Odisha, 1968). But researchers put their number at 180,000 (Pattanaik, Das and Mishra, 1987). Most of those who were not counted are tribal DP-PAPs inhabiting the CPRs that were their habitat for centuries before the colonial land laws turned them into state property. Their inhabitants thus became encroachers on land that they had inhabited for centuries (Ramanathan, 2008: 29–30). They were, therefore, 'evicted', not displaced under this law so they were not even counted among the DP-PAPs.

This anomaly can be better understood from Table 2 on the type of land used. The commons are high in states with a high tribal proportion. For example, in Odisha 22 per cent of the population is tribal and 58.19 of the land used for projects 1951–95 is commons. It includes 30.2 per cent forests that are tribal habitat. Not surprisingly. 40.38 per cent of its DP-PAPs are tribal. In Assam, only the 159,205.14 hectares recognized by the state as used for development projects between 1947–2000 are private and 55.71 per cent is commons. The legal status of 16.23 per cent is not known but there are indications that most of it is commons. Not surprisingly, tribals who are 12.4 per cent of the population are 40.6 per cent of the DP-PAPs whose caste-tribe is known.

Because of the role of the commons some states even changed the laws deliberately to facilitate tribal land takeover. For example, the Tripura Land Revenue and Land Reforms Act, 1960 (TLR&LRA) was enacted in order to facilitate tribal land acquisition to rehabilitate the more than 8,00,000 East Pakistani refugees and immigrants who had entered Tripura during the preceding decade. The Act recognized only individual registered land. Most tribal communities being illiterate and not familiar with the formal law did not register their land. The law in its turn did not recognize their right over the CPRs that were their sustenance for centuries. So their habitat became state property under the law based on the colonial principle of individual ownership (Deb Barma, 2009: 120–21).

More of their CPRs were acquired for other projects. For example, the Dumbur dam built in the 1970s counted 2,558 *patta* owning families as displaced and ignored 5,500 to 6,000 CPR dependent families (Bhaumik, 2003: 84). Because of the influx of East Pakistani refugees immediately after the partition and of immigrants later its tribal proportion that was more than 70 per cent in 1941 declined to 58 per cent in 1951 and 31 per cent in 2001. But they are 83 per cent of the 120,717 DP-PAPs between 1947 and 2000 whose caste-tribe is known. The caste-tribe of 56,111 DP-PAPs is not known (Fernandes and Bharali, 2010: 90). In Mizoram and Meghalaya, the proportion of the commons is low because of poor record keeping and because their land classification is different from that of the formal law. So it is not easy to record their sustenance in the language of the formal law (Nongkynrih, 2009: 34–35). As a result, much of the land they lost is not counted.

Table 2

Extent and Proportion of Private and Common Land Used (hectares)

State	*Private*	*Per cent*	*Common*	*Per cent*	*Forest*	*Per cent*	*NA*	*Per cent*	*Total*
Andhra Pradesh	684725.10	67.99	255077.73	25.33	67362.75	06.69	00	00	1007166.59
Assam	159205.14	28.06	316041.66	55.71	92034.49	16.23	567281.29		
Goa	12649.74	77.85	2880.00	17.72	720.00	04.43	00	00	16249.74
Gujarat	3126527.00	61.54	312653.00	6.15	1641427.00	32.31	00	00	5080607.00
Jharkhand	344952.75	55.11	141226.07	22.56	139710.67	22.32	00	00	625889.49
Kerala	66759.25	43.00	1222.32	0.79	40673.62	26.20	46608.33	30.02	155263.52
Meghalaya	43685.69	58.81	8022.07	10.80	22492.37	30.28	74200.13		
Mizoram	3471.11	16.48	1712.48	8.14	15874.42	75.38	21058.01		
Nagaland	1353.56	5.26	15985.47	61.97	1762.58	6.82	6668.50	25.92	25770.11
Odisha	399859.05	41.81	264648.15	27.99	288845.85	30.20	00	00	953353.05
Sikkim	47031.62	95.16	NA	NA	2184.67	4.84	00	00	49216.29
Tripura	51177.40	60.38	27762.45	32.76	5811.81	6.86	84751.66		
West Bengal	1600404.86	82.98	328340.08	17.02	00	00	1928745.94		
Total	6541802.27	62.23	3780529.48	35.96	189489.92	1.80	10511821.67		

* The forest-common revenue land division could not be got fully in Assam, Meghalaya, Mizoram and West Bengal. So the two are put together under common land.

Source: As in Table 1. Revenue commons not available in Sikkim.

Tribal land loss is much higher after liberalization. The statement of the Government of India that there would be more land takeover than in the past and that much of it would be in the tribal areas has turned out to be true. Much common land mostly tribal livelihood has been acquired during the last two decades or is planned to be acquired. The private sector is eyeing mining land in Jharkhand, Odisha and Chhattisgarh. Forty-eight mega-dams are being planned in the North-East during the present decade and more of them later. Most of the land they use will be tribal commons. So there will be more displacement than in the last 60 years, much of it tribal (IWGIA, 2004: 314).

Impact on the Tribes

The change of use in tribal land is bound to have many impacts on the tribal communities. Land in their economy is their sustenance, not primarily a commodity. So its loss forces them to change their lifestyle from their community based informal society to an individual based formal system. Most DP-PAPs, tribal in particular, belong to the informal sector and are not much in touch with the formal society and economy. Land loss pushes them without a transition into the new society with no preparation for the new society, economy and culture. In other words, the individual-based land that is used to acquire their land, changes their livelihood into a commodity that is valued at the market price. It deprives them of all rights over the CPRs by declaring that only individually owned land has value because it can be bought and sold at a market price. To facilitate the transfer of their sustenance to another class, the law thus turns their CPRs into state property, the people into encroachers and enables the state to 'evict' them from their sustenance with no respect for their future (Ramanathan, 2008: 31). By changing the nature of their sustenance the law denies them right to a life with dignity under Article 21 of the Constitution which is on right to life. The Supreme Court has interpreted it as every citizen's right to a life with dignity (Vaswani, 1992: 158). Their displacement is thus an attack on tribal culture and sustenance.

The attack on their livelihood begins from the moment a decision is taken to build a project because the assessment of their sustenance is based on the principle of individual ownership. For example, officials claim that the proposed Lower Subansiri dam in

Arunachal will submerge two villages and displace 38 families. One is aware of at least 12 more villages to be affected. The state insists that the 38 families will be rehabilitated on a land for land basis according to the state rehabilitation policy promulgated by the chief minister at the Independence Day celebrations on 15 August 2008. 'Land for land' according to it will be one hectare per family (*The Assam Tribune,* 17 August 2008). Ignored is the fact that the families to be deprived of livelihood are *jhum* cultivators using community land. In Lower Subansiri, for example, the 38 families counted by the project authorities cultivate 986 hectares of CPRs but they will be allotted only one hectare each. Jhum cultivation is not possible on it. By resettling them on one hectare each, the project is pushing them into settled agriculture with no preparation for the change of lifestyle (Menon, 2009: 133–36).

The situation of the DP-PAPs gets worse when no rehabilitation package exists. Till 2004 India did not even have a rehabilitation policy. A very poor quality policy was promulgated in 2004. The new one promulgated in 2007 made only marginal changes. The Land Acquisition Act, 1894 which is the enabling legislation for land takeover requires the displacing agency to compensate *patta* land but not to rehabilitate even individual owners. As a result, the resettlement ranges from 35 per cent in Goa to 9 per cent in West Bengal and is almost non-existent in the North-East (Fernandes et al., 2012: 20). That too applies only to individual land owners and ignores the CPR dependants. Absence of a policy or law is not the only reason for poor resettlement. The fact that most DP-PAPs are powerless may be a better explanation. Forty per cent of the estimated 60 million DP-PAPs are tribal, 20 per cent are dalit. Information from projects where data on the OBCs could be gathered shows that the weakest among them like fish and quarry workers form another 20 per cent of the DP-PAPs (Fernandes, 2008: 94–95). The fact that 80 per cent of them are voiceless may explain both the absence of a policy or law and poor resettlement.

These figures refer to resettlement, not to rehabilitation. Resettlement is one-time physical relocation with or without other economic, social and cultural support. Only the DPs need it but also the PAPs need rehabilitation which is a long process meant to help them to re-establish the livelihood lost. It requires replacement or rebuilding of their economic resources, cultural systems, social structures and community support mechanisms. It has to deal with the problems that begin as soon as a decision about a project is taken and continue for some years after resettlement. Long before the notification on land acquisition is issued merchants, moneylenders and the elite of the community who have access to more information than the ordinary people do, spread rumours in the area to be affected by the project in order to frighten the people into selling their land to them at a low price. When the state acquires it those who buy the land declare them DPs and get the benefits due to the original owners. That excludes even many individual owners from the powerless categories from the list of DPs. Those who survive this stage face other hurdles. Bank loans and development projects stop. The people to be deprived of their assets are prevented from cultivating the land earmarked for acquisition. That causes much insecurity among them and weakens the bond between the people and their sustenance. Slowly they internalize the concept of land as a commodity and begin to steal or cut trees because they see no future in it as sustenance. A sense of powerlessness and fatalism that overtakes many of them at this stage continues at the subsequent stages of identifying assets, fixing compensation, displacement and beyond it (Fernandes and Bharali, 2011: 253–68).

Lack of preparation ensures that the tribal, dalit and other subaltern DP-PAPs get no benefits. They get very few jobs and the ones they get are usually of a poor quality. Even for such jobs they have to make a transition from an agricultural routine to an industrial culture. Since they are not trained for the changeover many of them lose the job because of lack of punctuality or drunkenness (Viegas, 1992). The former is a result of lack of preparation. The latter is a coping mechanism meant to deal with the trauma of forced displacement. This combination ensures that they are unable to adapt themselves to the new environment. Land given to them is often of poor quality and they cannot sustain themselves on it. The combination of poor quality land and facilities and lack of training to deal with the new society enhances their trauma of forced displacement. As a result, very few DP-PAPs are rehabilitated even when resettled. Most of them are impoverished because the assets lost to the project are not replaced. Since these assets that are the basis of their economy, culture, social systems and identity are not rebuilt their resettlement does not result in rehabilitation.

Impoverishment as an Impact

Impoverishment and marginalization result from displacement and poor rehabilitation particularly of the powerless. Impoverishment is change in their economic status because of the project, not the state of poverty prior to it. A few PAPs from the better off sections living in 'advanced' districts may improve their lifestyle by getting a somewhat high compensation for their not very fertile land. But most tribal and dalit DP-PAPs are impoverished and also experience a deterioration of their cultural and social status. Impoverishment that begins with landlessness is followed by joblessness, lower income, and poor access to health, homelessness and malnutrition. For example, the 594 land loser families studied in Meghalaya, Mizoram and Tripura owned a total of 2,655.89 acres of *patta* land and 460.94 acres of CPRs and cultivated an average of 5.25 acres per family prior to the project. After the project *patta* land came down to 1,659.54 acres and commons to 162.44 acres or a total of 1,821.98 at an average of 3.07 acres. Private land declined by 37.52 per cent and commons by 64.76 per cent (Fernandes and Bharali, 2010: 103–04). Also other states studied show a greater decline in CPRs than private land ownership. Also the average area owned declines. For example, the proportion of the landless in Assam rose from 15.56 to 24.38 per cent but the average area declined from 3.04 to 1.45 acres per family. Most small and marginal farmers became landless and medium farmers became small and marginal farmers. Also support mechanisms like ponds, wells, poultry, cattle and draft animals that supplement agricultural income declined. Landlessness is higher among the tribals (ibid., 2011: 244–49).

The next step is joblessness because the land lost provided work to them. The project deprives them of that work but gives a job to very few DP-PAPs. For example, out of 266,500 displaced or deprived families studied in Odisha, the projects gave a job each to about 9,000. No job was given in Goa and very few in Kerala. West Bengal gave a job each to about 20 per cent of the displaced families of the 1950s and very few after it (Fernandes et al., 2011: 201). In Assam three projects gave some jobs and five resettled the DPs (Fernandes and Bharali, 2011). The resultant joblessness takes two forms. The first is lower access to work and the second is downward occupational mobility. Access to work declines by around 50 per cent in most states from around 90 per cent to around 45 per cent. Downward occupational mobility takes the form of around half of the cultivators who continue to have work becoming landless agricultural labourers or daily wage earners. In every case the decline is greater among the tribal and Dalit DP-PAPs than among the others. In Assam and West Bengal more than 60 per cent of them lost access to work (Fernandes, 2008: 93–94).

Liberalization has added to joblessness. The International Labour Organization estimates that 12 million jobs were lost in India during the first six years of liberalization (VAK Team, 1997: 167). Mechanization is one of its main reasons and its impact is visible, among others, in the coalmines. The average size of a mine rose from 150 acres in the 1970s to 800 in the 1990s (Fernandes and Asif, 1997: 74–75) and has risen further to 1,500 acres today. But they created fewer jobs. For example, Coal India gave a job each to 11,901 (36.34%) of the 32,751 families it displaced in 1981–85 (Government of India, 1985). After mechanization in the mid-1980s it began to transfer workers to other mines instead of giving jobs to new DPs. Moreover, most skilled jobs go to outsiders since very few land losers, even medium farmers have the skills that they require. For example, data from the Ministry of Commerce, Government of India show that with an investment of ₹ 100,000 crores on 400,000 acres the first few special economic zones (SEZs) created 500,000 jobs till 2006. That comes to an average of ₹ 20 lakhs per job. Studies show that on an average an acre of agricultural land provides work to two persons. The 4,00,000 acres would thus have been sustaining 8,00,000 persons. By creating 5,00,000 jobs the SEZs deprived 3,00,000 persons of work. Moreover, the peasants displaced by them lack the skills that the mechanized jobs require. So most jobs went to outsiders (Thakur, 2007). Despite Article 21 on right to a life with dignity the steps leading to land acquisition reduce these independent workers to the status of cheap labour.

That is the case of the relatively powerful medium and big farmers who are able to make their voice heard as one saw in Uttar Pradesh. Because of their agitation the Government of India promised a new Land Acquisition Act within a few months. But, the tribes of Niyamgiri in Odisha had to struggle for many years before the sanction of the project was withdrawn on environmental grounds, not because of loss of their livelihood. The tribals of Kalinganagar in

Odisha had to face state repression in the form of the police opening fire and killing 12 of them on 2 January 2006. In the North-East most persons to be displaced by the major dams are tribals. Their protests are ignored and the state goes ahead with the dams.

Marginalization as an Impact

Impoverishment is the first step. It is followed by marginalization particularly of the powerless like the tribes. Marginalization is deterioration of their social, cultural and psychological status. By depriving the powerless communities of their land, forests and other resources that are the centre of their economy, culture and identity the project dispossesses them of their cultural heritage, spiritual beliefs, history, legends and myths and disrupts their traditional lifestyle, social networks and cultural practices (Pamei, 2001). Since no alternative is provided to the social, cultural and psychological support that the commons used to provide them they are pushed with no preparation from their semi-monetized economy into the powerful formal economy and society. Unable to resist its imposition they internalize the commercial culture that accompanies it (Gaventa, 1980: 7–9).

That results in the development of a low self-image. Every step of land acquisition contributes to it. The state acquires their resources without their consent or a share in the decision concerning their survival. That confirms some of them in their self-image of being incapable of taking their own decisions. If they did not have a low self-image prior to it these steps create it in them. Its impact has already been alluded to. When they get no information about the threat of land loss, the powerful groups including their own elite use their ignorance to spread rumours and buy that land at a low price and later declare themselves DPs and get all the benefits meant for them. Knowledge is power. By keeping it away from the people the project renders the already weak further powerless. The insecurity and helplessness it creates results in fatalism and reduces their motivation for progress (Good, 1996: 1505). The denial of compensation confirms them in their low self-image because the law does not respect their livelihood and by implication their right to a life with dignity. The *patta* land losers are paid a meagre compensation in the 'backward' areas and the CPR dependants are evicted even without that meagre compensation. Their land ceases to be their sustenance and becomes only a commodity to be sold and bought at the market price. The CPR dependants who have least assets are dispossessed of the little they own without alternatives. Some even think that the project goes deliberately in search of the commons or the 'backward' areas in order to reduce its investment by paying very low compensation or none at all (Singh, 1989: 96).

Those DP-PAPs thus come face to face with the dominant society in a state of disarray and crisis. This unequal encounter with the 'advanced' society confirms them in their feeling of helplessness and fatalism. Mechanization and labour-saving devices add to their low self-image both because their traditional techniques are ignored and because the technology used is not accessible to them. Lack of rehabilitation and its poor quality confirm it. Its nature and extent depend on power relations in the area or in the community. Some of them respond to it through violence as one sees in so many tribal struggles for protecting their sustenance. Niyamgiri in Odisha, the army test range in Jharkhand and the Dumbur dam in Tripura are among its examples. The Dumbur dam in Tripura was announced after the tribes had lost 20 to 40 per cent of their land to the East Pakistani immigrants. They resisted the project but it was implemented and the unrest in that state began after it (Bhaumik, 2003: 85). Even the resettlement package can add to low self-image if it is viewed as welfare, not as a right.

The combination of lack of respect for their livelihood and low compensation thus confirm them in their low self-image. The remaining inputs devalue their culture and social life, treat them as people without rights and their sustenance as commodity. These steps give them the message that they and their sustenance are dispensable commodities. Cultural changes add to it. For example, the tribal tradition treated forests and the rest of their sustenance as renewable resources that had come down from their ancestors, meant to be used according to present needs and environmental imperatives and preserved for posterity. Shortages after their loss weaken that culture. For sheer survival they overexploit the resource by cutting trees for sale as firewood or as labourers of timber contractors and smugglers and through other abuses. This change symbolizes loss of hope in their future. They can think only of the present and cannot preserve the resources for the next generation. That results in further impoverishment and loss of the social and psychological infrastructure that had sustained them till then. They internalize an ideology of their sustenance being a commodity or a source of income and their community being incapable of developing itself (Fernandes, 2008: 101).

Women and Children Worst Hit

Even these impacts are felt more by women and children than by men. Alcohol is the coping mechanism of many men and its result is a rise in domestic violence. Both drinking and wife beating did exist in the past. But drunkenness as a coping mechanism increases domestic violence. A majority of tribal women in Assam and Odisha mentioned more drinking and violence than in the past as a major problem they faced (Fernandes and Bharali, 2011: 315–17). One understands it better when one realizes that tribal women enjoyed a slightly higher social status than women in caste societies did. But no tribe treated them as equal to men. That relatively high status was linked to their land and forests. As long as their sustenance was community owned, women had some decision-making power since in most tribal societies they were in charge of the family. These resources were thus the locus of their work that made them economic assets. That was the foundation of their relatively high social status. When the project alienates the resources from them, women lose access to work but do not get access to work in the project. But for exceptions, tribal women who want to work are forced to take up low paid unskilled daily wage jobs. Others are reduced to being housewives alone living on the man's single salary. However, they have to continue to play their role of providers of the family even after losing the resources (Thukral and Singh, 1995).

Tribal women resort to three coping mechanisms to deal with these changes. The first is to treat their sustenance as a commodity. As stated above the communities that had till then treated the natural resources as renewable, begin to destroy them as a source of income for sheer survival. The second is change of attitude towards children. In the absence of alternatives, 56 per cent of the displaced families in Assam and 49 per cent in West Bengal pulled their children out of school or did not send them to school in order to turn them into child labourers to earn an income for the family. The proportion of such children was more than 75 per cent among the tribal DP-PAPs. The third is a new view of women's bodies. Many women cope with their impoverishment by earning some income to maintain their families by selling their bodies. Prostitution grows enormously among displaced women in general and tribal women in particular (Fernandes and Bharali, 2011: 318–20). These coping mechanisms can be summarized as internalization of the dominant ideology. The renewable natural resources are treated as a commodity for present income. Children cease to be providers of future livelihood. They as well as women's bodies are used as sources of present income. Thus the DP-PAPs internalize the commercial value system as a source of survival.

Equally important is internalization of the upper caste ideology of women being fit only for the home. That legitimizes the new roles assigned to them. For example, the project employs a few men as maintenance staff in the office and some women try to supplement that income by doing unskilled work in the mines or as domestic helps. However, many such men internalize the dominant value of women's subjugation and of their improved social status and object to their wives doing domestic or other unskilled work because 'it is against an office worker's dignity to have his wife doing menial work' (Menon, 1995: 105). In many cases tribal women too internalize the dominant ideology of their subordination. Around two-thirds of the displaced tribal women interviewed in Odisha and many in Assam and West Bengal said that women's place is in the kitchen or that they are not intelligent enough for skilled work (Fernandes, 2008: 101). Internalization of dominant values by the subalterns is essential to maintain an unjust society. No unequal society can survive without the subalterns internalizing the dominant ideology (Gaventa, 1980: 27–30). Tribal men accept these values when they come face to face with the formal society with a different value system, by beginning to believe that they are incapable of being active economic agents. Tribal children are forced to accept it by becoming child labourers and depriving themselves of a better future. In the process they internalize the ideology that they are made only for a life as labourers. The whole tribe internalizes the ideology of the natural resources being not the centre of their social system and identity but only a commodity. Women are the worst victims of the cultural changes based on an economic model to which they are only commodities (Bharali, 2009).

Conclusion

This paper is a bird's eye view of the impact of displacement on the DP-PAPs in general and on the tribes in particular. Their proportion among the DP-PAPs is higher than their share in the population. They live in resource rich regions. These resources are monopolized for the benefit of another class. In the process, the fact that the resources are the centre of their culture and identity is ignored. Also the need to prepare them for the transition to a new society is ignored. They are forced into the new society with no preparation and without alternatives to the material assets lost to the project. That begins the process of their impoverishment and marginalization. All the DP-PAPs feel its negative impact. But because of their distance from the formal society tribal DP-PAPs feel it more than the others do. Even among them women and children are the worst affected. As most studies have shown, the tribes in general and women and children among them in particular pay the price of the development of another class. That is bound to lead to conflicts and repression. A solution to it requires a new look at the development paradigm that depends on their impoverishment.

References

Areeparampil, Mathew (1996). *Tribals of Jharkhand: Victims of Development*, New Delhi: Indian Social Institute.

Bharali, Gita (2009). *Social and Environmental Cost of Development-Induced Displacement: An Appraisal of Cost-Benefit Analysis in Assam*, PhD Thesis, Department of Economics, Dibrugarh University, Assam.

Bhaumik, Subir (2003). 'Tripura's Gumti Dam Must Go', *The Ecologist Asia*, Vol. 11, No. 1, January–March, pp. 84–89.

Deb Barma, Sukhendu (2009). 'Refugee Rehabilitation and Land Alienation in Tripura', in Walter Fernandes and Sanjay Barbora (eds), *Land, People and Politics: Contest over Tribal Land in Northeast India*, Guwahati: North Eastern Social Research Centre and IWGIA, pp. 88–112.

Ekka, Alexius and Mohammed Asif (2000). *Development-Induced Displacement and Rehabilitation in Jharkhand: A Database on its Extent and Nature*, New Delhi: Indian Social Institute (Mimeo).

Fernandes, Walter (2008). 'Sixty Years of Development-Induced Displacement in India: Impacts and the Search for Alternatives', in Hari Mohan Mathur (ed.), *India, Social Development Report 2008: Development and Displacement*, New Delhi: Council for Social Development and Oxford University Press, pp. 89–102.

Fernandes, Walter and Mohammed Asif (1997). *Development-Induced Displacement and Rehabilitation in Orissa 1951–1995: A Database on its Extent and Nature*, New Delhi: Indian Social Institute (Mimeo).

Fernandes, Walter, Nafisa Goga D'Souza, Arundhuti Roy Choudhury and Mohammed Asif (2001). *Development-Induced Displacement in Andhra Pradesh 1951–1995: A Quantitative Study of its Extent and Nature*, New Delhi and Guwahati: Indian Social Institute and North Eastern Social Research Centre (Mimeo).

Fernandes, Walter and Niraj Naik (2001). *Development-Induced Displacement in Goa 1965–1995: A Database on its Extent and Nature*, Guwahati: North Eastern Social Research Centre and Panjim: INSAF (Mimeo).

Fernandes, Walter and Gita Bharali (2010). *Development-Induced Displacement 1947–2000 in Meghlaya, Mizoram and Tripura: A Quantitative and Qualitative Database on its Extent and Impact*, Guwahati: North Eastern Social Research Centre (Mimeo).

—— (2011). *Uprooted for Whose Benefit? Development-Induced Displacement in Assam 1947–2000*, Guwahati: North Eastern Social Research Centre.

Fernandes, Walter, Thejanuo Fidelia Sekhose, Medonuo Pienyu, Alibo Achumi, Sungtemmenla Aier, Mhonthung Yanthan and V. Sherpa (2011). *Development-Induced Displacement and Deprivation in Nagaland 1947–2008 and in Sikkim 1975–2008: A Quantitative and Qualitative Database on its Extent and Impact*, Guwahati: North Eastern Social Research Centre (Mimeo).

Fernandes, Walter, Shanti Chhetri, Sherry Joseph and Satyen Lama (2012). *Progress: At Whose Cost? Development-Induced Displacement in West Bengal 1947–2000*, Guwahati: North Eastern Social Research Centre.

Ganguly Thukral, Enakshi and Mridula Singh (1995). 'Dams and the Displaced in India', in Hari Mohan Mathur (ed.), *Development, Displacement and Resettlement: Focus on Asian Experiences*, New Delhi: Vikas Publishing House, pp. 93–121.

Gaventa, John (1980). *Power and Powerlessness: Quiescence and Rebellion in an Appalachian Valley*, Oxford: Clarendon Press.

Good, Byron J. (1996). 'Mental Health Consequences of Displacement and Resettlement', *Economic and Political Weekly*, Vol. 31, No. 24, 15 June, pp. 1504–08.

Government of India (GoI) (1985). *Report of the Committee on Rehabilitation of Displaced Tribals due to Development Projects*, New Delhi: Ministry of Home Affairs.

Government of Odisha (GoO) (1968). *Report on the Benefits of Hirakud Irrigation: A Socio-Economic Study*, Cuttack: Bureau of Statistics and Economics.

International Work Group for Indigenous Affairs (IWGIA) (2004). *The Indigenous World 2004*, Copenhagen: IWGIA.

Lobo, Lancy and Shashikant Kumar (2009). *Land Acquisition, Displacement and Resettlement in Gujarat 1947–2004*, New Delhi: Sage Publications.

Menon, Geeta (1995). 'The Impact of Migration on the Work and Tribal Women's Status', in Loes Schenken-Sandbergen (ed.), *Women and Seasonal Labour Migration*, New Delhi: Sage Publications, pp. 79–154.

Menon, Manju (2009). 'Land Alienation due to Large Hydro-Power Projects in Arunachal Pradesh', in Walter Fernandes and Sanjay Barbora (eds), *Land, People and Politics: Contest over Tribal Land in Northeast India*, Guwahati: North Eastern Social Research Centre and IWGIA, pp. 128–41.

Ministry of Rural Development (MoRD) (1994). The Draft National Policy for Rehabilitation of Persons Displaced as a Consequence of Acquisition of Land, New Delhi: MoRD, Government of India (Second Draft).

Murickan, Jose, M.K. George, K.A. Emmanuel, Jose Boban and R. Prakash Pillai (2003). *Development-Induced Displacement: Case of Kerala*, Jaipur: Rawat Publications.

Nongkynrih, A.K. (2009). 'Privatisation of Communal Land of the Tribes of North East India: A Sociological Viewpoint', in Walter Fernandes and Sanjay Barbora (eds), *Land, People and Politics: Contest over Tribal Land in Northeast India*, Guwahati: North Eastern Social Research Centre and IWGIA, pp. 16–36.

Pamei, Aram (2001). 'Havoc of Tipaimukh High Dam Project', *Economic and Political Weekly*, Vol. 36, No. 13, p. 1045 and 1148.

Pattanaik, S.K., B. Das and A.B. Mishra (1987). 'Hirakud Dam: Expectations and Realities', in PRIA (ed.), *People and Dams*, New Delhi: Society for Participatory Research in Asia, pp. 47–59.

Ramanathan, Usha (2008). 'The Land Acquisition Act 1894: Displacement and State Power', in Hari Mohan Mathur (ed.), *India, Social Development Report 2008: Development and Displacement*, New Delhi: Council for Social Development and Oxford University Press, pp. 27–38.

Singh, Chatrapati (1989). 'Rehabilitation and the Right to Property', in Walter Fernandes and Enakshi Ganguly Thukral (eds), *Development, Displacement and Rehabilitation: Issues for a National Debate*, New Delhi: Indian Social Institute, pp. 91–103.

Thakur, Debdulal (2007). 'Budget and Policy Tracking of the Union Government', *Budget Track*, Vol. 4, No. 2, February, pp. 3–5.

VAK Team (1997). 'The New Economic Path: Trends and Impact', in Ajit Muricken (ed.), *Globalisation and SAP: Trend and Impact*, Mumbai: Vikas Adhyayan Kendra, pp. 151–80.

Vaswani, Kalpana (1992). 'Rehabilitation Laws and Policies: A Critical Look', in Enakshi Ganguly Thukral (ed.), *Big Dams, Displaced People: Rivers of Sorrow, Rivers of Change*, New Delhi: Sage Publications, pp. 155–69.

Viegas, Philip (1992). 'The Hirakud Dam Oustees: Thirty Years After', in Enakshi Ganguly Thukral (ed.), *Big Dams, Displaced People: Rivers of Sorrow Rivers of Change*, New Delhi: Sage Publications, pp. 29–53.

4

Development-Induced Displacement

Future Fortunes

RAMESH S. MANGALEKAR

The term 'nation-state' refers to the fusion in one political community of the idea of the nation and the idea of the state. The process is generally considered to have begun around 200 years ago, though the term itself did not enter into common use until after the First World War (McIver, 1999: 2). As a nation, the nation-state is ideally a homogeneous cultural community, with a common language and common values, sentiments and attachments. It is based not just on common interest but also, and more fundamentally, on assumed common historical characteristics: it provides or aspires to provide its' members with their dominant source of collective identity. The story of nation building and state formation over the past 200 years is the story of the coming together of these two ideas in a mutually reinforcing union, which has become the universal political organizing principle of the modern era. They were in a sense, 'made' for each other (Jenny, 2002).

India became free from British rule in 1947. After that, this independent and free country has its own 'nation-state' identity. Since then like elsewhere the planners of our nation made several efforts to achieve development in different fields. Such developments will raise the standard of living, and provide rich and wide opportunities for the life and livelihood of its citizens. Towards this end, they planned and implemented several small, medium and mega projects relating to the different field such as the agriculture, irrigation, water and power supply, industries, transport and communications, rural, urban and tribal development, etc. Thus, through five-year plans, India, as an independent 'nation-state', made efforts for infrastructure development. Mahapatra (1994: 37) also write in the same line: 'since independence of our country, there has been sustained efforts to develop the infrastructure through major industrial, power generation and water management projects. Projects of such large scale were not established during the British colonial regime. However, soon after independence, free India was in a great hurry to make up the shortfall in development to catch up with the advanced countries of the world'.

This shows that India's freedom and independent 'nation-state' identity has played a significant role in its overall development. However, all such kinds of developmental efforts have some meaning only when the particular 'nation-state' is free, independent and secured. For the independent 'nation-state' like India the national security is important. On one side, it helps for the continuity of building the Indian nation-state and, on the other side, its citizens will enjoy the fruits of nation building in real sense. Therefore, along with infrastructure development for socio-economic progress Indian 'nation-state' made effort towards the infrastructure development for national security. The nations like USA, Russia and England are strong and dominant in the global world because, on one side, they have developed countries infrastructure and technology, and on the other side, they are having powerful armed forces. Thus, nations like India are forced to develop their own defence force.

Defence Development-induced Displacement: Sensibility of 'Gains' and 'Pains'

An attempt to achieve modern integrated development in national defence has been based on two interrelated processes: one, the unchecked use of the earth's natural resources; and two, the transformation of people, often against their will, into a dispossessed working class. These processes were not new. They had their antecedents in India's history of colonial and pre-colonial extraction, and they continued after independence, though they were legitimized in different ways. The project of national 'development' is not limited to the Indian State alone, but is embedded in contemporary global structures such as the arrangement of the world into nation states, and the expanding system of international capitalism (Baviskar, 1995: 35).

Hence, the development of a common identity is seen as necessary to enable the state to mobilize and control its citizens.

Therefore, on the one hand, we have a situation where the nation-state fixes people to a particular place or territory, but on the other hand, as an all-encompassing spatial division of the world into like units, the system of nation-states enables the movement of people and things across those divisions to become predictable and routine. Thus, the fundamental goals of the nation-state project are in conflict. The figure of the forced resettlers, 'displaced' in the 'national interest' to make way for large-scale development projects, highlights a related tension within the idea of the nation-state (Jenny, 2002: 6).

The problem under this study, the development of Sea Bird Project (SBP), Karwar and displacement of coastal habitats from west coast also raises same kind of issue. Due to this the paradoxical situation encountered by our 'nation-state'. Because, on one hand, our independent nation-state is democratic and welfare state, whose aim is to achieve the welfare of all citizens, and on the other hand, due to land acquisition for the establishment of the SBP, the coastal habitats of Karwar region had to be uprooted from their hearths and fields. As a result, the uprooted people lost the symbiotic relation with their habitats. The paradox here is the nation state's 'gain' is some citizens 'pain'.

Jenny (2002: 6) has also highlighted the paradoxical situation of the nation-state and how the state exercises the idea of 'eminent domain' to overcome from it. He writes: 'The development-induced displacement is tension between the nation-state as the ultimate source of legitimate political control over a given territory and as a community of equal citizens. For, in development-induced displacement and resettlement projects the state exercises its monopoly of legitimate force to uproot a group of its own citizens, usually as we shall see, a relatively impoverished and powerless group of citizens and usually with disastrous consequences for their socio-economic well being.'

Thus, after independence, the idea of 'eminent domain' as main tool is used by our planners to attempt the development of national infrastructure, even though they are contradictory to displacement of indigenous people. At the same time, the contemporary citizens resisted such kinds of contradictory developmental attempts. As a result, the debate between the supporters and opponents of developmental projects are highly controversial in nature, for example, the development projects like Sardar Sarovar in Narmada basin, Upper

Krishna Project, Nagarjunsagar dam, Koyana dam, etc. The project supporters highlight the positive aspects of the project such as growth in irrigation, agricultural production, electricity, urbanization, transport and communication, national security, etc. Whereas the opponents of such projects highlight the consequences of development particularly the socio-cultural and ecological-economic impacts on the uprooted indigenous population. Such population is mostly found in almost remote and self-sufficient rural and tribal communities. In addition, majority of them belong to socially, economically, educationally and politically backward sections. Such kind of poor and powerless uprooted people always look towards the welfare state to reconstruct their disintegrated life patterns and livelihood systems.

Fisher (1997: 8) summarizes this entire controversial debate in following words: 'The proponents and opponents seem sincere in their commitment to goals of sustainable development and social justice, but what they mean by these terms differs. Sharing the same rhetoric to describe profoundly different goals and means disguises fundamental philosophical differences and maintains confusion in the global debate about development. While widespread commitment to the term "sustainable development" might suggest a growing worldwide consensus on the need for development that is sustainable, there is no agreement about the specific goals of development or the appropriate means to achieve them.'

This shows that development is required but what is required more is that it should be 'sustainable' in nature. The 'gains' from the development should be much more than the 'pains'. Jenny and Cernea have focused these arguments in different way. Jenny (2002: 7) states: 'The main objectives of development-induced displacement projects are to benefit a much wider population than that of the displaced themselves. In addition, the key characteristic of this wider population is that it shared with the displaced population membership of the same nation-state.' Co-membership of the nation-state, therefore, makes legally and morally legitimate a situation in which, as Cernea (2000: 12) has put it 'some people enjoy the gains of development while 'others' bear its pains'. However, who are these 'others', who are also fellow citizens? In what sense are they 'others'? Is it just that they are 'not us' or is it, more fundamentally, that are 'not like us', that they, have a different and systematically inferior relationship with the sources of state power? If the later position is correct, the figure of the forced resettler challenges not only policy makers and planners to come up with better-planned and implemented schemes, but also the ideology of the nation-state itself as community of equal citizens and as principle agency of development'.

Historical and Physical Background of Study Area

The Uttar Kannada district is one of the socio-economically backward but naturally rich districts of Karnataka state. It is one of the three coastal districts of the state and stretches itself along the coastline of the Arabian Sea. The Uttar Kannada with its long silver white beaches, fertile green paddy fields, cool palm groves, picturesque river valleys and rich hilly forest tracts, is one of the most beautiful regions in India, endowed with most captivating landscapes. Its waterfalls have attracted men far and near. It is richest forest district of Karnataka, endowed with a beautiful variety of fauna and flora. The British named this district as 'Canara' when they acquired it from Tipu in 1799. Of late, the state government discontinued the English nomenclature and named the district as 'Uttar Kannada' from 1977 (Kamat, 1995: 1).

Positive Aspects of SBP Displacement: A Critical Analysis

Until the decade of the 1970s geo-strategic situation placed greater emphasis on the continental strategy. However, the changes in geo-political environment thereafter, necessitated the shift in the emphasis. Accordingly, Indian Navy also started evolving a viable and credible maritime strategy to meet demands of both present and the future (Sampathgopal, 2000: 1). As a result, the third naval base code name 'Project Sea Bird', Karwar is planned and implemented on the west coast of India. This project will meet all the naval requirements, which were hitherto not available in both Mumbai and Kochi naval bases.

The 'Sea Bird' is the most prestigious national defence project of India, when complete it will be the largest naval base in Asia. The SBP has underlying assumption that it would bring human as well as financial capital to this region. This in turn would help to change and develop the socio-cultural and economic life and living conditions of the local population (communities) in general and displaced in particular. This will help the people of Uttar Kannada district as well.

The Uttar Kannada district is comparatively least urbanized district of the Karnataka state. The district has a rich human and natural resources. However, it is industrially backward with very poor trade and business linkages. As a result, there is absence of urban centres, small and large-scale industries, trade and commerce, well-developed transportation and communication, professional educational institutions, modern medical centres, technical experts, scope for entrepreneurship, etc. Hence, the establishment of Sea Bird Project (SBP) in such a backward district will help structural change and development in the region. In coming decades, the people of this region will enjoy the fruits of development. The foremost benefit of this project is that it will provide some direct as well as indirect employment opportunities to the local communities.

The direct employment opportunities of the project can broadly be divided into two sub-categories such as:

(a) Skilled (engineers, doctors, software and hardware technicians, strategic experts, naval commanders, soldiers, mechanics, administrators, etc.).
(b) Unskilled (physical labourers/manual wage labourers).

The indirect employment opportunities in various fields that SBP can create in this region are:

(a) Transport and communication
(b) Small-scale industries
(c) Boarding and restaurants
(d) Educational institutions
(e) Healthcare and medical centres
(f) Large scale trade and business
(g) Consumer goods
(h) Fruits, milk and vegetable markets
(i) Mechanical and electrical goods and services, etc.

The people of this region particularly the SBP displaced are eagerly looking for such job opportunities. These will fulfil their hopes of getting alternative sources of livelihood. These jobs are more significant for them because, after displacement every occupational group lost its source of earning. The agrarian community rejected the land-for-land resettlement offer provided under the SBP rehabilitation package. They rejected this livelihood offer mainly due to certain problems related to offered land such as the low fertility of land, lack of irrigation and long geographical distance. As a result, they adopted the cash compensation for land and rehabilitation grants. However, none of them invested this money in agricultural land due to insufficient amount to purchase alternative land. As a result all the landowners (haves) turned into landless labour (have-nots) category. This disturbed the livelihood network of families dependent upon the agriculture. Sinha and Rao (1998: 147) have also noticed the same, in their study. They write: 'Agricultural employment has disappeared in the post-displacement phase. Once the people are taken out of the agricultural production system, their employability in the sector also declines. They may then have a status as a migrant labour, where they have to compete with others in output and in the wages. Only persons in certain age group can sustain themselves as migrant labourers.' The condition of fishermen is also not much different from this. Though they resettled in fishermen resettlement colonies (RCs) close to seacoast, more than 65 per cent families have discontinued their fishing occupation, due to lack of availability of fish, sharp flow of water, unsuitable area for traditional fishing, more distance between dwelling place and sea, etc. This indicates that during the transitory phase of involuntary resettlement families face the employment and livelihood problems. Particularly, on one side, they lose their productive system and another side the alternative productive system is not yet developed. Only those who are in public and private services, the skilled workers like masons, carpenters, drivers, blacksmiths, etc., somehow manage to maintain their livelihood condition.

Thus, the wide-open options remain before the displaced groups. Some of them are: (a) migration in search of livelihood, (b) to get employment (in the project or outside the project), (c) earning through self-employment. The field observation and experience reveals that the displaced people of this coastal area may not migrate to other places in search of livelihood. Because prior to displacement, more than private property, the common property resources played significant role in earning their livelihood. Everywhere there is shortage of CPR. Hence, they may not take the risk of migration. It is difficult for them to adapt and adjust with altogether new kinds of jobs or occupations. The other reasons are: they are less mobile, more rigid about the food habits (fish curry), lack of skills. Moreover, they know that everywhere there is dearth of employment opportunities. Further, they are aware that the construction of SBP creates varied types of job opportunities.

The field data reveals that people from different parts of India and the world have migrated to this area in search of employment and livelihood. During the first stage of the construction of SBP, various group of engineers and technical experts are involved in the project. They belonged to Engineers India Limited, Messrs REDECO of Australia, Messrs NEDCO of Netherland, Larsen and Turbo, etc. A number of people from different parts of India have also come to work in the SBP. They are contractors, sub-contractors, supervisors, technicians, clerks, lorry owners and drivers, unskilled labourers, etc. On the other hand, the resettlers are repeatedly raising the issue of livelihood problems in the RCs established close to the SBP construction area. They do not realize that the knowledge, skills, and job experience they have is not suitable for the available jobs in the project. They even do not understand that the main and sub-contractors of the project have their own group of permanent and temporary employees. They only know that they have sacrificed their original sources of livelihood for national development. Hence, they believe that the fruits of development should reach to those who have made sacrifice.

The project contractors are worried about the completion of their work within a given time, while maintaining the standard and quality. Hence, they prefer to use their permanent human skill and resources. On the other side, the displaced people were unaware about the nature and types of job opportunities that SBP would create. They were also not much alert about the skills and training required to avail those opportunities. It is the moral duty of the planners to make the project-affected people aware about the future job opportunities and to provide appropriate training to them. This helps them to avail the new jobs and sources of livelihood soon after the displacement.

The project is expected to provide more than 10,000 direct (skilled and unskilled) jobs of different types after its completion. The local people, more particularly, the displaced youth will be the beneficiaries. Such regular jobs in the project will help them to re-establish their life and livelihood. The success of human resettlement and rehabilitation is probably more dependent upon the quick adaptation of the alternative sources of livelihood. Hence, the resettlement and rehabilitation (R&R) of SBP affected families will be determined by the number of job opportunities made available to the displaced people. Hasan (2006: 99) has emphasized the significance of any kind of job to the displaced people particularly during the initial stage of resettlement. 'The benefit generally valued most by resettlers is wage employment, which yields a steady income flow and a sense of control over their lives. Even temporary wage earning during project construction ensures much needed income during transition period'.

The funding agencies like the World Bank, Asian Development Bank, etc., issued their own policy statements on the involuntary resettlement. They insist the local governments and project planners to provide job resettlement and alternative livelihood systems for the uprooted people. As a result, today the government and project planners are giving some serious thought to the job resettlement of displaced people. The R&R policies of Maharashtra Electricity Board, Indian Railway (Konkan Railway Project), Kudaremukh Iron Ore Project in Karnataka, NTPC in Sangruali region, etc., added job provisions in their respective plans.

Hasan (ibid.: 100) has summarized the project-wise position of employment provided to displace as follows: 'In Rihand and Vidhyachal projects 890 project-affected families (PAFs) are working with contractors. Similarly, out of identified 10,099 eligible persons under the coal sector environment and social mitigation project, 2,736 PAFs had been absorbed in regular mine jobs and about 316 were working with contractors (up to May 1999).' Almost all the eligible persons displaced by the National Aluminum Company were given regular jobs in the company (Mahapatra, 1994). Warren has also noticed this trend in his study. He states: 'The R&R policy of Odisha Water Resources Sector reserved five per cent of all government jobs in class III and IV categories for the displaced people. Similar provisions are available to the displaced families of the Upper Krishna Project in Karnataka. Most of these permanent jobs are highly prized and are often passed as inheritances within families' (quoted in Hasan, 2006: 100).

Likewise, at the time of evacuation the R&R authorities of SBP also promised to absorb the displaced youth in the project gradually. However, it is difficult for Indian Navy to recruit one youth from each SBP displaced family. The other infrastructure development projects like industries, railways, transport and communication can absorb one youth. The SBP being a defence project, the criteria of selection are different from other project. The age, gender, physical fitness, educational skills, confidentiality, etc., are more important. Hence, youth with all such qualities may not be available in each and every displaced family. Probably, because of such reasons displaced people of Bombay naval base got fewer jobs in the project. In

Jawaharlal Nehru Port, 91 per cent families lost all their land to the project, but less than 33 per cent of them got employment (Parsuraman, 1996). Field study has brought out that during the transitory stage of resettlement some displaced youth got permanent and temporary jobs in the project. To some extent, this helped them to re-established livelihood soon after relocation in the colony. Table 1 below gives clear picture about this:

Table 1

RC-wise Distribution of Job Resettlement Families

RC	*No Job*	*Got Job*	*Security of Job*		*Nature of Job*		*Total*
			Permanent	*Temporary*	*Skilled*	*Unskilled*	
Chittakula	70	16	2	14	9	7	86
	81%	19%	2%	16%	11%	8%	100%
Toddur	69	19	1	18	4	15	88
	78%	22%	1%	20%	5%t	17%	100%
Belekeri	33	0	0	0	0	0	33
	100%	0%	0%	0%	0%	0%	100%
Total	172	35	3	32	13	22	207
	83%	17%	2%	15%	6%	11%	100%

This shows that only 17 per cent resettled families managed to get jobs during first phase of SBP construction. It is interesting to note that no family of Belekeri RC was able to avail any kind of job in the project. The reasons for this are many. This RC is established in Ankola taluka, little away from the main construction area. Also, the resettlers of this RC are socially, economically and educationally backward. They are also politically powerless, and have weak managerial skill. The most important factor is, by generations, they have developed the habit of suffering and survival of adjustment with problems. Some of them have adopted the sharecropping, wage labour and CPR based livelihood after displacement. Like other projects, in general, in this project also among the displaced the 'haves', elites, educated, comparatively powerful, those who have managerial skills have grabbed all the job opportunities created by the project. However, most of the jobs are temporary and unskilled in nature.

The local youth settled in urban areas (Karwar, Ankola, Kumta, Honawar, Sirsi, etc.) have availed more number of jobs in the project. This is mainly because they are comparatively more qualified, and have acquired the technical and managerial skills pertaining to jobs available in the SBP. The problems of the displaced youth is that they come from the background of rural coast, not well qualified and never got any kind of expose to the modern/technical professions. As a result, they develop some kind of negative attitude towards the entire process of SBP development. During the focused group discussion, they expressed their helpless condition and negative approach. They said that: 'those who give the bribe, they only get jobs in the project. After displacement we are dying every day without livelihood. Instead of that, they should put bomb on us so that we can sacrifice our life also to the project along with the livelihood'. Some youth also expressed some positive points of the project. According to them this project helps the nation and national security; some regional youth may get certain opportunities to show their talent. The project will bring lot many developmental activities. Ashok Naik resettled in the Toddur RC after division in his joint family. His mother and two brothers, one among them is polio victim, are staying outside the RC. He raises basic question of development: 'What we gain from the project? Our families have been divided, neighbourhood relationships are disintegrated, occupational groups are scattered due to non-availability of productive system in the RC. Of course nation got security, state and region got prosperity but our long learned skills and hands have no work other than to beg'. This is mainly because after resettlement in the RC's, the traditional livelihood skills handed down from one generation to another have lost their relevance. Hence, they are suffering to sustain their families. This is only a 'technical unemployment' problem. Once the necessary technical skills are acquired, then slowly Navy will recruit the eligible displaced youth through direct recruitment.

The project planners are giving requisite training to the displaced youth according to their individual interest and educational qualification. Particularly the youth who have passed the tenth and above exam are selected for the ITI and computer training. One member of displaced family is eligible for such kind of training. The cost of training is entirely borne by the project. Every such candidate also gets a stipend of ₹ 1,000 per month for two years. The local ITI has given a grant of ₹ 36 lakhs for upgradation and augmentation of their training facilities. This aims at creating a better-equipped ITI in the region with additional trades included in the curricula. This would result in enhancement of the skill levels of the local people, which would in turn create better job opportunities and also would create trained manpower to meet the future requirements of the Navy (Shashidhar, 2000: 17). Project has also provided free self-employment training to men and women belonging to displaced community. This includes training in bar binding, plumbing, photocopying, photography, beauty parlour, service and repairs of TV, computer, refrigerator, washing machine, AC, making of candles, papad, pickle, etc. The field data regarding this is given in the Table 2.

Table 2

RC-wise ITI/Computer and Self-employment Training Obtained by the Youth

RC	*No Training*	*Got Training*	*Total*	*No Training*	*Nature of Training*		*Total*
					ITI/ Computer	*Self-employment*	
Chittakula	57	29	86	57	23	6	86
	66%	34%	100%	66%	27%	8%	100%
Todur	57	31	88	57	26	5	88
	65%	35%	100%	65%	30%	5%	100%
Belekeri	28	5	33	28	5	0	33
	84%	15%	100%	84%	15%	0%	100%
Total	142	65	207	142	54	11	207
	68%	32%	100%	68%	26%	6%	100%

Though the government was ready to provide free training to all displaced families, only 32 per cent families have been trained. There are several reasons for it. In some families, the children are below the age and educational qualifications required for the training. Some other families are having members above the age limit. Some of them dropped out of self-employment training after getting work on wage basis either in the project or outside the project. However, some of them who have undergone such trainings are given suitable jobs either on permanent or on temporary in project. They are absorbed particularly in the jobs like bar binding, motor winding, welding, computer operator, attender, storekeeper, etc. Some of the trained youth have taken self-employment like small-scale industries such as making of kokum drinks and other soft drinks, making of candles, papad, pickles, etc. However, due to lack of experience of marketing the product and proper business linkages, they are unable to continue the self-employment activity gainfully. This shows that simply giving the training and pushing them into wide open, highly competitive and liberalized private market is not the real justice to the displaced. The continuous follow-up measures are required. The R&R authorities should provide continuous support and guidance until the successful pursue of their business. At initial stage, it is moral responsibility of the government to provide financial and technical support to start self-employment. Hasan (2006: 99) has rightly pointed out the important aspects of success of self-employment scheme. He opines: 'The package should include skill training, investment support (both infrastructure and working capital), and establishing required market linkages for raw materials and sales of produce.' However, R&R authorities feel that such aspects, on one hand, consume more time and, on the other hand, required to generate the social, human and financial capital. The authorities working under the formal bureaucratic system are bound with their respective duties and government rules. Moreover, they are in transferable job. Hence, long before actual displacement government must seek the advice of experts and introduce well-planned R&R package.

The study strongly recommends two things. One, every key government officer who is directly or indirectly involved in R&R process should not be transferred for minimum 8 to 10 years of period. Second, instead of giving the self-employment training to individual member they should organize individuals and give specific training to such organized group. It has more chances of success. When particularly the project like sea bird is at the first phase near future it will create lot many entrepreneurship opportunities. At that time, these well-trained organized displaced youths will dominate over the local self-employment market.

Future Fortunes for Self-employment (Entrepreneurship)

The transportation and communication are expected to receive boost with the commencement of the naval base. There will be increase in the frequency of trains, road traffic and shipping is expected to grow. This kind of growth will provide number of job opportunities, particularly, in services sector like autorickshaws, taxi, heavy vehicles, automobile shops, workshops, petrol and diesel pumps, etc. Recently, a Bangalore-based businessman has started 'Sea Bird' travel agency. These buses are run between Karwar and Bangalore and Karwar and Mumbai. The area of business in the radio, TV, phone, mobile and internet services will also expand rapidly.

The demand for modern restaurants and lodgings will increase. People from different parts of India and world will be attracted towards SBP area. Naturally, there will be a demand for variety of quality food dishes and lodgings. This industry will provide number of jobs to local youth from supplier to manager.

At present, there is no medical and engineering college in the district. Such professional colleges are likely to be started in near future. Indian Navy is also going to start some educational institutions likes Kendriya Vidyalaya, Dockyard apprentices' school and other vocational training institutes (Shashidhar, 2000: 18). As a result, there will be increased teaching, non-teaching and certain professional jobs. Moreover, local people will get excellent opportunities to have professional education.

Indian Navy has already prepared a plan for the establishment of Naval Hospital at project area. This hospital will have modern medical equipments and highly qualified doctors. After its establishment, the requirement of medical practitioners, medicine and drugs suppliers will increase. Outside the project also, some health care clubs and hospitals are likely to be established.

There is also scope for improvement in trade and business, which, in turn, will open number of jobs, particularly in the banking, financial institutions, insurance companies, chit funds, share market, etc.

A mass migration of people to SBP area will increase demand for consumer goods. To fulfil such demands, the variety of cloth shops, janata bazaars, electronic showrooms, shoe shops, laundry, LPG suppliers, etc., will start on large scale. As a result, local youth will get job opportunities.

When the SBP becomes fully functional with its full strength (10,000 Naval Staff), it will require not less than 10,000–12,000 kg food grains, 4,000–5,000 kg vegetables, 20,000 eggs, 5,000–7,000 litre milk per day. Outside SBP, also there will be increase in demand for such goods. There will be a substantial increase in the non-vegetarian market particularly, fish, chicken and mutton.

Locals will also get wide employment opportunities in the mechanical and electrical goods and service field such as TV, radio, computer, watch, mixer, grinder, aquaguard, washing machine, tape recorder, and water pumpset repairs.

This indicates that in future, plenty of self-employment opportunities will be created by SBP. The displaced youth will enjoy the real developmental 'gain' for their present 'pain'. What is required is the development of proper plan, organization and action. Their major worry is requisite skill, knowledge and finance. Only time will tell how many displaced youth will avail these opportunities.

Note: The situation has changed since the study was conducted.

References

Baviskar, Amita (1995). *In the Belly of the River: Tribal Conflict Over Development in the Narmada Valley*, New Delhi: Oxford University Press.

Cernea, M.M. (2000). 'Risks, Safeguards and Reconstruction: A Model for Population Displacement and Resettlement', *Economic and Political Weekly*, Vol. XXXV, No. 41, pp. 3659–78.

Fisher, W.F. (Ed.) (1997). *Toward Sustainable Development: Struggling Over India's Narmada River*, Jaipur: Rawat Publications.

Hasan, Mohammed (2006). 'Creating New Economic Opportunities for Displaced People: Approaches to Income Restoration', *Social Change*, Vol. 36, No. 1, pp. 87–108.

Jenny, Robinson (Ed.) (2002). *Development and Displacement*, New Delhi: Oxford University Press.

Kamat, Suryanath U. (1995). *Uttar Kannada District Gazetteer*, Bangalore: Government Central Book Depot.

Mahapatra, L.K. (1994). *Tribal Development in India: Myths and Reality*, New Delhi: Vikas Publishing House.

Parsuraman, S. (1996). 'Development Projects, Displacement and Outcomes for Displaced: Two Case Studies', *Economic and Political Weekly*, Vol. XXXI, No. 24, 15 June.

Sampathgopal, S.R. (2000). 'Naval Base at Karwar: A Dream Come True', *Navy Week: Project Sea Bird, Karwar*, Manipal: Manipal Press Limited.

Shashidhar, L.K. (2000). 'Sea Bird: The Harbinger of Fortunes to Karwar', *Navy Week: Project Sea Bird, Karwar*, Manipal: Manipal Press Limited, pp. 17–18.

Sinha, B.K. and Srinivasa Rao (1998). 'Rehabilitation and Resettlement the Gopalpur Way: To What Extent Ideal?', *The Administrator*, Vol. XLIII, No. 2, April–June, pp. 125–76.

5

Development through Displacement and Marginalization of Tribal Community

An Overview

NARENDRA K. BEHERA

The building of large multi-purpose river valley projects and large-scale industries has ushered the path of infrastructural development in post-independent India as a euphoria of sacrifice for the building of a newly-born nation. But, all these mega projects have left an imprint of untold misery upon a section of population through displacement which has resulted in loss of land, home, livelihood and, many more by the affected people of there. Out of various projects, dams rank at the top of the list in displacing people. A conservative estimate puts that a total of 2,13,00,000 have been displaced by various projects like dams, industries, mines, etc., out of which only 53,80,000 people have been rehabilitated so far. A significant section of the displaced is tribal and economically marginal rural population, who are dependent on common property resources (CPRs) or the natural resources like forests and rivers for their livelihoods. The 29th report of the Commissioner for Scheduled Castes and Scheduled Tribes (1990) makes very interesting revelation. The report pointed out that till 1990, out of the total displaced persons, 40 per cent were Scheduled Tribes (STs). Their share in the total population of India, however, is 7.5 per cent, Scheduled Caste (SC) people who constitute about 16 per cent of the country's population constitute 20 per cent of the total displaced persons. The concept of inclusive growth is of little importance for these displaced people who have sacrificed a lot for the cause of country's economic development and it is the best example of development deficit. The space of democracy is squeezed, the voice of marginalized section created through the process of development and the draconian evils of laws has failed to reach the highest podium of executives and legislature in many a way at various level of the society and the tribal in particular. Let development be people-centric instead of corporate-centric. In recent time the issues of Kalinganagar, POSCO, Nandigram, Singur, Vedanta, Polavoram, etc., have become the focal points of attraction due to the culmination of violence against the tribal and marginalized farmers of those areas. Displacement begets further inequality and discrimination.

'Economic development is a process whereby in economy's real national income increases over a long period of time. And, if the rate of development is greater than the rate of population growth, then the per capita real income will increase. "Process" implies the operation of certain forces; these forces operate over the long period and embody changes in certain variables. Details of the process vary under diverse conditions in space and time. But there are some basic common features. And, the general result of the process is growth in an economy's national product – in itself a particular long run change' (Meir and Baldwin, 1957: 2). To carry out development process building of projects and industries is common in any set of economic system. These projects bring serious problem for the project-displaced people. In addition to development projects, there is another aspect of displacement due to conservation such as sanctuary and parks. The extent of sufferings and miseries of human beings caused due to the implementation of developmental projects is more serious in case of developing countries like India where the tribal population depends largely on CPRs and agriculture, and lives in their traditional way of living. The era of liberalization has coined development terminology like sustainable development, inclusive growth to focus on a broader framework of economic development. The concept of inclusive growth is of recent origin, with the beginning of the 11th Five-Year Plan. In India it has become a popular terminology on the lips of the politicians and policy makers alike. Without going much deep into the concept of inclusive growth, the government has tried to focus on numerous strategies to bring the economy into the arms of inclusive growth. Inclusive growth should connote the attainment of equity with social justice. It is necessary to emphasize the Gandhian ideas on inclusive development, which is a decentralized and nature-friendly approach, and aims at the 'happiness' of mankind.

The United Nations Development Programme (UNDP) defines inclusive growth by laying emphasis on the production and income side of the gross domestic product as 'the process and outcome where all groups of the people have participated in the organization of growth and have benefited equitably from it'. Thus inclusive growth represents an equation with organization on the left-hand side and benefits on the right-hand side. The deputy chairman of the Planning Commission Montek Singh Ahluwalia provides the following interpretations: (a) 'achieving a growth process in which people in different walks of life ... feel that they too benefit significantly from the process, and (b) 'poverty was one-dimensional, but lack of inclusion now is multidimensional; and interlinked with regional and caste issues... The plan is no longer a whole lot of forces and impulses ... An inclusive strategy should provide for health, education and agriculture' (in Suryanarayanan, 2008: 94). These definitions have over scored the gains of development without an adequate touch to the cases of those people who had been the initial target of the left-hand side of development. They are termed as internally displaced people (IDP) or oustee in their homeland. The pauperization, inequality and discrimination inflicted upon this section have received least attention throughout the process of development over the past decades. The aggressive 'development terrorism' of neo-liberalism in the name of industrialization is going to create more of IDPs and devastation to environment life system of tribal, ultimately leading to climate change than ever before. 'The key question, however, is common to all involuntary displaced persons. Given that industrial transformation is necessary to shift surplus workers from agriculture to industry, and that this involves dams, mines, factories, etc., all of which requires changes in land use, how can this be brought in inclusive manner?' (Nathan, 2009: 22). The provision job for the displaced people of different projects have failed to accommodate them such development projects concerned as a result there is marginalization of large scale tribal population in the process of development.

While modernization has been a force for well-being in third world and has brought in some of the expected economic, political and other advantages, also it has revealed its ugly side. It has failed to produce the much vaunted trickle-down effect to reduce vast economic and social inequalities and to empower the poor. As development projects are not 'space-neutral', displacement of human population becomes inevitable. And, the end result leads to inequality, discrimination, disparity within and among various sectors and regions of the country. These are the outcome of political, social and economic circumstances and the system has not been able minimize it effectively.

Industrial development has compounded the situation enormously by completely displacing many thousands of *adivasis* from their land to make dams and mines – a process of displacement which claims much further what the British began by 'reserving' large areas of forest and carving others into coffee and tea plantations. Overall, the present situation in tribal India has aptly been called internal colonialism (Padel, 2009: 288).

In the absence of organized movements, low level of mass political consciousness of continuance of relations of traditional dependence and domination, there is hardly any concerted effort to challenge the sources and forces of mass destitution. The state's efforts from above in terms of land reforms and tribal and rural development schemes in crucial respects have failed to yield the desired results. ... Land legislation are made not simple as a question of human rights and social justice to ameliorate the living conditions of the poverty stricken majority or to eliminate feudal exploitative relations but rather to accelerate the face of capitalism, both in agriculture and industry (Pathy, 1988).

It is the devastating findings of N.C. Saxena Committee which have revealed that the state government of Odisha and Vedanta and its associate companies had both engaged in the acts of omission and commission. The mining company had violated the Forest Conservation Act by illegally occupying 26 hectares of village forest land in the area. It had equally brazenly embarked on construction activity to expand its production capacity at its aluminium refinery complex from 1 to 6 million tonnes per annum without obtaining clearance under the Environment Protection Act. The Committee also found that the refinery was now obtaining its ore from 14 mines, 11 of which did not have environmental clearance. The state government on its part had not ensured that consent of Gram Sabha had been obtained as required under the Panchayat (Extension to the Scheduled Area) Act (PESA), through the Kondh hamlets are in a Schedule V area. And most important, mining would violate sections of the Forest Rights Act that are meant 'to ensure that the habitat of the forest peoples is preserved from any of the destructive practices that affect their cultural and ecological heritage' (Editorial, *EPW*, 2010).

The issue of tribal land or specially that of tribal land alienation has always been a matter of great concern to planners, policy makers, academicians and activists. This is so because, despite progressive and protective legislations, tribal people all over the country are perpetually threatened over their land rights. The process of alienation of tribal land began with the stabilization of the British rule in India. This process was accelerated by the development of transport, establishment of individual rights over agricultural lands, commercialization of agriculture and spread of English judicial system. At present, the threat has become more compounded than ever due to the onslaught of industrialization, urbanization, commercialization and infrastructure development. It is also evident from the Odisha High Court judgment and Saxena Committee's report over Vedanta mining and Vedanta University cases the state has become a gross violator of land rights and perpetuated the policy of land alienation in a more aggressive manner. The traditional mode of securing their livelihood is seriously threatened without any appropriate alternatives in sight. In Odisha the tribals are the worst sufferers over the land question. Their communities did not have a tradition of being landless labourers. The existence of this category among them at present is a sign of land alienation (Ambagudia, 2010: 60–61) Italics are mine.

In addition to STs, there is another group of tribes in India called 'Denotified Tribes' or 'Criminal Tribes' who have experienced a different crisis through the development projects. The Britishers notified around 150 tribes as 'Criminal' by enacting the Criminal Tribes Act, 1871. The Government of India denotified these tribes in 1952. Now, these denotified tribes comprise 126 tribes with a population of about 20 million spread all over the country. They are primarily nomads, pastoralists, hunter and performing age-old religious practices. They have faced severe crisis due to deforestation and destruction of their traditional source of livelihood. The present paper is not going to deal with their problem but the problem in general.

Under the present neo-liberal market-driven paradigm of development, hundreds of industrial, mining, irrigation or infrastructure projects are being proposed and memoranda of understanding (MoUs) are being signed by the central or state governments which, if and when they materialize, may change the landscape of urban/rural India. For instance, as many as 341 SEZs to be set up in the public and private sector across the country have been approved by the central government. If these projects take shape, they would require lands to the order of 1.49 lakh hectares (Mehra, 2007). And most of the MoUs relate to the mineral states like Jharkhand, Bihar, Chhattisgarh and Odisha where the percentage of tribal population in such mineral rich areas is high enough.

If the flat-topped hills are destroyed, the forest that clothes them will be destroyed too. So will the rivers and stream that flow out of them and irrigate the plain below. So will the Dongria Kond. So will the hundreds of thousands of tribal people who live in the forested heart of India, and whose homeland is similarly under attack. 'In our crowded cities, some people say "so what"? Someone has to pay for the price of progress'. Some even say, let's face it these are people whose time has come look at any developed country, Europe, the US, Australia they all have a 'past'. Indeed they do. So why shouldn't we? ... In the name of operation Green Hunt about 70,000 paramilitary forces are closing in on India's tribal homelands. Hundreds of thousands of people have begun to flee their homes. Not unlike US 'strategic hamleting', using random police terror to force people to move off their lands into roadside police camps. But behind this police and military offensive is an elaborate financial structure which links the mining corporations, international banks, NGOs, aid agencies, and the media, all of whom collude to rip bauxite all of the mountains (Arundhati Ray's Foreword in Padel and Das, 2010).

The robber barons are described as the model of corporate wealth and power in the US, which is still being copied and carried to new lengths by leading Indian businessman such as Anil Agrawal, Laxmi Mittal and Sir Ratan Tata, whose impact spans London, New York and the remotest adivasi villages of Odisha, Jharkhand, Chhattisgarh, Andhra Pradesh and West Bengal. India's robber barons, like those in the US, are projected as national heroes. Perhaps their ruthlessness is part of their appeal, like the love-hate relationship of Americans with the self-made tycoons who made 'America great'. These men claim to be leading India's development, and benefiting the lives of thousands of the poor (Padel, 2010: 15).

A Brief Review of Studies

Although the study of basic problem of displacement lies with economists, it has largely been dominated by sociologists and social anthropologists. Despite negative effects of displacement the economic study relating to displacement/resettlement is inadequate basically due to externalization of social and economic costs of the affected people/area. 'Basic research by professional economists on population displacement, to the best of my knowledge, currently is not carried out anywhere. Development economics still has to respond in full to the challenge of analysing not only the economic dimension of dislocation, but also the economic content of other social development ... population displacement is just another one of those "social" costs; however, the economic book on displacements costs has yet to be written' (Cernea, 1999: 9).

Studies made by various scholars at different point of times (Vidyarthi, 1970; Sengupta, 1979; Joshi, 1982; Despande, 1989; Fernandes and Thukral, 1989; Areeparamipli, 1989; Centre for Science and Environment, 1985) have shown that displacement has brought with it economic, social and cultural malady among the uprooted sections of the society and the tribals are the worst victim of development-induced displacement that has been set in the post-independence and post-economic reform period of the state.

The aggregate analysis of recent social research glaringly reveals and factually documents the new impoverishment taking place now in Africa. This must be recognized as the biggest paradox and the most unacceptable, in induced development: the fact that some development programmes, although launched, financed, and designed to reduce poverty, end up causing more poverty to segment of their population. And nonetheless, this paradoxical outcome is ineptly and immorally tolerated, and it occurs again and again. It is predictable, yet it is not pre-empted. Impoverishment from displacement becomes a strange and routine outcome of most projects that displace a number of people but do not provide effective safeguards to precede their livelihood. The risk to livelihoods can be avoided or much mitigated. But investments in safeguards measures are not made and the risk of pauperization materializes again and again into disastrous actual impacts (Cernea, 2006; Adivasi, 41).

In India economists have devoted much to the study of poverty and its alleviation programme. But analysis on impoverishment arising out of land acquisition and displacement due to development projects has been missed. Solid, extensive research by Indian economists on the economics of resettlement is surely missing. Nor are current mainstream economists concerned with the economic and financial dimensions of restructuring displaced persons livelihoods. It is, as if, the development projects they studied did not result in the displacement of any people (Mahapatra, 1999: 199).

The problem is that very little work has been done on non-reservoir displacement and this not-so negligible area has been completely swamped by the excessive emphasis on dams. This is not to say no work has been done (Dhagamwar et al., 2003: 30). There is enough reason for study of displacement due to dam projects, that dam projects have completely shattered the lives of displaced people in a much wider area than any other development projects and top the list of involuntary displacement.

The Hirakud dam across the river Mahanadi has been built over the tears of 18,000 families who were displaced from the most fertile track of western Odisha. A total of 22,144 families with a population of about 1.1 to 1.6 lakh spreading over 249 villages in the then Sambalpur district, Odisha and 36 villages of Raigarh district of Chhatisgarh have been badly affected due to its reservoir. The data on the exact number of effected tribal is not available. The problem of displacement attracted a poor attention of the planners. They have been treated badly by the politicians and bureaucracy time and again. While laying the foundation stone, Nehru told the villagers, if you are to suffer, you should suffer in the interest of the country (Viegas, 1992: 53). The construction of IB thermal power station, sponge iron plants, iron and steel, thermal power plants, aluminum industries and coal mining around the Hirakud reservoir, particularly in Jharsauguda and Sambalpur belt in the 1980s and post-liberal era has again uprooted them for the second time and still struggling for their rights and livelihood.

Another post-independent euphoria of sacrifice lead to the construction of Bhakra dam across the river Sutlej in Punjab. It displaced 7,206 families from 371 villages and affected 36,000 persons. Even today 50 years after their displacement they are still struggling to put their lives back on line. The entire economic and social structure of this population was completely disrupted with displacement. Long arduous years were spent trying to scrap up enough for minimum sustenance (Dharmadhikari et al., 2005: 209, 216).

The displaces of Bhakra dam and Ranjit Sagar dam at Pong on the river Beas are going to face the second displacement due to the construction of Special Economic Zones (SEZs) at Gagret in Una districts in Himachal Pradesh. Here the state violates the basic concepts that fertile agricultural land will not be diverted for non-agricultural purposes. It is also a fact that in Himachal Pradesh the Una district has large plain areas while the rest of the state is covered with hilly tracks. This implies that to show favour and preference the state attach least care to the former oustee, who have yet to regain their lost status and farmers who will be land losers for the SEZs.

A few studies of displacement arising out of industrial projects have also set a milestone in this regard. To mention a few here are B.K. Roy Burman on Rourkela Steel Plant (RSP), S. Parsuraman on National Thermal Power Station (NTPC) in Korba, K.C. Samal on National Aluminium Company (NALCO), etc. The studies on displacement arising due to industrial projects also do not show a much encouraging findings. The findings on RSP shows that although the benefits accruing to the nation from the multiple effects of the RSP are immense, the local tribal are affected by the 'backwash effects' of industrialization to a great extent. Most of the direct and organized sector jobs generated by steel plant have been monopolized by outsiders hailing from different parts of the country, and also by the people from the relatively more advanced coastal districts of Odisha. Whereas the backward tribal people of the region and people from other depressed categories of adjacent tribal districts mostly landed up with informal and contractual category jobs of an exploitative nature (Meher, 2001: 290).

Mahapatra in *Development-Induced Displacement* (1998), a prominent Indian Administrative Service officer of Odisha cadre and Member of Parliament, candidly admits, little attention was given to the adverse affects of displaced people over their social, economic and community disruption, although they have sacrificed for the building of the nation. The bureaucracy or the civil servants obstructs the implementation of any beneficial schemes announced even by the chief minister of the state. In the case of Rourkela Steel Plant land acquisition the displaced suffered as the land has been allotted to outsiders and employees at a price 100–400 times more than what the government paid as compensation to the displaced people. The displaced people were deprived of land and commercial complexes by the authority.

'A cost-benefit analysis of the major development projects implemented in the country brings us to the stunning discovery that the Planning Commission criterion of 1:1.5 cost-benefit proportions has rarely been realized in any of them' (Murickan et al., 2003: 346). The Environmental Impact Assessment (EIA) is hardly carried out properly to guard against the cause of global warming and climate change, which has become a threat to the human and other living species. The industrial waste adversely affects the productivity agricultural field nearer to industrial units, to which the affected farmers are never compensated. The anti-pollution laws seldom operate in favour of the affected population. Lip service continued to be paid to the issues of environment, social and human concerns but development dominates other issues. There is 'lack of human touch' to the victims of development projects in general. Further 'studies show that a very large number of projects do not fulfil the norm on which they are sanctioned' (Lobo and Kumar, 2009: 290).

Thus, the studies made for the major industries and dams show that the affected population in general and the tribal in particular have not become a part of development process and have been marginalized in the process of current approach to economic development. The general conviction of the people that these people get much through compensation is a fallacious one. On this count they are marginalized and become the anti-development in the eye of general public. This sentiment of the people is largely exploited by the politicians against those who face the wrath of displacement through the engine of economic development. Sometimes the decision of putting a date line in availing compensation and R&R measures for various projects creates not only discriminations but also a sense of marginalization among the affected population. Marginalization is created through development and policy measures as well. Whatever the policy may the implementation is always half-hearted.

Estimate of Displacement

Among all the displacing agents such as dams, mines, industries, sanctuaries dams constitute the single most important displacing agent. And in the process among the people the tribal are the worst sufferers. They have experienced displacement more than once in their life time. But it is a fact that accurate data on the number of people displaced and affected by the projects is still not available. Here, a few cases of estimates have been presented.

By the end of the 20th century the world governments had build more than 45,000 large dams, possibly as many as 48,000. The overwhelming majority of these, around 40,000, were constructed after 1945. These dams, and the reservoirs behind them, had cumulatively pushed somewhere between 40 and 80 million people from their homes and lands. These are dams on approximately 60 per cent of the world's rivers, and nearly every larger river (Klingensmith, 2007: 1). In fact, dams have become the symbol of conquest over nature and strength of politico-bureaucratic power structure of developing countries like India. In this process the livelihood of millions of people was completely shattered only to provide benefit to a limited few thousands.

Asian countries record the highest incidence of displacement. In India, around 21 million people were affected during the last four decades (Fernandes, 2004). Among the displacing agents like dams, industries, and mines, dams occupy the top position. During the last two decades of the previous century, the magnitude of force population displacement caused by development programme was of the order of 10 million people each year or some 200 million people globally during that period (Cernea, 2000: 11). An estimate of nine states, viz., Andhra Pradesh, Assam, Gujarat, Goa, Jharkhand, Kerala, Odisha and West Bengal, show that 19,781,109 people have become displaced/project-affected people during 1947 to 2004. If other states of the country will be added the figure will become more than double.

In India 461 tribal communities have been identified which constitute about 8.08 per cent of total population in the country. Although they are unevenly spread across the country but large concentration is seen in the central India and north-eastern states. Roughly 92 per cent of the tribal live in hilly, dry and forested areas of rural India where there is the high availability of most of minerals. In Odisha, tribals account 22 per cent of the population, but 42 per cent of DPs-PAPs. The data is more or less similar in the states of Jharkhand, West Bengal and Chhattisgarh.

Significant section of the displaced is tribal and economically marginal rural population, who are dependent on natural resources like forests and rivers for their livelihoods. The 29th report of the Commissioner for Scheduled Castes and Scheduled Tribes (1990) makes very interesting revelation. It pointed out that till 1990, of the total displaced persons, 40 per cent were scheduled tribes. Their share in the total population of India, however is 7.5 per cent, SC people who constitute about 16 per cent of the country's population constitute 20 per cent of the total displaced persons (Kar, 1999: 19). The relocation and rehabilitation of these people varies in many respect from other categories of displaced people. No longer they can be deceived and deprived of economic development. They have also started demanding their jal, jungle and jamin (water, forest and land) for their survival and livelihoods. The incidence of Maoist violence is recording a high level, in various parts resource rich states for the growing inequality in the process of development.

In India, for instance, under the Sardar Sarovar Dam Project built in a mountainous region, no less than 95 per cent of the population displaced from Gujarat submergence area were tribals (the Tadvis, Bhils and Ratthwa), while in Madhya Pradesh about 40 per cent are tribals and the rest are caste Hindus (Mores and Berger, 1992; Modi, 2004; quoted by Cernea, 2006: 1). The percentage of tribal people displaced due to large dams is very high in the cases of Maheswar, Madhya Pradesh 60 per cent, Bodhghat, Madhya Pradesh 73.9 per cent, Chandli, Bihar 87.92 per cent, Keol Karo, Bihar 88 per cent, Polavaram, Andhra Pradesh 52.90 per cent, Upper Indiravati, Odisha 89.2 per cent, Pong, 56.25 per cent. These data reveal the extent of tribal affected through various development projects. The conservation projects also largely displace the tribal population.

The estimate made by Fernandes, Das and Rao (1989) shows that between 1950s and 1980s the number of people displaced in India not rehabilitated properly is over 11.5 millions or roughly 1.45 per cent of India's population. Another estimate shows that since independence, development projects of the five-year plans have displaced about 5 lakh persons each year, primarily as a direct consequence of administration and land acquisition (Maloney, 1991).

According to Fernandes (2007), since independence, as many as 60 million persons have been displaced, of whom a large majority have not been properly rehabilitated as yet. According to Reddy (1994: 4), seven government-based industrial projects, viz., the Bhilai, Bokaro, Rourkela and Vishakhapatnam Steel Plants, Hindustan

Aeronautics, Heavy Engineering Corporation, and National Aluminium Company, acquired 1,23,409.54 acres of land affecting 41,652 families. About 33,645 jobs were provided by these public sector projects to the affected families. The Krishna Irrigation Project (the reservoir and two major dams) displaced about 3,00,000 people. The controversial Sardar Sarovar Project has affected 297 villages, with at least 1,63,500 people getting displaced (ibid.: 179). According to another estimate (quoted in Kothari, 1996: 1476–85) based on a comprehensive study of 110 projects, of the 16.94 lakh people displaced by these projects, almost 50 per cent (8.14 lakhs) are tribal (Sharma and Singh, 2009: 62–63).

Industrialization has already displaced 60 million of India's villagers with the last 60 years, 3 million in Odisha alone, around 75 per cent of whom are adivasi and dalit. Very few indeed have been properly compensated, let alone improved their standard of living (Padel, 2009: 320).

With the adoption of New Economic Policy, 1991 the domestic private sector and multinationals have assumed the role of industrializing the state mainly through mineral based industries by getting the cheap minerals through an unholy alliance of politicians-bureaucrats-corporate. The mining scams of Odisha, the 2G spectrum scam are the burning examples. The era of liberalization is going to see more of tribal displacement in future.

Resistance and Violence

When you are transferred from one place to another place for a short time of one to three years you are doing all possible means either to cancel or to change the place of transfer, in case it is not to your choice one. And, when we are leaving our birth place and being snatched away from all social and economic means, will we not raise our voice against this forced eviction? This was the straight, simple truth told by a displaced person to the official, when he was asked that in spite of number of provisions why you are reluctant to leave the area for a particular project. This naked truth need to be understood by the politicians and bureaucrats in its human sense. Once they are out of the original habitations they are marginalized and their grievances remain unresolved forever.

Displacement induces the affected people to voice against displacement on account of several factors, like disruption of economic and social fabric, inadequate and improper resettlement and rehabilitation measures, denial of project benefit to the displaced people. It has been an observed fact that the project authorities and the displaced people have no economic compulsion to 'work together'. The oustees organize public processions *rasta rookos* (road block) *gheraos* and *bandhs* which are often brutally suppressed by police force. The political leaders and media often act on self-interest and political directions without promoting the cause of the oustee. Once they are physically removed, whatever, little attention was initially paid, their grievances are completely isolated.

A significant number of people have gradually refused to become silent sufferers of the ill effects of development and are now raising their voices collectively to counter development plans that they feel go against their interest and existence. In the process, they are profoundly influencing the emergence of an alternative development paradigm for India and the North-East (Hussain, 2008: 22).

The causes of displaced people have been brought to the light more successfully by the Narmada Bachao Andolan (NBA) against the construction of Sardar Sarovar Project. The history of struggle against development project has shown a little record of success, in cases like Silent Valley Project, Tikarpara dam across the Mahanadi, BALCO at Gandhamardan. The long march in October 2007 of more than 25,000 displaced, landless dalits and tribal from Gwalior to New Delhi to pressurize the central government to form a national lands commission and formulate a national land reforms policy was the culmination of many years of struggle, despaired and hope thousands of land less people (Pai, 2007: 10).

The history of police firing goes back to Colonel Dyer ordering Gurkha troops to open fire at Jallianwalla Bagh in 1919, and several large-scale firings in Odisha during the Quit India Movement 1942, as well as a pattern of more recent firings on Adivasi protestors, including 11 killed at Mandrabaju (Gajapati District) in December 1999 (Padel and Das, 2009: 128).

In the recent past the cases of Kalinganagar, Singur, Nandigram, and Kashipur are worth mentioning. The police firing at Kalinganagar killed 13 tribal people (January 2006) due to construction of Tata Steel which is likely to displace 443 families. In 2001, 10 tribal people were killed in a police firing in the protest against the Koel Karo Hydro Power Project. Similarly, on 6

December 2008 one person was killed and several people were injured in a police firing near Dumka, Jharkhand. A recent release of the people's tribunal on Nandigram has described the police firing and killings of 14 March in Nandigram as nothing less than a 'state-sponsored massacre'. The report of the people's tribunal, headed by Justice S.N. Bhargava, finds that 'there was unprovoked, indiscriminate firing without sufficient warning and without following the established procedure in accordance with law against a peaceful religious and lawful gathering of mostly women and children from Nandigram'. The report named 14 people, including two women, who were killed by police and one person who is missing. Further, it described the unsavoury collusion between the government agencies and the ruling CPI (M) party. Thus, the motive behind this massacre seems to be the ruling party's wish to 'to teach a lesson' to the poor villagers in Nandigram by terrorizing them for opposing the proposed Special Economic Zone (SEZ) project (Chaudhuri and Sivaraman, 2007: 4103).

Martyr's days to mark the fallen are becoming a routine. January 2, 2007 was the first anniversary of the shooting of 13 people resisting a steel plant on their land in Kalinganagar in Odisha. In Maikanch, Kashipur, also in Odisha, three tribal men were killed in 2001 during a protest against an ALCAN/Hindalco bauxite mine, and women were lathi charged and brutally beaten in 2005. In Nandigram, West Bengal, 14 were killed by police tried to enter barricaded villages scheduled to be displaced by a chemical hub (Temper and Martinez-Alier, 2007).

It is in the light of these 'power plays' of corporations that one needs to view events like Kalinganagar massacre at the outset of 2006, where, in one of the most startling incidence of state excess under a supposedly democratic government, 12 tribals laid down their lives while protesting specifically against the construction of work by Tata Steel – but generally against that area's reckless 'industrialization' that entailed their forceful eviction (Mishra, 2010: 49).

The formation of 'Salwa Judum' (purification hunt) in Chhatisgarh as a brainchild of a tribal leader in the assembly in 2005 has been designed to counter naxalite activities in the state. But the operation of Salwa Judum is principally against the tribal facing displacement due to the mining operation made by Tata and the US companies in Dantewada areas. The level of brutality, adopted by this agency, is to terrorize the tribals of these mining areas so that they will be forced to leave the mining belt to have easy extraction of mineral resources by the corporate giant.

The state-sponsored tribal militia called Salwa Judum was launched to fight the Maoists or Naxalites, with another major iron and steel project signed with Essar steel a few days later. Since then, over 600 tribal villages have been burnt by Salwa Judum, thousands of people have been raped and killed by both sides, and an estimated 2,00,000 tribal people have become refugees...yet this model is presently being copied in Odisha (Padel, 2009: 118).

The growing euphoria on the part of the state to create more mineral-based industries in the state is going to witness the ugly face of development-induced tribal displacement along with serious consequences to the environment in the days to come. In the name of economic development the developed countries have successfully transferred the most pollutant industries to the developing countries and the brunt of pollution have to be carried by the people of these developing countries through the destruction of natural livelihood of the tribal. The alarm of climate change has already warned the people of the planet.

Impact of Displacement

Is sacrificing people like this really development? And, is India's majority really benefited at all? Or, is the benefit simply the creation of further economic wealth for already privileged elite? And, can we say we know the relative values of what is gained and what is destroyed? Do we fully comprehend what is being sacrificed where tribal people's culture and quality of life are destroyed (ibid.: 310).

The Land Acquisition Act fails to address several economic, social, cultural, psychological and physical aspects of the displaced people. Once displacement takes place successfully, whatever may be the policy of R&R, they become marginalized; their voice remained unheard, they become rootless and suppressed ruthlessly. The democratic rules of right to equality and right against exploitation fail to operate for the victims of development. Their sacrifices for the cause of development become the forgotten story of the past and they slip down the economic and social ladder. Experiences show that development process creates a marginalized section of the people who become exclusion rather than inclusion to the process of development. The economic structure of the displaced people collapses. Based on the issues of resettlement Michael M. Cernea has evolved eight major impoverishment risk factors arising out of displacement. These are: (a) landlessness, (b) joblessness, (c) homelessness, (d) marginalization, (e) food insecurity, (f) increase in morbidity and mortality, (g) loss of access to common property, and (h) social disarticulation. Other risks like the risk of education in shift of occupation and risk of loss of livestock may also be added. The consequence of the insufficient and poorly conceived compensation and the resultant failure to recreate livelihoods is impoverishment (Cernea, 2003).

Many things in the modern power structure are the opposite of what they seem and a claim to be – a form of contrast which should excite any anthropologist interest. For instance, the World Bank often claims that its main aim is to eradicate world poverty. Yet, in the eyes of the people affected by dam and industry projects it has funded, it has vastly increased poverty, displaying huge numbers of people. Shattering their previous standard of living and reducing them to a desperate level of existence (Padel and Das, 2010: 21).

The net effect of lopsided development upon the displaced people has not only become impoverishment at the social and economic level but also lead to disempowerment in political sphere. 'Expropriation of land removes the main foundation upon which people's productive systems, commercial activities and livelihoods are constructed. This is the principal form of de-capitalization and pauperization for most rural and many urban displaces, who lose this way both natural and manmade capital' (Cernea, 1999: 17).

The draft National Tribal Policy (NTP), 2006 also admits the alienation of tribal land is the single most important cause of pauperization of tribal. The differed investment in the affected areas and the non-access to the collateral assets like land, in the pre- and post-displacement periods adversely affects their economic and social fabric for long time. The clothing of economic security becomes a dream for them.

In addition to this economic disruption there arises break of family and social relation. The women in the society of displaced community burnt the burden of displacement to a high level. There arises problem of health, plant and life in the process of industrialization. Deterioration of air, water, soil becomes obvious pollution that affects agricultural production, which again deteriorates the peasant community. Depletion of mineral resources, deforestation, dumping of industrial waste, pollution, haphazard and unplanned human settlement ... This is the stark evidence of the peril of mining and industrialization (Dhagamwar et al., 2003: 189). Various studies have marked out that all cases of involuntary displacements sub-serving development projects are inequitable in which the displaced are not the targeted beneficiaries (Mahapatra, 2006: 62).

'At the planned rate of extraction (3 million tonnes of bauxite per annum) the Vedanta mine will last 26 years. Yet most of the environmental effects are irreversible. If one side represents the past and the next the future, it is heartbreakingly obvious that after the minerals are gone, there will be no Dongria Kondhs left to enjoy the upswing of the Environmental Kuznets Curve (EKC) if it comes' (Temper and Martinez-Alier, 2007). The concept of EKC is only myopia of development via destruction without restoration of nature.

There exist no systematic data on the migration of people due to development projects but it has happened largely in the case of dam projects. As for example the displaced people of Hirakud have settled in various parts of western Odisha and neighbouring Chhattisgarh without availing the irrigation of Hirakud's water. On the other hand, there is in large number an influx of farmer from Andhra Pradesh to the command area of Hirakud. This is also with the displaced people of Bhakra, Sardar Sarovar Project and other dam projects in the country. Once the land-based livelihood system is shattered by these projects, they have no alternative except to move to other places in search of jobs and shelter. No systematic measure has been taken to prevent migration of displaced people of various development projects in the country. This creates subaltern in the economy through the process of economic development.

Again, in the context of RSP, it is pointed out that Raurkela achieved 91.06 per cent growth in population between 1961 and 1971, and a further 87.02 per cent between 1971 and 1981; it declined to 23.58 per cent between 1981 and 1991 because of the normalization of population. Who were these migrants and what role did they play in the distribution of the privileges? The majority of them were upper castes of the advanced coastal parts of Odisha and plain land of Madhya Pradesh, Bihar and West Bengal. They occupied more than 50 per cent of white-collar jobs in the plant. The tribes were then left with the low paid unskilled jobs (Rath, 2009: 84).

Industrialization, in fact, became a blessing to many who converted their land in to market complexes and gave houses on rent. But, for majority, industrialization became a curse. One can see this gloomy scene throughout the tribal settlement areas of the city (ibid.: 85).

Development-induced displacement leads to tribal deprivation of natural resources, culture, and social structure. The common property resources (CPRs) system of tribal livelihood get disturbed and the tribal women are the worst victim of this deprivation. In the context of tribal women, Fernandes concludes this somewhat sketchy discussion on tribal women's change in status after development-induced deprivation focuses on the fact that impact of displacement and deprival is felt in a graded manner. Most tribal communities suffer its negative consequences more than others. Even among them, women pay a higher price than men. This situation can be better understood when one realizes that displacement and rehabilitation are not one time event but a process that begins long before land is acquired and continues much after physical resettlement (Fernandes, 2009: 113).

The health aspect of the displaced tribals suffers due to change in habitation and dependence on natural vegetation. As a result, the cases of untimely death become more in such tribal areas. Least attention has been paid to this aspect of marginalized displaced tribals.

Policy Towards Displacement

In the matter of government influence upon the right of the tribal communities the Britishers were collecting land revenue from the tribal but the settlement of the outsiders in the tribal areas were not allowed. The tribal policy in India goes back to 1940, had an influence over the policy of United Nations Organization (UNO) and International Labour Organization (ILO). But Indian policy contains many contradiction in itself as a result a lot of gap between theory and practice is experienced in course of implementation of such policy.

Over the last 20–25 years, the international level has been incessantly trying to draw the attention of the world's leading power blocs to save them from perennial miseries. Currently, there are about 300 million indigenous people living in over 70 countries. They have come together to seek help from the United Nations to put an end to their poverty as well as to social discrimination against them (Rath, 2009: 15).

The declaration of the International Decade of the World's Indigenous People by United Nations had the objectives to make their life more of human in nature through better health, education and environment. Various committees, such as Elwin Committee (1959), Dhebar Committee (1961), Shilu Committee (1969), Shivaraman Committee (1981), etc., have examined the problem of different development programmes and suggested means or new programmes for the tribal communities. In India, several general and specific tribal development programmes have been launched through the creation of Tribal Development Blocks in the Second Five-Year Plan. Tribal sub-plans like Large Agricultural Multipurpose Societies (LAMPS), Juang Development Agency (JDA), in Keonjhar, Bonda Development Agency (BDA) in Koraput and many others. Along with these plans, the tribal communities get threatened due to proactive developmental adventures of the neo-liberal state policy.

To carry out the process of expropriation the state is well equipped with a set of colonial law called the Land Acquisition Act, 1894, as amended in 1984. 'The British were all set to modernize the then capital city, Calcutta but they were ill equipped, without acquiring the state rights over individual land. The first All India Act VI of 1857 was passed where land owners may be required by the legislature to surrender some of their rights they possess over their land for a purpose of public utility. Subsequently, a well-defined, all-comprehensive Land Acquisition Act covering the whole of British India came into force on 1 March 1894 as the Act 1 of 1894. In addition to the Land Acquisition Act, the Coal Bearing Act, 1956, the Wild Life Protection Act, 1972, 1982, are used as instrument of displacing people. Under the clauses of 'eminent domain' and 'public purpose' the state is empowered to acquire privately owned land. Till now with minor amendments this Act is being followed by the state as well as Government of India in the matter of land acquisition and distribution of compensation to the oustee. It is matter of concern that there was no proper R&R measure for long time in the country. Maharashtra is the first state to formulate a policy in 1976, which was followed by other states after much struggle by the affected community. Still the policy is to receive a legal status in the land where millions of people have been thrown out of development orbit of inclusive growth.

In Japan, in order to ease tension and conflict due to land expropriation and relocation, land acquisition has been substituted by the land leasing for land required for the reservoir. In Canada, the local indigenous communities who are affected by the dams have become the direct investors in hydro projects, by contributing their land. So also in case of Columbia 20 per cent of the project revenue is allocated towards providing benefits to the displaced reservoir population.

These cases of benefit sharing measure adopted in other countries can also be practised in India provided the age-old Land Acquisition Act is replaced by a new set of law with adequate provision of benefit sharing mechanism to the victims of development projects. There is lack of uniform policy for various displacing agencies. The mining sector, industrial sector, water resource sector have their own policies to deal with displacement differently. The displaced people are dealt with an iron law but treated with a soft policy which is not at par with the status of the law.

The compensation had to be paid for the land or property taken over based on historical cost plus a solatiums but the concept of replacement cost was unknown. The compensation amount was not a negotiated sum but a figure fixed by the government officials under certain rules ... enhancement of valuation in some cases (by the Court), but this was nowhere near replacement cost (Iyer, 2007: 3104). No profit-making activity should be termed as development activity and hence does not deserve land allocation on priority basis or concessional rates (Reddy and Reddy, 2007: 3239).

The Ministry of Rural Development, Government of India, has framed the National Rehabilitation and Resettlement Policy to deal with the problem of involuntary relocation in a better way. The incorporation of the provision of Ombudsman in R&R policy is a welcome step. But the power and function of this body need further strength. The concept of replacement cost, a long standing demand of the activists and researchers had found a place in the policy. This reflects the voice of the people to certain extent.

The 2006 Odisha R&R policy is somehow an improved version and shall apply to all projects for which private land has been acquired under Land Acquisition Act, 1894 as well as for which land is acquired through negotiation under the policy. This policy provides a better deal in comparison to earlier policies. However, certain areas of concern still prevails. Inadequate provision of agricultural land for the displaced people from mining and industrial projects may lead fettered away of cash compensation in a very short time period. Thus, there is the need of providing displaced people with replacement of agricultural land. The cases of multiple displacements need a far better treatment than the prescribed additional compensation amounting to 50 per cent of the normal compensation. The Scheduled Tribes and Other Traditional Forest Dwellers (Recognition of Forest Rights) Act, 2006 is a law to protect the livelihood of the tribal community. But the spirit of the law fails in its implementation sphere in many respects before the corporate lobby of mining and industrialization.

The multi-faced engagement of District Collector has led to half-hearted implementation of R&R policies. This has raised the eye-brow of the affected population over the imperfect implementation of the much talked R&R policy. A separate body for the purpose needs to function properly. An institution like Ombudsman should be instituted to check malpractices, corruption and discrimination prevailing in the present day political and bureaucratic culture of the country.

Conclusion

The time scale involved before the poor people in this country can benefit from industrialization by moving into industrial jobs is too long. It involves several generations that would have lost their land, livelihood and home in the mean time. How would they survive, how would their children face eventually the industrializing and globalizing world without education, health and without a community to impact social values? To sacrifice the weakest members of several successive generations in the name of development is unacceptable and incompatible with basis democratic values and economic goals of equity (Bhaduri and Patkar, 2009: 10).

While dealing with development of the economy the issue of displacement and environment cannot be relegated to background. The concepts of Pareto optimality and inclusive growth will be far away from reality in case of lopsided development where, development is made at the cost of a section of population. The sacrifice made by the displaced people as a whole for the development of the country is in no way less than the sacrifice of the freedom fighters. To achieve sustainable development or inclusive growth there is the need to deal displacement and environment properly to overcome risks arising out of development process without leaving them as the by-product of development. There is no substitute to development but we must have a comprehensive economic policy without undermining the social, cultural and institutional values.

The landmark judgment of the Supreme Court in the case of Menaka Gandhi vs. Union of India (AIR SC 597) and subsequent cases the right to life have included a life more than the mere animal existence to education, to safe and healthy environment and a 'good quality of life'. The implementation of this judgement will ensure a decent living for the displaced tribal.

The alternative way of industrializing would involve the poor, mostly uneducated and illiterate people as a propelling face for the creation and distribution of wealth. This involves (a) their participation through moving towards productive full employment in the shortest possible time, and (b) not destroying existing livelihood, which, in the present context, means that industry must come up on vacant/uncultivable land. Economic growth would be the outcome of this strategy, rather than employment and other benefits being the 'trickle down' outcome of growth. This is a fundamental difference between our and the official economic perspective in the formulation of Indian economic policies (Bhaduri and Patkar, 2009: 11).

Displacement should be avoided or to be as minimum as possible. The fertile land and populated areas should be out of the industrial establishment. The displaced people should be provided with the replacement cost of land rather than market determined price for the acquired land. R&R measures need to precede the construction of projects. Education and training must be imparted to the affected population before the commencement of the projects so as to prevent hijack of jobs and other benefits by the outsiders. A proper socio-economic survey is a prerequisite to carry out proper R&R operation. A time-bound measure is needed to achieve an all-round and higher level of development of the affected population/areas. Above all, a corruption-free administrative mechanism is highly essential to percolate the desired economic and social benefits to the bottom of the society. The industrial and mining units should allot share to the affected people so as to maintain a regular source of income. Social security measures like family pension, unemployment allowance, health insurance, and ensuring education to students irrespective of their level of schooling and category of caste or creed, food security during and after displacement need to be introduced to all categories of displaced people irrespective of the nature of the projects. Insurance coverage in respect of health, life and property should be provided to the affected population of all development projects. Land in the command area of irrigation projects must be acquired to resettle and rehabilitate the displaced people of that project before the project starts. The corporate houses must adhere to their commitment by discharging the corporate social responsibility in a vigorous way particularly towards the displaced people and environment of project areas. The displaced people of other projects should also be taken in a normative manner so that their deprivation and marginalization in the face of economic development is minimized and brought back to mainstream. To finance displacement, measure like collection of special assessment from the project benefit area, particularly in case of irrigation projects can also be taken. This unique measure requires courage on the part of the government for its introduction. The R&R policy should be accorded the status of an Act. Last but not the least, before chanting the mantra of development; let the inclusive growth not become exclusive growth for displaced people in general and the tribal in particular of the nation.

References

Ambagudia, J. (2010). 'Tribal Rights, Dispossession and the State in Orissa', *Economic and Political Weekly*, Vol. XLV, No. 33, 14 August.

Baboo, B. (1992). *Technology and Social Transformation: The Case of Hirakud Multipurpose Dam Project in Orissa*, New Delhi: Concept Publishing.

Baxi, U. and B. Parikh (Eds) (1995). *Crisis and Changes in Contemporary India*, New Delhi: Sage Publications.

Bhaduri, A. (2007). 'Alternatives in Industrialization', *Economic and Political Weekly*, 5 May.

Bhaduri, Amit and Medha Patkar (2009). 'Industrialization for the People, by the People, of the People', *Economic and Political Weekly*, Vol. XLV, No. 1, 3 January.

Cernea, M.M. (Ed.) (1999). *The Economics of Involuntary Resettlement: Questions and Challenges*, Washington, DC: The World Bank.

—— (2003). 'For a New Economics of Resettlement: A Sociological Critique of the Compensation Principle', *International Social Science Journal*, Vol. 55, No. 175, March.

—— (2006). 'International Dimension of Tribal Displacement', *Adivasi: Journal of the SC and ST Research and Training Institute*, Bhubaneswar, Vol. 42, No. 2.

—— (2007). 'Financing for Development: Benefit Sharing Mechanisms in Population Resettlement', *Economic and Political Weekly*, 24 March.

Chaudhuri, D.R. and S. Sivaraman (2007). 'Nandigram Six Months Later', *Economic and Political Weekly*, 13–19 October.

Debarajan (2008). 'Is the Struggle for Livelihood a Criminal Offence?', *Economic and Political Weekly*, 12–18 January.

Dhagamwar, V., Subrata De and Nikhil Verma (2003). *Industrial Development and Displacement: The People of Korba*, New Delhi: Sage Publications.

Dharmadhikari, S. et al. (2005). *Unravelling Bhakra*, Badwani: Manthan Adhyaayan Kendra.

Editorial (2010). 'Niyamgiri Triumph', *Economic and Political Weekly*, Vol. XLV, No. 35, 28 August.

Fernandes, W. (2004). 'Rehabilitation Policy for the Displaced', *Economic and Political Weekly*, 21–27 March.

—— (2009). 'Development-Induced Displacement and Tribal Women', in G.C. Rath (ed.), *Tribal Development in India*, New Delhi: Sage Publications.

Fernandes, W. and E.G. Thukral (Eds) (1989). *Development, Displacement and Rehabilitation: Issues for a National Debate*, New Delhi: Indian Social Institute, p. 4.

Fernandes, W., J.C. Das and S. Rao (1989). *Displacement and Rehabilitation: An Estimate of Extent and Prospects*, New Delhi: Indian Social Institute.

Government of Odisha (GoO) (2006). Odisha Resettlement and Rehabilitation Policy 2006, Bhubaneswar: Revenue Department.

Guha, A. (2007). 'Peasant Resistance in West Bengal: A Decade before Singur and Nandigram', *Economic and Political Weekly*, Vol. XLII, No. 37, 15 September.

Hussain, M. (2008). *Interrogating Development*, New Delhi: Sage Publications.

Iyer, R. (2007). 'Towards a Just Displacement and Rehabilitation Policy', *Economic and Political Weekly*, Vol. XLII, No. 30, 28 July and 3 August.

Kar, G.C. (1999). 'Displacement, Resettlement and Rehabilitation', *Orissa Economic Journal*, Vol. XXXI, Nos 1 and 2, January–June and July–December, p. 19.

Klingensmith, D. (2007). *'One Valley and a Thousand': Dams, Nationalism and Development*, New Delhi: Oxford University Press.

Lasgercaix, A. and A. Kothari (2009). 'Displacement and Relocation of Protected Areas: A Synthesis and Analysis of Case Studies', *Economic and Political Weekly*, 5 December.

Lobo, L. and S. Kumar (2009). *Land Acquisition, Displacement and Resettlement in Gujarat, 1947–2004*, New Delhi: Sage Publications.

Mahapatra, L.K. (1999). 'Testing the Risks and Reconstruction Model on India's Resettlement Experiences', in M.M. Cernea (ed.), *The Economics of Involuntary Resettlement*, Washington, DC: The World Bank.

—— (2006). 'Displacement of Tribal People with Land Resources for Development Projects: Their Risks and Entitlement for Rehabilitation', *Adivasi: Journal of the SC and ST Research and Training Institute*, Bhubaneswar, Vol. 46, No. 2, December.

Maloney, C. (1991). *Environmental and Project Displacement of Population in India*, Report No. 14, University Field Staff International, Indianapolis.

Meher, R. (2001). 'Degeneration of the Periphery under Hegemonic Development: The Case of Marginalisation of the Aboriginal in a Tribal Region', *Indian Social Science Review*, July–December.

Mehra, Puja (2007). 'SEZ Controversy: Course Correction', *India Today*, Vol. XXXLI, No. 5, 30 January–5 February.

Meir, G.M. and R.E. Baldwin (1957). *The Economic Development*, New Delhi: Allied Publishers.

Ministry of Rural Department (MoRD) (2007). National Rehabilitation and Resettlement Policy, 2007, New Delhi.

Mishra, B. (2010). 'Agriculture, Industry and Mining in Orissa in the Post-Liberalization Era: An Inter-District and Inter-State Panel Analysis', *Economic and Political Weekly*, Vol. XLV, No. 20, 15 May.

Mohanty, S.C. (2006). 'Involuntary Displacement and Rehabilitation of Project-Affected Persons in Upper Kolab Project, Koraput', *Adivasi: Journal of the SC and ST Research and Training Institute*, Bhubaneswar, Vol. 46, No. 2.

Murickan, Jose, M.K. George, K.A. Emmanuel, Jose Boban and R. Prakash Pillai (2003). *Development-Induced Displacement: Case of Kerala*, Jaipur: Rawat Publications.

Nathan, D. (2009). 'Social Security, Compensation and Reconstruction of Livelihoods', *Economic and Political Weekly*, Vol. 44, No. 30, 25–31 July.

Padel, F. (2009). *Sacrificing People: Invasion of a Tribal Landscape*, New Delhi: Orient Blackswan.

Padel, F. and S. Das (2010). *Out of This Earth: East India Adivasis and the Aluminium Cartel*, New Delhi: Orient Blackswan.

Pai, S. (2007). 'Janadesh 2007: The Land Question', *Economic and Political Weekly*, Vol. XLII, Nos 45–46, 10–16 and 17–23 November.

Panda, D.K. and N.K. Behera (2008). 'Development and Displacement: An Orissa Experience', *Journal of Rural Development*, Vol. 27, No. 1, January–March.

Panwar, T.S. (2008). 'Nailing the Himachal Pradesh Government's Lies', *Economic and Political Weekly*, Vol. XLIII, No. 50, 13 December.

Pathy, J. (1986). *Underdevelopment and Destitution*, New Delhi: Inter-India Publication.

Rath, G.C. (2009). 'Nehru and Elwin on Tribal Development: Contrasting Perspective', in Rath (ed.), *Tribal Development in India*, New Delhi: Sage Publications.

Reddy, V.R. and B.S. Reddy (2007). 'Land Alienation and Local Community', *Economic and Political Weekly*, Vol. XLII, No. 31, 4–10 August.

Sharma, R.N. and S.R. Singh (2009). 'Displacement in Singrauli Region: Entitlements and Rehabilitation', *Economic and Political Weekly*, Vol. XLIV, No. 51, 19 December.

Sharma, R.N. (2003). 'Involuntary Displacement: A Few Encounters', *Economic and Political Weekly*, Vol. XXXVIII, No. 9, 1–7 March.

Singh, S. (1997). *Taming the Waters*, New Delhi: Oxford University Press.

Suryanarayanan, M.H. (2008). 'What is Exclusive about 'Inclusive Growth'?', *Economic and Political Weekly*, 25 October.

Temper, L. and J. Martinez-Alier (2007). 'Is India Too Poor to be Green?', *Economic and Political Weekly*, Vol. 42, No. 17, 28 April.

Viegas, Philip (1992). 'The Hirakud Dam Oustees: Thirty Years After', in Enakshi Ganguly Thukral (ed.), *Big Dams, Displaced People: Rivers of Sorrow Rivers of Change*, New Delhi: Sage Publications, pp. 29–53.

6

Water for Power

Debating New Trends of Water Development in the Sikkim Himalayas

VIMAL KHAWAS AND DEEPA JOSHI

A small and beautiful state, Sikkim situated in the Eastern Himalaya spreads below the world's third highest mountain Kangchendzonga (8,598 m). The state is separated by the Singalila range from Nepal in the west, Chola range from Tibet in the north east and Bhutan in the south east. Rangit and Rangpo rivers form the borders with the Darjeeling district of West Bengal in the south. Sikkim Himalaya measures a total geographical area of 7,096 sq km with 349.3 km of international border – China border: 220 km, Bhutan border: 32.8 km, Nepal border: 96.5 km. It has a national border of 30.3 km with West Bengal. This also means 92 per cent of Sikkim's border is with neighbouring countries. About 100 kms from the border town Rangpo in South Sikkim lies the Bangladesh. The state of Sikkim has four districts – North, South, East and West – with the capital city of Gangtok located in the east district. The north district is largely a tribal district inhabited by about 56 per cent tribal population. Sikkim merged with Indian Union in 1975 and became the 22nd constituent state (Map 1).

Sikkim Himalaya is strategically located. It is wedged between Nepal in the west and Bhutan in the east and China in the north and north east. Measuring just 65 km east to west and 115 km from north to south, it ranges from sweltering deep valleys, with a mere 300 metres above sea level to lofty snow peaks such as Kangchendzonga. The state being a part of inner ranges of the Himalaya has no open

Map 1
Administrative Division of Sikkim

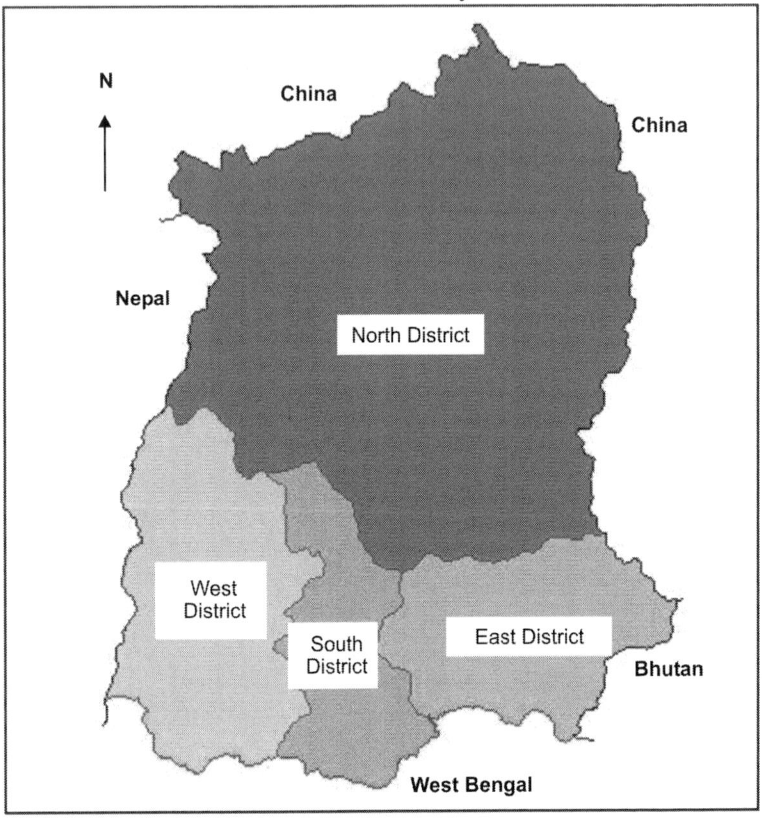

valley and plains but varied geographical elevations ranging from 300 to 8,598 metre above mean sea level consisting of lower hill, middle and higher hills, alpine zones and snow bound land; the highest elevation 8,598 metre being the top of the Kangchendzonga itself. On the north-western side of the Sikkim Himalaya lies the massive 31 km long Zemu glacier. Sikkim's botanical and zoological affluence is truly impressive and profusely fascinating.

Society and Economy

Different social, religious, linguistic and ethnic groups co-exist in the Sikkim Himalaya practising different types of agriculture and pastoral activities. The present population of Sikkim primarily consists of Lepcha, Bhutia, Nepali and plainsmen. The records of the Gazetteer of *Sikkim* (1891) throws us light that in the late 19th century Nepalis with 56 per cent constituted majority of the population followed by the Lepchas with 19 per cent and Bhutias constituting 16 per cent. There were also other groups like the Khambus and slaves. A little over century later, the share of Lepcha population has gone down to 14 per cent whereas that of the Nepalis climbed to almost 70 per cent with the Bhutias constituting more or less the same share.[1] These ethnic groups traditionally have their own language, culture and social practices although homogenization of such practices has gradually been taking place in recent times.

All the ethnic groups are characterized by specific ecological adaptations as well as by the social organization of the region where they live.[2] Majority of the social groups are found throughout Sikkim Himalaya although some areas are dominated by Lepchas and Bhutias. The Dzongu and Lacheng/Lachung regions of North Sikkim are the strongholds of Lepchas and Bhutias respectively. Lepchas, traditionally nature worshippers, are now mainly Buddhist by religion. Bhutias are also Buddhist and follow a form of *Lamaism* while majority of Nepali speakers are Hindus. Geographically, the northern Sikkim is very scarcely populated while the eastern part is densely populated followed by southern and western region.

Sikkim is primarily a rural and agricultural economy where over 60 per cent of its population are directly engaged in agriculture and allied activities while 85 per cent of the population is in one way or the other linked with agriculture and allied activities including livestock. The state has limited industrial potential due to its geologic and geomorphic constraints. More recently small and medium scale industrial units like fruit processing, pickle making, jewels, distillery, etc., are, however, gradually penetrating in the region. Sikkim is also a well-known producer of alcoholic beverages (Bhasin and Bhasin, 1996: 279). Notably, the contribution of agriculture and allied activities on the gross domestic product (GDP) of Sikkim has drastically reduced over the years while that of secondary and tertiary sector has increased. Conversely, however, the proportion of Sikkimese dependant on agriculture and allied activities has remained constant or decreased negligibly during the same period.

Table 1

Economic Arrangement in the Himalaya

Region	*Major Economic Activity*	*Other Sources of Economy*
Jammu & Kashmir	Agriculture and allied activity (about 70%)	Household industry, manufacturing, tourism
Himachal Pradesh	Agriculture and allied activity (about 90%)	Forest, hydropower, tourism
Uttaranchal	Agriculture and allied activity (more than 80%)	Forest, hydropower, tea, tourism, small-scale and cottage industry
Darjeeling	Agriculture and allied activity (about 26%)	Tea, tourism, forest
Sikkim	**Agriculture and allied activity (more than 85%)**	**Hydropower, tea, tourism, forest**
Arunachal Pradesh	Agriculture and allied activity (more than 90%)	Forest, hydropower, tourism, cottage industry and handicrafts
Nepal	Agriculture and allied activity (more than 91%)	Forest, hydropower, tourism, manufacturing, Household Industry
Bhutan	Agriculture and allied activity (93%)	Forest, hydropower, tourism

Source: Khawas, V., 2008.

Growth and Development of Power in Sikkim: A Review

Sikkim has innumerable streams and rivers flowing down the glaciers, which provide abundant potential of hydroelectric power projects. It is estimated that Sikkim has a potential to produce 8,000 MW seasonally and about 3,000 MW power during winter months.[3] The river Teesta, which is one of the major rivers originating in the state, has tremendous potential for promoting power generation as the river descends from an elevation of about 3,600 m to about 300 m over a distance of 175 km.

Power sector is the key input to the economic sustenance of any state. Sikkim is no exception in this, largely because here power industry, unlike other industries, is not only the propelling instrument but in itself a revenue generating sector for the state. The land locked hilly terrains marred with long rainy season may be inhibiting factors for the growth of industrial developments, but the same two natural features bestow the state a concentration of hydro potential.

Sikkim was declared a 100 per cent electrified state in 1995 as per definition of Rural Electrification Corporation of India (a federal government enterprise). However, the foundation of power was established in 1927 with the commissioning of first hydel project at Lower Sichey Busty on the bank of Ranikhola River near Gangtok with the installed capacity of 50 KW. This was distributed through 3.3 KV overhead transmission line to the Royal Family and Gangtok town. The Ranikhola hydel station was further augmented in the year 1935 by adding 60 KW generating set. In 1957, keeping in view of growing demand for electricity and as a standby measure, a diesel power house was established and commissioned with a capacity of 257 KW. This was upgraded to 4 MW from the previous capacity in 1998. Though the first generating unit was installed in the State as early as in 27 May 1927, it was only in 1962 that the electricity was made available to the general public in Gangtok. Till the end of 1975, the state was having a generation capacity of only 3 MW from its small hydel projects (SHP) like Jali Power House, Rimbi Micro Hydel, Rothak Micro Hydel, Manul Micro Hydel Power House and Diesel Power House at Gangtok.

The 60 MW Rangit Hydel project in West Sikkim was commissioned in 1999. A 2 MW Kalez Khola hydel project in Dentam in West Sikkim and 3 MW Rabomchu power project in North Sikkim were commissioned in 1995–96 and 1998, respectively. In the meanwhile, the demand started growing at a rather slow pace and the state government added some meagre capacity by installing diesel generator sets and microhydel units progressively. In 1979–82, when 12 MW LLHP was commissioned, the state could take up Rural Electrification Schemes, thereby more villages were electrified and the demand started growing.

At present, the peak load during winter is of the order of 61 MW[4] and it is expected to grow rapidly. The state nodal agency for renewable energy has installed 1,000 solar home lighting systems and five solar water heating systems. Till 31 March 2007, a total of 16 solar home lighting systems, 162 solar street lighting systems, 720 solar lanterns, 15 KWP aggregate capacities of solar photovoltaic plants, five solar water heating systems of 156 sq. m. area and 20 solar cookers have been installed in the state.

Existing Power System in Sikkim

With the launching of liberalized power policy by the Government of India and the opening of the sector for private developers, Sikkim was poised to gain in a big way and has been looking forward to earn significant revenue by exploiting its huge potential. The national planners and economists realized that the country cannot sustain a loss making power sector. Therefore, a new concept of providing quality power both to urban and rural populace alike at a reasonable rate arose which heralded emerging of the Electricity Act, 2003.

Further keeping in pace with recent development in power sector in the country the state government has launched its ambitious plan of developing the hydro potential giving due diligence towards environmental safeguard. Based on their viability a number of mega, small, mini and micro hydel projects have been identified and are being developed under state, public, private and joint sector in the state.

Sikkim, at present, has a total installed capacity of 100.70 MW. The per capita consumption of electricity in the state is calculated a little over 182 KWh.

Table 2

Existing Power Generation in Sikkim

Name of the Power House	*Installed Capacity in MW*
Lower Lagyap Hydroelectric Project	12.00
Jali Power House	2.10
Rimbi-I	0.60
Rongnichu-II	2.50
Chaten	0.10
Rimbi-II	1.00
Lachung	0.20
Meyonchu	4.00
Upper Rongnuchu	8.00
Diesel Power House	5.00
Rothak	0.20
Kalez Khola	2.00
Rabomchu	3.00
Total Under State Sector	40.70
Rangit-III under NHPC	60.00
Total installed capacity in the state	100.70

Source: Annual Report 2008–09, 2009. Energy and Power Department, Government of Sikkim, Gangtok.

Of the total capacity of 40.70 MW installed on 31 March 2004, 35.70 MW is hydro and the balance 5 MW is a diesel generating plant. All the projects being run of the river schemes have no dam or major reservoir for generation of rated capacities during the lean period. In Sikkim, the peak demand occurs during the winter months when the hydro generation drops down to less than 50 per cent of the installed capacity. In addition to the available capacity of 40.70 MW, the state also has a share of 77 MW in central sector generating stations and 10 MW seasonal in Raman HEP belonging to West Bengal State Electricity Board. This makes the total capacity availability of 127.70 MW.

Ongoing and Proposed Power Infrastructures

Projects under the State Sector

There are four on-going small/mini/micro hydel projects in the state sector currently under development with capital subsidy support from MNES; of which Mangley (2 MW) and Lachung Phase II (3 MW) HEP are expected to be complete by the year 2006–07. Other two ongoing hydroelectric projects, i.e., Relli Khola (6 MW), Rongli Khola (5 MW) are in the varying stages of construction. These projects have been transferred to Sikkim Power Development Corporation Ltd. (SPDC) for completing them through market borrowings. Besides, the department also awarded implementation of the following mini/micro hydel projects during the financial year 2005–06, by arranging fund through market borrowings.

Table 3

Projects under the State Sector

Project	*Installed Capacity in MW*	*Amount (Crore)*
Hee Khola	3	23.59
Kalez Khola II	6	47.79
Upper Rimbi	7.5	58.91
Barmelee Khola	3	21.23
Kissim Khola	2	15.35
Ringyang	1	9.02
Chatten II	2	12.02

Source: Annual Report 2008–09, 2009. Energy and Power Department, Government of Sikkim, Gangtok.

However, the government estimates total hydro-power potential at 8000 MW. Out of which, a total capacity of 5,248 MW from 26 projects have been formulated (see Table 3). The vision document of the state enshrines the fulfilment of this hydro potential. Under the Prime Minister's 50,000 MW initiatives, the Central Electricity Authority (CEA) have prepared Preliminary Feasibility Report (PFRs) of 162 schemes which are located in 16 states. Under this scheme, the Sikkim government has been allocated 10 schemes of 1,469 MW of installed capacity.[5]

Development of Hydel Projects under Public, Private or Joint Ventures

Considering the huge untapped hydel potential of the Teesta, Rangit and their tributaries and in keeping in view of the urgent need to harness the water resource of the state efficiently, there is opportunity to mobilize flow of capital investment through public, private or joint sector. Therefore, apart from development of various small, mini and micro hydel projects, the state has also awarded 26 projects to National Hydroelectric Power Corporation (NHPC) and other private developers. The total capacity of these projects stands at 5,248 MW. These projects are being developed under private, joint or public sector schemes. The list of the projects so far awarded is presented in Table 4.

A total of 5,188 MW capacity hydel power generation is expected to be added by the end of 11th Five Year Plan. From these projects, the State Power and Energy Department will get 12 per cent of free power.

The below projects after completion will fetch 12 per cent free power for the first 15 years and 15 per cent free power after that for a period of 35 years. After this, these projects shall be reverted back to the state free of cost in good operating condition. The Sikkimese government hopes to yield approximately ₹ 2,000 crore[6] per annum by tapping into 'the enormous hydroelectric potential from the run of the two snow-fed perennial rivers Teesta and Rangit'. The state expects to fully utilize the potential of one of the major resources of the state, i.e., the Teesta river. Besides, contribution at the national level, the state of Sikkim visualizes of a 'prosperous Sikkim with an effective public sector, thriving trade, abundant hydroelectric power, tourism, horticulture and floriculture and without poverty, illiteracy and unemployment'.

Table 4
Hydro-power Projects Allotted to Private and Public Sectors

Name of the scheme	*Installed capacity (MW)*	*Year of commissioning*	*Being developed under*
Teesta I	280	2011–12	JV
Teesta II	330	2011–12	JV
Teesta III	1,200	2011–12	JY
Teesta IV	495	2011–12	JV
Teesta V	510	2006–07	CPSU
Teesta VI	500	2011–12	JY
Lachen	210	2011–12	CPSU
Panan	300	2010–11	JV
Rangyong	117	2011–12	Private
Rongnichu	96	2010–11	Private
Sada Mangder	71	2010–11	Private
Chujachen	99	2009–10	Private
Bhasmey	32	2010–11	Private
Rolep	36	2009–10	Private
Chakhungchu	50	2010–11	Private
Ralong	40	2010–11	Private
Rangit II	60	2010–11	Private
Rangit IV	120	2010–11	JV
Dikchu	54	2010–11	Private
Jorethang Loop	96	2010–11	Private
Lingza	120	2010–11	MoU not signed
Thankgchi	40	2010–11	Private
Bimkyong	99	2011–12	Private
Bop	90	2011–12	Private
Ting Ting	70	2010–11	Private
Rateychu Bakchachu	40	2010–11	Private
Tashiding	60	2011–12	Private
Total	5,215		

JV: Joint Venture, CPSU: Central Public Sector Undertaking Annual Report 2008–09, 2009, Energy and Power Department. Government of Sikkim.

With the commissioning of a number of upcoming projects in the north-eastern region and Sikkim, the Ministry of Power, Government of India is working and an integrated transmission network for large scale evacuation of power to the prospective buyers in the power-deficit regions so as to facilitate independent power producers (IPPs) for marketing their energy.

Hydel Power Development and Conflict

Sikkim at present is at the summit of infrastructure development ventures. Up to March 2003 an estimated 834 hectares of forestland was diverted for development related activities. The share of hydro-electric projects, construction of roads, buildings, complexes and playgrounds, transmission line, etc., has been prominent in this regard.

Indigenous Community

The state government's hydel spree of more than two dozens of projects on the Teesta river basin has been facing severe protest in the tiny Himalayan state. Various community organization led by Affected Communities of Teesta (ACT), along with the Concerned Lepchas of Sikkim (CLOS) and the Sangha of Dzongu are protesting projects proposed in North Sikkim, particularly in Dzongu, the holy land and exclusive reserve of the Lepcha indigenous community.

Mention should be made here that the Sikkim government's plans to construct many of the hydroelectric projects in the Teesta river basin is meeting with stiff resistance in recent times. Protestors have joined together in an organization called the Affected Citizens of Teesta (ACT) and have been on *satyagraha* against these plans since 20 June 2007. The ongoing protests are focused on projects proposed in North Sikkim, particularly in Dzongu, the holy land and exclusive reserve of the Lepcha tribe. The protesters want the seven proposed projects in Dzongu scrapped and others in Sikkim reviewed. The ACT protest has received commendable support from the activists and environmentalists from across the country and outside.

While Sikkim has seen dam-related protests before, there have never been any on this scale. The 1990s saw the construction of the 60MW Rangit project, clearances for the 510 MW Teesta V project and the scrapping of the Rathong Chu project following protests about its impact on a sacred landscape. Further, in May 2008, the Chief Minister of Sikkim decided to cancel the Teesta IV Hydropower project, the Lingza Hydropower project, the Ringpi Hydropower project, the Rangyong Hydropower project and the Rukel Hydropower project, all expected to affect the Lepchas of the Dzongu region in North Sikkim in view of the persistent protests.

The cultural impacts of the dam constructions are immense. Imagine a situation where the locals are merely 300 individuals and more than 600 individuals come from outside to construct and operate the dam. Inundated by something exotic, the locals are bound to be influenced and may end up losing their culture and lifestyle altogether in the long run. Further, some of the areas where dams have been proposed are protected under Article 371 of the Indian Constitution, in order to protect these areas from outside influence; however, this does not seem applicable to dam proponents. Majority of the people living in these areas have always lived sustainably and they are not yet exposed to many diseases. The chances of the locals acquiring diseases like AIDS, cancer, and tuberculosis are multiplied significantly with increase in the number of outsiders visiting these areas.[7]

Environment

The degradation of the Himalayan ecosystem/environment is emerging as one of the major concerns for ecologists and environmentalists across the country. It has been observed that the creation of reservoirs, fluctuation in natural river discharge and diversion of river waters through closed tunnels would completely change the ecological conditions of the river systems. Along with the submergence of rivers and valleys by hydro power plants, deforestation, pollution of fresh water sources and improper sewage disposal are some of the major factors which are affecting the Himalayan ecosystem directly.

The most burning environmental issue faced by Sikkim currently is the installation of dams on Teesta and adjoining rivers and submergence of valleys for the construction of hydroelectric projects. The biggest concerns are the impact on the surrounding environment, the glacial behaviour, the river system and the occurrences of floods. These seem to have either been overlooked or their impacts underplayed in the Environment Impact Assessment (EIA) reports. The proposed sites are already unstable and a number of active and dormant landslides of different dimensions are present in the region. After impoundment of the reservoir, the water level in the reservoir area will rise considerably. As a consequence, the strength parameters of the slope mass will decease and it may become susceptible to destabilization. Thus triggering of new landslides and further destabilization of already active slides cannot be ruled out.

The EIA reports make a cursory mention of impending hazards but little is known of how the project authorities propose to tackle the problems. This is no great news for a region already facing the cost of short-sighted mountain development.

Box 1

Dam of Chuzachen Hep Collapses

At least 12 labourers were washed away in East Sikkim when an under-construction dam of 99 MW Chuzachen HEP collapsed at about 9 pm on 16 April 2009. At least 12 bodies were trapped in a tunnel between Lamaten and Rolleck areas and 10 bodies have been recovered, but the toll could mount as it was not clear how many labourers were at work at the site. Since a 1 km tunnel was flooded after the collapse. Superintendent of Police M.S. Tuli said that they have registered a case under Section 304(A) of the IPC against the private developer and another company to which the dam construction work was awarded for causing unintentional death of the labourers. As per the preliminary information, the labourers were working in the coffer dam in the night shift when the dam suddenly burst 'due to a rise of water level of Rongli River triggered by heavy rainfall'; it is not known if there was any heavy rainfall in the area recently. The dam was being built by Gati Infrastructure Limited, a courier company that has no experience in dam building. The project has two intakes one on Rangpo Chhu and another in Rongli Chhu and each with a dam and headrace tunnel and then join together to a common headrace tunnel. Chief Minister of Sikkim laid the Foundation Stone for the Chuzachen Hydroelectric Project on 6 February 2007. The project got environment clearance on 9 September 2005. In September 2008 the project applied for CDM under UNFCCC status. In fact, during the public hearing for the project on 30 September 2004, 'Several people expressed fear about disaster that may happen due to the tunnel passing through Rongli bazaar as the area is vulnerable to landslides. They desired that tunnel should be shifted', as noted at the Project Design Document submitted for the CDM status. This incident shows that the feat expressed by people then was timely and by not heeding it the project authorities, the Sikkim Pollution Control Board and the Union Ministry of Environment and Forests, have invited this disaster. They all must be held accountable for this disaster, along the contractor building the project.

Source: http://www.indiaenvironmentportal.org.in/files/Chuzachen_Hydro_Dam_Collapse_in_Sikkim_April_2009.pdf (accessed 20 March 2011).

Further, huge physical and financial damages were caused to the Nathpa Jhakri (Himachal Pradesh) and Rangit (Sikkim) projects by glacial lake outbursts in recent years. These outbursts caused sudden increase in the flow into the respective river systems. But there is no mention of such a phenomenon in the EIA reports of the projects on the Teesta, which is sustained by glacial melt, snow melt run-off and monsoon rainfall. Information on glacial behaviour and its impacts is, therefore, necessary to analyse the impacts on downstream population and the environment, and to gauge the economic viability of projects in these regions. The information on melt water yield and its chemical and sediment characteristics is vital to the safety and maintenance of the hydroelectric installations and reservoirs in the Himalayas.

According to noted environmentalist, Sunderlal Bahuguna,[8] 'construction of several hydel projects in Sikkim amounted to a "destructive act" against the ecology of the "greenest" state of the country. The hydropower projects in Sikkim are a destructive act against the ecology and environment of Sikkim which is a part of the Himalayan mountain range. Power generation by disturbing water resources emanating from the Himalayans cannot be justified for seeking to commercially tap them, through 'destruction of the forest cover and the fragile landscape'.

The Comptroller and Auditor General (CAG) of India, in its 2008–09 report, recommended the state government to strengthen the monitoring and vigil aspects of the hydel power projects execution by setting up a system of independent power projects (IPPs). After reviewing the performance of the hydel power thrust of the state government, it was said that the 'monitoring of execution of projects was virtually non-existent' in the state.

The CAG also called it necessary to make adequate provisions in the environment plans for designing suitable measures to mitigate the effect of hydel power projects on aquatic life of Sikkim. Sikkim has 63 species of phytoplanktons, 17 species of zooplanktons and 48 species of fish inhabiting state's river systems.[9]

It was reported by the CAG that there were many gaps in the proposed Environment Management Plans (EMP). The CAG said that the EMPs for the projects had been prepared through assessment of secondary data without any diligent study or observation and no proper time series research of prevailing ground realities was done. The Catchment Area Treatment (CAT) plans for the various power projects was prepared without taking into account the field requirement for survival of the plantations and were therefore said to be arbitrary and inadequate.

Cross-Border Concerns

Researchers and activists from Bangladesh and India have also raised concerns about the impacts of dam building activity on the Teesta on the water flows into Bangladesh. The problem is aggravated due to official secrecy. Data of international rivers is not accessible to the public and this limits water-related research and water resource planning. Lack of river flow data also causes conflicts and unjustified claims by different parties. Due to lack of any data about river flows in upstream parts of rivers (like the Teesta), it is impossible for downstream communities to ignore these claims or verify them.

The Controversy of Stay Order to Some Projects

In an interesting twist in the late 2008, the Ministry of Environment and Forests (MoEF) issued a letter to the Government of Sikkim that no activities related to dams (even investigations) should be taken up north of the Chungthang region in North Sikkim, home to the Lepcha and other communities. It was seen as a critical step forward for the struggling Lepcha community members. The Centre directed the state government not to proceed with construction of six projects with projected capacity of 1047 MW.

Various formalities like land acquisition and survey works by the developers at the six projects were stopped after the union environment ministry wrote a terse letter suggesting that these projects were unviable citing a study report by an independent body. The environment ministry took the report by the New Delhi-based Centre for Inter-Disciplinary Studies of Mountains and Hill Environment (CISMHE) and derailed six proposed hydel projects in North Sikkim adding that the state government has no option but to put the project on hold. The projects affected by the Centre's directive included Teesta Stage I (300 MW), Teesta Stage II (480 MW), Lachen (120 MW), BOP (99 MW) and Bimkyong (99 MW) and Lachung (99 MW).[10]

The Government of Sikkim was, however, not deterred. In January 2010 meeting of the Expert Appraisal Committee (EAC), it argued that the project developers were willing to take on board the concerns raised in the CISMHE study and address them, and exploratory work in North Sikkim should therefore be permitted to determine if projects there could be carried out. In February 2010, the EAC gave permission to Teesta I and II projects to conduct investigations, based on revised location and parameters. As the projects were close to the Kanchandzonga National Park, the Government of Sikkim was also asked to take the permission of the National Board of Wildlife (NBWL). In March 2010, members of the EAC visited Sikkim and were hosted by the government, and local activists allege, by the project authorities themselves.[11] In April 2010, the remaining three projects in North Sikkim were also allowed to carry out investigations. These were the Lachung, Bhimkyong and Bop hydroelectric projects.

In the judgement of the group that visited the sites of the above projects, the sites at Bop and Bhimkyong, do not have any rehabilitation issues and the 10 km stretch of the tunnelled river is intercepted by several perennial streams. Using modern technology the impact of tunnelling on land slide prone areas may be reduced. These and other technical considerations noted in the minutes of the April 2010 meeting allowed the project authorities to invade into the ecologically fragile North Sikkim. Recommendations from MoEF's own processes, as well as large scale protests by affected people were just brushed aside.

Consequently, hydropower corporations, supported by the processes and persons of government, are left free to exploit the resources of a region, with little regard to the wishes of the local people or even normal considerations of common sense in the management of an ecosystem.

Voices from the Field

'We first welcomed this project as it was supposed to bring development to the state. But until now we have only seen the negative impacts of the project. So we cannot speak positively about the project now. We have been dealing with the negative impacts phase wise. First was the issue of compensation, now it is of the impacts of blasting…' The residents of Lower Samdong, Sikkim, reacting to the hydel dam constructed near their village.

Dawa Lepcha, general secretary, Affected Citizens of Teesta (ACT), said, 'The entire Teesta River is being tunnelled. The main river of Sikkim is disappearing underground. Is this development? Sikkim is a very small state, but very rich in biodiversity. If they are allowed to go ahead with the hydel projects, they will ravage, plunder and destroy everything.'

'By building seven dams in the Lepcha-protected (Dzongu) area, and allowing such a large influx of migrant labour, the government is violating its own laws. There are only 7,000 Lepchas in Dzongu.[12] With just one project, we will be outnumbered. Our culture is under threat.'

'The blasting of rocks to build the tunnels has resulted in the drying up of water sources and landslides in villages near the 23 km long stretch. A lot of mud and debris has been dumped along the river banks.'

According to Jung Bahadur Chettri, 'Owing to the blasting, there are so many cracks in my house that it is not in a condition to live in. There are 20 of us in my family. We had to move to another person's house during the monsoon. What's even worse is that our farms are destroyed because the streams have dried up. We used to sell fruits and vegetables in the market. Now, there's none for us to eat.'

Box 2

Impact of large-scale tunneling across the hills: villagers' perception

Pamphok is a village located in the rain shadow area of South Sikkim. It is inhabitated by about 100 households mainly agrarian in nature. Major crop in the village include maize. According to the villagers, forest has been degrading rapidly in the last 20 years.

LANCO (Langarapati Amaraappa Naidu and Company), a private hydel company, has dug several underground tunnels at the foot of the Pamphok village. These tunnels cross the village from beneath it and reach *Sirwani* near Singtam where hydel dams are have been constructed.

Complaints of cracking houses, drying up of water resources and landslides have been streaming in from local people living above the tunnelling area.

The villagers believe that ponds and natural springs are gradually drying up because of the construction of tunnels beneath their village. They lament 'the company is digging from the base of the village and surface water in and around the village are drying up. If a vessel has a hole from inside at the bottom, it can never be filled or hold water. It will leak definitely'.

In Bhim Prasad's opinion, 'This dam has destroyed Sikkim. Water used to spring out of the earth here. Now, it's all gone – the trees, the farms, and the grass. All the villages are hungry.'

'If the land is taken by industrialists, we will be refugees in our own land. It hurts us to see Dzongu being destroyed,' says Onchuk Lepcha.

'On the one hand, the Lepchas have been declared a primitive tribe by the State Government, and on the other, they are assisting capitalist companies to bulldoze, plunder and devastate in the name of development of the land that had been protected for decades,' says Dawa Lepcha.

'The projects involve diverting up to 85–90 per cent of the river flow in the lean season through long tunnels before the water is dropped downstream. Not only will this destroy the riverine ecology

Box 3
Press Release
Tseten Lepcha, Working President

Affected Citizens of Teesta, Gangtok, Sikkim Dated 13 October 2010

The demand for scrapping of various mega hydro-electric power projects raised for a very long time by the people of North Sikkim particularly from Dzongu through the *Affected Citizens of Teesta, Sangha of Dzongu and the Concerned Lepchas of Sikkim* and supported by various individuals and organizations has reached the highest International forum, the United Nations Organization (UNO).

The issues raised in the memorandum submitted to the General Body of World Mountain Peoples Association (WMPA) by the representatives of the North-East India were discussed, accepted and then passed as the motion by the General Body and then submitted to the UNESCO by the WMPA on the 4 October 2010.

The meeting at the UNESCO, Paris was presided by Mr Thomas Schaaf, Secretary of Commission and present on the occasion were Mr S. Panikar, the Indian Government representative in the UNESCO, The Ambassador of Equador, Peru and Mr Jean Lassale the Chairman of WMPA read the Motions and submitted to the Secretary of Commission. The North-East was presented by Ms Mayfereen Ryntahaing, President Grassroots (Meghalaya) Mr Anthony Debberma, Borok Peoples Human Rights (Tripura) and the undersigned. The copies of the motion and letters attached for your kind reference please.

but a cascade of projects will mean the Teesta is in full flow only in brief stretches between the two hydel projects,' says Pemzang Tenzing, a civil engineer and ACT member.

Discussion

The hydel dams proposed for Sikkim are part of the Government of India's programme of dam construction to create another 200 billion cubic metres of storage through the 50,000 MW Hydroelectric Initiative, launched in May 2003.[13] It is part of the central government's master vision of the north-eastern region as 'India's Future Power House', with around 168 dams planned. The projects are being cleared at any cost. The potential for hydro development in India as proposed by the government is immense and a modest estimate of the same has been assessed at 84,044 MW at 60 per cent load factor – if about 1,48,000 MW is the installed capacity. The north and north-eastern regions contain the lion's share of this, with 54,000 and 59,000 MW respectively.[14]

The arguments put forward to justify hydel projects in Sikkim are: exploitation of the state's perennial water system to produce power for the nation; economic benefits to the state through power export; employment generation and low displacement of local communities.

However, critics lament several unique features of the state including its ecological and geological fragility, its indigenous communities, their cultural and spiritual association with the river system and the landscape pose a challenge to these ambitious plans.[15] The Carrying Capacity Study of the Teesta basin in Sikkim, commissioned by MoEF, Government of India urged caution in relation to the Teesta projects on environmental safety and cultural grounds.

The six-member Independent Committee on Big Hydro Projects that visited the Dzongu region in May 2008 stressed that the development of small and micro hydropower projects would economically benefit the people of Dzongu and in addition help Sikkim generate additional electricity. The Committee headed by Himanshu Thakkar suggested the state government to develop small and micro hydropower projects in the Dzongu region. Nonetheless, in the last many years, the state government has signed MoUs for no less than 27 large hydroelectric projects in the state. It is alleged, Sikkim government has committed itself to develop these hydropower projects, without much consultation with the Sikkimese people or without considering the implications of the projects for the local people, environment, culture, future generations and even return on investment for the state or the people.

One wonders how the MoEF cleared the dam projects after reading the carrying capacity report. The report recommends that there should be no large-scale development in the geologically sensitive and biodiversity-rich regions of North Sikkim because there is the danger of glacial lake outburst floods, massive landslides and flash floods. Dam-building activities should not be carried out upstream of Chungthang, a town situated at the confluence of the Lachen and the Lachung Chu, tributaries of the Teesta, which is the starting point of the river. It is also a town imbued with Buddhist legend. Guru Padmasambhava, the revered founder of Tantric Buddhism in Tibet, is said to have rested here and left his footprint on a rock. There are seven projects planned north of Chungthang.

Further, considering that the Teesta basin is in an earthquake-prone area,[16] the report also recommends more surveillance of seismic activity. It recommends small-scale projects south of Chungthang rather than large projects. The report also warns that the views of local communities should not be undermined or neglected. Besides warning about the dangers of dams, the carrying capacity report also focuses on local development measures such as reviving agriculture, organic farming and minor irrigation projects, infrastructure for floriculture, improving schools and healthcare facilities, protecting biodiversity and endemic species, and restricting commercial taxis.

However, the Government of Sikkim insists that they (hydel dams) are harmless. Representatives of the state government persevere:

> It is the most eco-friendly. There is no pollution, only a little during the construction; we have got all the environmental clearances from the Central government. These are not big dams, just small diversion dams. They are not within the Kanchenjunga National Park. The entire Himalaya is a sensitive zone but the Central government has planned hundreds of dams across the mountain ranges, not only in Sikkim. No one can prove that people's homes were damaged owing to the blasting. It could be for other reasons such as earthquakes or landslides.

Unfortunately, the proposal of the hydel dams in Sikkim have not looked into the economic and livelihood impact on this region, the forests destroyed, biodiversity affected and the impact on riverine flora and fauna, once Teesta is tamed and flows like a timid stream, with less discharge and becoming a stagnant pool of water chained in reservoirs. A whole civilization will get badly impacted, resulting in newer forms of trade and marketing relations coming up facilitated and promoted by a large influx of people from outside disturbing the tranquility of this otherwise sleepy region. The identity and culture of the region is going to change for bad.

Further, there has been no employment for the locals. Even unskilled work is being done by migrant labourers from outside.

Lastly, the question that is often being raised today by the critics from various fronts is development for whom and for whose benefit? It is clear that the hydropower projects are proposed not for development of Sikkim or the Darjeeling but for meeting the huge demand of the northern states of India including the big cities and metropolis. The excess power that will be produced will be evacuated to meet the above demand-supply gap and the affected people have to sacrifice – their home, their land, their identity, culture and livelihood to meet demands of people at faraway places.

Notes

1. M.P. Lama. 2001. *Human Development Report: Sikkim.* Gangtok: Government of Sikkim.
2. Veena Bhasin and M.K. Bhasin. 1996. 'Sikkim Himalayas: Ecology and Resource Development', *Journal of Human Ecology*, 7(4): 270.
3. *Annual Report 2008–09.* 2009. Energy and Power Department, Gangtok: Government of Sikkim.
4. Ibid.
5. Avilash Roul. 2007. 'God's Own Garden in Peril: Hydel Projects Threaten Lepcha Community in Sikkim', *Ecoworld: Nature and Technology in Harmony*, December 33. http://www.ecoworld.com/energy-fuels/hydro-electric/sikkims-teesta-river.html (accessed on 16 March 2011).
6. Kerry Little. 2008. 'Lepcha Narratives of Their Threatened Sacred Landscapes', *Transforming Cultures eJournal*, 3(1): 232, February. http://epress.lib.uts.edu.au/journals/tfc.
7. Upendra Mani Pradhan. nd. 'The Dam and the Damned'. http://www.mountainforum.org/rs/ol/counter_docdown.cfm?fID=1629.pdf (accessed on 27 March 2011).
8. *The Sikkim Time.* 2009. 'Bahuguna Criticizes Sikkim Government on Hydel Projects', 13 November.
9. Pragya Lama. 2010. 'Ill Planned Hydroelectric Projects: The Burning Environmental Issue in Sikkim'. http://www.negreens.com/2010/10/

27/ill-planned-hydroelectric-projects-the-burning-environmental-issue-in-sikkim (accessed on 27 March 2011).

10. PTI. 2009. 'Six Hydel Projects in Sikkim Put on Hold', 19 July.
11. Kanchi Kohli. 2010. 'Damming and Damning the Teesta', *India Together*, 22 June.
12. Dzongu, the holy land of the Lepchas, was a protected area even when Sikkim was an independent kingdom (Sikkim merged with the Union of India in 1975). Any outsider, even a Lepcha living outside Dzongu, has to apply for a permit to enter it. Only Lepchas from Dzongu can own land here.
13. Shripad Dharmadhikary. 2007. 'Have River, Will Dam', *Himal Southasian*, September 2007 (accessed on 20 March 2011).
14. Upendra Mani Pradhan. nd. 'The Dam and the Damned'. http://www.mountainforum.org/rs/ol/counter_docdown.cfm?fID=1629.pdf (accessed on 27 March 2011).
15. Neeraj Vagholikar. 2007. 'Satyagraha for the Teesta', *Tehelka*, 20 September. http://www.tehelka.com/story_main34.asp?filename=cr290907SATYAGRAHA.asp (accessed on 20 March 2011).
16. The area falls under seismic zone IV with a history of moderate to high intensity earthquakes during the last 200 years. The NH 31A to Gangtok connecting Siliguri in West Bengal and Assam is dotted with highly unstable landslide-prone areas and sinking zones. Because of a comparatively young Himalayas, unstable slopes and turbidity of the river Teesta, it carries heavy sedimentation and silt load during the monsoons changing the colour of the water completely. It erodes its banks consistently and changes its course especially in the downstream.

References

Annual Report 2008–09 (2009). Energy and Power Department, Gangtok: Government of Sikkim.

Bhasin, Veena and M.K. Bhasin (1996). 'Sikkim Himalayas: Ecology and Resource Development', *Journal of Human Ecology*, Vol. 7, No. 4, pp. 265–99.

Bhatt, S.C. and Gopal K. Bhargava (2005). *Land and People of Indian States and Union Territories*, Vol. 34, New Delhi: Kalpaz Publications.

Bunsha, Dionne (2008). 'Teesta's Tear', *Frontline*, 3 June.

Choudhury, Maitreyee (nd). *Carrying Capacity Study of Teesta Basin in Sikkim: Socio-cultural Environment*, Vol. X, Commissioned by Ministry of Environment and Forests, Government of India, Sponsored by National Hydroelectric Power Corporation Ltd., Faridabad, Executive Summary (the report is undated however the references date as late as 2002).

Dharmadhikary, Shripad (2007). 'Have River, Will Dam', *Himal Southasian*, September (accessed on 20 March 2011).

Government of Sikkim (GoS) (2003). *Sikkim: A Statistical Profile-2002*, Gangtok: Government of Sikkim.

Khawas, Vimal (2008). *Environmental Issues and Human Security in the Himalayas: A Comparative Study of Eastern Nepal and Sikkim*, Unpublished PhD. New Delhi: Jawaharlal Nehru University.

—— (2007). 'Environmental Challenges and Human Security in the Himalaya', Paper presented at National Seminar on 'Himalayas in the New Millennium: Environment, Society, Economy and Polity', Centre for Himalayan Studies, North Bengal University, Darjeeling, 11–12 January.

Khullar, D.R. (2000). *India: A Comprehensive Geography*, New Delhi: Kalyani Publishers.

Kohli, Kanchi (2010). 'Damming and Damning the Teesta', *India Together*, 22 June.

Lama, M.P. (2001). *Human Development Report: Sikkim*, Gangtok: Government of Sikkim.

—— (2007). *Sikkim Economic Survey 2006–07*, Gangtok: Government of Sikkim.

Lama, Pragya (2010). 'Ill Planned Hydroelectric Projects: The Burning Environmental Issue in Sikkim', http://www.negreens.com/2010/10/27/ill-planned-hydroelectric-projects-the-burning-environmental-issue-in-sikkim (accessed on 27 March 2011).

Little, Kerry (2008). 'Lepcha Narratives of Their Threatened Sacred Landscapes', *Transforming Cultures eJournal*, Vol. 3, No. 1, February, http://epress.lib. uts.edu.au/journals/tfc.

Majumdar, Tapas (nd). *Teesta, Condemned to Death: A Synopsis*, A Short Documentary, Kolkata.

Pradhan, Upendra Mani (nd). 'The Dam and the Damned', http://www.mountainforum.org/rs/ol/counter_docdown.cfm?fID=1629.pdf (accessed on 27 March 2011).

Press Trust of India (2009). 'Six Hydel Projects in Sikkim Put on Hold', 19 July.

Roul, Avilash (2007). 'God's Own Garden in Peril: Hydel Projects Threaten Lepcha Community in Sikkim', *Ecoworld: Nature and Technology in Harmony*, 3 December, http://www.ecoworld.com/energy-fuels/hydro-electric/sikkims-teesta-river.html (accessed on 16 March 2011).

The Hindu (2004). 'Testing Times for the Teesta', 6 June.

—— (2007). 'Protest against Hydel Projects in Sikkim', 25 July.

The Sikkim Time (2009). 'Bahuguna Criticizes Sikkim Government on Hydel Projects', 13 November.

Vagholikar, N. (2007). 'Satyagraha for the Teesta', *Tehelka*, September 20, http://www.tehelka.com/story_main34.asp?filename=cr290907SATYAGRAHA.asp (accessed on 20 March 2011).

7

Giving with One Hand, Taking Away with the Other

Land for Industry via Land Distribution Programme in Andhra Pradesh

PATRIK OSKARSSON

Andhra Pradesh has been one of the most active states in India in pursuing industrialization via Special Economic Zones (SEZs), power plants, ports and many others forms of large-scale projects. As elsewhere in the country most SEZs are in Information Technology and concentrated in the main urban areas of the state but a number of projects across the state are attempting to acquire larger areas of land and these are the ones where most concerns relating to displacement exist. Land acquisition in Andhra Pradesh becomes especially interesting since the state has managed to divert major areas of land for SEZs largely without the protest movements of, for example, Maharashtra or West Bengal. This has been achieved despite Andhra Pradesh not having followed the proactive policy of states like Tamil Nadu and Gujarat where state industrial development corporations acquired large areas of land over decades and recently converted many of these into SEZs.

This paper presents one answer to how the Government of Andhra Pradesh manages to acquire land largely without protest. The account is based on a disturbing pattern noticed during PhD fieldwork at an upcoming alumina refinery in Vizianagaram district where a disproportional part of land now provided to investors had been part of earlier government campaigns to distribute agricultural land to poor, landless households. The paper begins with an overview of policies for land acquisition in Andhra Pradesh with special focus on compensation and for local democratic deliberations. The second part of the paper provides details about the case study at a site in coastal Andhra Pradesh. The following section shows how land acquisition proceeded, focusing on the differences between what was presented in official planning documents and what was actually happening on the ground. Finally, some conclusions are made as to why the case study is likely to have a much wider relevance in the state and what the implications are for the possibilities of just land acquisition.

Policies for Land Acquisition in Andhra Pradesh

Land acquisition and compensation in Andhra Pradesh as in the rest of India relies on the Land Acquisition Act, 1894. Here, as in basically any other part of India, there is no land vacant waiting for an investor to construct a plant on it. Most land, whether officially classified as agricultural, waste land or government land, will already be in use for agricultural purposes or at least provide support to livestock or other livelihood supporting activities. Forests can also not easily be used for large industrial projects both for its environmental and livelihood benefits. The end result is that when land is acquired for industry land used for agriculture is removed, sometimes including patches of forest.

The acquisition of farm land with subsequent displacement of farmers has become a very sensitive political issue as well as an expensive proposition across India in recent years. Some states have avoided this by planning ahead to acquire large tracts of land for industrial parks but Andhra Pradesh is not one of them. Instead, the availability of pockets with large concentrations of so called 'assigned land', which on paper already belong to the government, has come to be favoured for industrial plants and other land hungry projects (Seethalakshmi, 2009). Assigned land is legally land belonging to the government but assigned to a poor, landless person. It cannot be sold but only inherited to the children of the original assignee. Since 1969 successive Andhra Pradesh governments have distributed 42 lakh acres of land as a welfare measure and it is now a significant portion of the state's total 368 lakh acres of cultivable land (Government of Andhra Pradesh, 2006).

There are a number of reasons why assigned land has come to be preferred for industrial purposes, none of which seems to serve the project-affected persons and their interest of getting a fair deal from industrialization. The government 'Land Committee' report acknowledges that about 25 per cent of all assigned land has ended up in the hands of unintended non-poor recipients. An amendment in 2006 allows the government to take back this land with the main purpose to assign it to a new landless farmer. But, the government may choose to use it for a different purpose if it so wishes, such as for industrialization. More land becomes 'available' for re-assignment from another clause which demands land to be brought under cultivation within a certain time frame or the government can take it back. Since the land assigned is often of poor quality and the poor recipients lack funds to develop the land, including levelling it to make it suitable for agriculture, it is common that the land remains uncultivated leaving it opens for re-assignment (Balagopal, 2007).

When the state government is acquiring its own land, even though assigned to (and used by) a farmer, it claims there is no need to pay compensation. This is currently challenged in a court case but has put pressure on assigned land title holders to accept low amounts of compensation. Another issue with assigned land is how sometimes the assignee has been forced to sell the land making the new occupant illegal in the eyes of the state.[1] In yet other cases the *patta* was not provided for new farming but given to people who had been cultivating the land for decades as a substitute for a proper private *patta*.[2] 'In practice the government pays or does not pay according to the pressure the landholders are able to put up' (personal communication, K. Balagopal).

To summarize 42 lakh acres have been distributed to poor farmers in Andhra Pradesh and at least 10 lakh acres of this land is in hands other than the intended recipient. There is further a significant portion of the land which has not been brought under cultivation. Thirdly, the amount of compensation to be paid is unclear. From this we realize how the larger the land for the poor programme is, the greater the possibilities for the government are to later acquire land for industry. As long as it remains a 'public purpose' for the government to allow a poor farmer to till the land this is allowed to go on but when a new 'public purpose' arises, such as providing land to industrialists, the land can be taken back.

Compensation and Rehabilitation

Compensation for land acquired for industrial projects is based on the by now arcane Land Acquisition Act of 1894 (with amendments). This Act empowers the government to take over land for a 'public purpose' and pay compensation according to an estimated market value which includes the land, potential buildings, crops and other assets. This procedure has come under a lot of criticism for its deficiencies in general as well as specific concerns related to the Scheduled Areas. Land is always undervalued in India to avoid stamp tax. For industrial projects the market value is on the date of notification of land acquisition and will thus not take in the expected price increase due to industrial development and its influx of people, nor the fact that people in the surrounding area may hike the prices of agricultural land knowing demand is likely to go up. In tribal areas the market value may be particularly unclear since the market is restricted to only members of the community, and the land is held even more often without papers and on nominally illegal land (Iyer, 2007; Sampat, 2008; Fernandes, 2007; Singh, 1986). It is often the case that companies or state governments offer better compensation rates than what the law requires but this tends to be on a case-by-case basis wherever the opposition is strong enough to be taken seriously (Newell and Wheeler, 2006).

Beyond the issues of whether land estimates are correct and include all those affected, movements across India have been built around the inadequacy of only providing monetary compensation. The Narmada Bachao Andolan has been especially at the forefront of highlighting the difficulties people face when they are uprooted from the land, water and forests of particular areas they have depended on for generations (Baviskar, 1995; D'Souza, 2002). Slowly it has come to be accepted across India that displacement should lead to rehabilitation including land for land compensation (Iyer, 2007). But with the continued deferment of a national rehabilitation bill, it is the Andhra Pradesh Rehabilitation and Resettlement (R&R) Policy of 2005 with amendments which applies to all forms of large-scale acquisition of land in Andhra Pradesh. Large-scale acquisition is here defined as 100 families affected by any one project in the plains, or 25 families in the Scheduled Areas. The AP R&R policy importantly defines displacement as losing your house plot if you are living in the plains, but shows better official concern for tribal land by allowing any type of land acquired in the Scheduled Areas to account for displacement (Government of Andhra Pradesh, Irrigation and CAD Department, 2005).

A second important benefit for the displaced in the Scheduled Areas of Andhra Pradesh is contained in an amendment to the policy which makes land for land compensation mandatory (ibid., 2006). For people on the plains new land is only provided if land is available with the government, a clause which in similar cases has tended to work against rehabilitation of the displaced since it would mean that the government had to acquire new land thus creating even more displacement (Iyer, 2007; Nathan, 2009). A special 'compensation package' was announced by Jindal South West (JSW) for its refinery in addition to what the AP R&R policy demanded. It offered one job according to qualification for each of the estimated 600 families affected irrespective of the type of land they had lost, or a onetime payment of ₹ 3,00,000. The displaced (following the state government's definition), estimated at 30 families, got additional incentives with a new house and infrastructure, transportation costs paid (up to ₹ 5,000) for and a new cattle shed (₹ 3,000). 'Encroachers', those without official land titles, and whom revenue officials could testify, had been present for more than five years, would receive the same land compensation as those with land titles (Government of Andhra Pradesh, Revenue Department, 2007b).

It is evident from this that a wide number of Acts and policies exist both at central and state levels meant to safeguard against negative consequences of industrialization and there are special benefits for members of the Scheduled Tribes (STs). What is also clear, however, is that a lot of criticism has been levelled against government implementation of this legislation, both at the planning and at the monitoring stages.

Panchayat Raj

Possibilities for wider deliberations on local natural resources and land use are possible via the Panchayat Raj legislation with its vision of democratically elected panchayats as part of a move towards decentralization and self-governance. Though earlier forms of panchayats have been in place in Andhra Pradesh since 1957 (Srinivasulu, 2002) the main difference came about with the 73rd

Constitutional Amendment in 1993 which formalized local governance in rural areas across India via Panchayat Raj. Panchayats exist in a three-tier system from the village (Gram) Panchayat to the sub-district Panchayat Samithi (in Andhra Pradesh known as the Mandal Parishad) and the district-level Zilla Parishad. At the village level not only do direct elections every five years function to hold panchayat members to account, there is also the Gram Sabha, the village assembly, consisting of all eligible voters and meant to work as a public forum for transparency and accountability (Johnson et al., 2003). There is extensive reservation for members of Scheduled Castes (SCs), Scheduled Tribes (STs) and Other Backward Castes (OBCs) according to their proportion of the population. Additionally 33 per cent of the seats are reserved for women both as part of the above three minorities and for the general category. The difference in these reservations compared to state and national elections is that they only last for one session after which the constituency becomes open for competition again. The empowerment impact of reservation policies was found to be limited by Johnson et al. (2003), since most reserved candidates tended to lose their seats in open competition.

Three main critiques have been made against panchayat institutions over the years; states have been unwilling to devolve significant power to the panchayats; a resistant bureaucracy has limited actual effectiveness; and local elites have influenced outcomes (Johnson, 2003; Srinivasulu, 2002). In Andhra Pradesh the panchayats have in recent years often seen themselves being bypassed in influence and allocation of development funds through the creation of a number of other institutions such as water user associations, self-help groups and joint forest management committees, while much of actual control over programmes has remained within the bureaucracy. This process was particularly apparent during TDP rule leading to interpretations that it was aimed at bypassing the traditionally Congress-dominated panchayats (Johnson et al., 2003).

The right of panchayats to be consulted in relation to land acquisition has been established in Andhra Pradesh after much protest and litigation. Both the Gram Panchayat and a Gram Sabha meeting will have to provide their consent according to the Andhra Pradesh panchayat regulations. But once consultation has been secured, as happened in the High Court case of the Surampalem dam in Andhra Pradesh, the underpinning of the judgement can be removed by changing the law. The Andhra Pradesh government introduced its R&R policy and thus made the government order invalid (Ravi Rebapragada of NGO Samatha at public meeting in Visakhapatnam, 26 March 2010). The right for consultation via Panchayats is thus an ongoing struggle where pressure has to be continuously re-asserted on the authorities.

Following this discussion of policies, the next section presents the site proposed for the alumina refinery in Vizianagaram district of coastal Andhra Pradesh including details of the affected people and their livelihoods.

Case Study

In 2005 an agreement was signed between the Government of Andhra Pradesh and Jindal South West (JSW), part of the Haryana-based Jindal Group, to set up a bauxite mining[3] and refining project. According to this agreement, the government would mine bauxite via its mining company the Andhra Pradesh Mineral Development Corporation (APMDC) from deposits available in the Scheduled Areas of Visakhapatnam, while JSW would build a refinery where the ore would be processed. Part of the agreement was also an aluminium smelter but to date no further plans have been presented on this component of the project making it highly uncertain (MoU between GoAP and JSW, 2005).

Due to the tribal land rights legislation in AP,[4] affirmed in the 1997 Supreme Court 'Samatha judgment',[5] the privately owned refinery could not be located in the Scheduled Areas of the State. This meant that it instead had to compete for land on the intensively cultivated plains in direct competition with farmers. Initially a site was announced at Sabbavaram close to Visakhapatnam city. Shortly after the environmental public hearing was held in late 2006 the location was abandoned however. It was never clarified why this move was made though possibly it had to do with the higher land prices close to urban areas and the shorter distance to the proposed mines at the new site in S. Kota (short for Srungavarupukota) Mandal of Vizianagaram district which would cut down on transportation costs.[6]

The area chosen as the location for JSW's refinery close to S. Kota town had seen an influx of outsiders for decades to acquire the best land from what was only a few decades ago described in interviews as a forested area inhabited almost exclusively by tribal communities. Or as one tribal villager explained it:

> We have been here for a long time, earlier we used to go to (the) hills and depend on forest products. Once this land was uncultivable, but later we made it cultivable. With borrowing we dug bore wells and got water at 50–60 feet. We are farming this land with the help of loans. These coconut trees were planted in my childhood stage and now they are giving us some income. It took a lot of time to make this land cultivable and these trees to give us some income. At this moment some people came and asked us to give up these lands. They want to cut down these trees but if this is done how much time will it take to bring up new trees. (interview with local refinery opposition group member, S. Kota Mandal, 26 January 2008)

Some of the villages now losing land to the refinery, had lived there for generations but were for some reason never included when the Scheduled Areas were demarcated despite the people in them being recognized as tribal (and at least nowadays having tribal caste certificates). Other tribal villages were displaced when the Tatipudi irrigation reservoir (approximately 2 km from the proposed refinery site) on the Goshtani river was built in the 1960s. At the time they were rehabilitated with new houses and land only a few kilometres away from the original habitations and on good (but then forested) land. Since the exact border between scheduled and non-scheduled land is not known, it might even have been the case that the displaced were rehabilitated from scheduled to non-scheduled land.

A number of villages affected by land acquisition had only tribal groups in them whereas others were a mix of Scheduled Tribes, Scheduled Castes and a handful from Backward Caste communities, mainly as a result of illegally bought assigned land (see Table 1). Yet there was no particular awareness during interactions in the villages of how Scheduled Area land transfer legislation could at least to some extent have kept more land in the hands of long-term tribal settlers and even would have made the refinery impossible. The local protest group never raised the issue of tribal land loss or displacement other than to highlight the unfairness of displacing some people first for the irrigation dam in the 1960s, and then again for the refinery.

The people losing land to the refinery officially lived in four revenue villages but the habitations of the estimated 600 land-losing families were spread out in about 15 smaller villages and hamlets. Each small village would be about 100 people, or 20 households in size, while hamlets only consisted of a few households. The land acquisition site represented a dramatic contrast to the general population in the Mandal since overall tribals are not very well represented. A survey by Reddy and Mishra (2010) of six villages found the break-up of castes affected by land acquisition in S. Kota to be 290 tribal, 33 dalit, 105 backward caste and 10 households of other castes. S. Kota Mandal had 74,500 people according to the Census 2001 with 5,749 ST (8%) and 6,629 SC (9%) (Office of the Registrar General, India, 2001a). There was also 170 acres of private land acquired for the refinery but the social composition of this land is unknown. None of the people met at the site had private land, and since negotiations for the purchase of this land was held directly between the company and the landowners the details are excluded from available government documents.

Of particular concern for tribal rights to land were the several villages of Gadaba tribals whose land was acquired for the refinery. The 36,000 Gadaba in Andhra Pradesh (ibid., 2001b) form a small and almost exclusively rural community with a unique language remotely related to other Dravidian languages. Also present in southern Chhattisgarh and Odisha three out of seven sub-groups are officially defined as primitive and traditionally subsisting as hunterer-gatherers. How and when Gadaba came to settle down as farmers in the S. Kota area is not well known but interviews testified that 10–12 villages existed in the area since the 1950s, which is significantly longer than the dam displaced who were resettled in the late 1960s.

The refinery required a significant amount of land for not only the central ore refining activities but also a thermal power plant, a housing site for its office staff and displaced people, and its two waste ponds (see Table 1).

Table 1

Proposed Land Use for the Alumina Refinery

Particulars	*Land Use in acres (hectares)*
Alumina refinery and co-generation (including storage and green belt)	750 (303)
Residue disposal area and ash pond	500 (202)
Township and miscellaneous	50 (20)
Railway lines	50 (20)
Total	1350 (550)

Source: Vimta Labs, 2007, Table 2.1.

Land use in the refinery Environmental Impact Assessment (EIA) was determined remotely via satellite imagery and secondary statistical sources. This analysis focused on the 10 km prescribed study area and not the actual site. The conclusion was that 25 per cent of all land was double crop and 15 per cent was single crop agricultural land indicating significant agricultural activities at least in the surroundings of the site. Forest was 38 per cent while 16 per cent was classified as wasteland (Vimta Labs, 2007). At the particular plant site however the EIA described the land use as 'wasteland with agricultural activities in patches' (ibid., 2007: C1–2). Ownership was also not an issue according to the EIA:

> [The] site near Boddavara village near S. Kota is selected and finalised as no Forest Land, approximately 85 per cent of total land is government/assigned dry land and marginal Resettlement and Rehabilitation (R&R) issues are involved. (ibid.)

A visit to the site gave a very different impression of the possibilities for agriculture and the effect of land acquisition. Being located close to an irrigation dam meant good local availability of groundwater in the area even though not directly served by the irrigation canals further east.[7] It was possible to grow rice and sugarcane on much of the land. Land slightly further away from the dam had cashewnut plantations (see Table 2). Because of the way statistics are collected it is not possible to separate the acquired villages from those

Table 2

Agricultural Land in the Revenue Villages of the Upcoming Alumina Refinery in S. Kota

Revenue village	*Rice*[a]		*Sugarcane*[b]	*Mango*	*Cashew*	*Total Land*[c]
	Irrigated	*Unirr.*	*Irrigated*	*Unirr.*	*Unirr.*	
M.B. Vara	45	28	43	350	392	858 (5,142)
Cheedipalem	26	0	37	15	28	106 (378)
Chinakandepalli	68	21	76	13	0	178 (729)
Kiltampalem	81	0	782	55	0	918 (1,611)

Notes: a: All units in acres.
b: A minor part of sugarcane production is lower yielding ratoon cultivation.
c: Total area of revenue village within brackets.

Source: Government of Andhra Pradesh, Revenue Department (2008a).

nearby who are grouped into the same revenue village, but it is assumed that productivity will vary significantly between cultivators depending on the possibility to use various inputs. Rice dominates cultivation along with sugarcane in S. Kota Mandal. In Kiltampalem revenue village this is even more pronounced indicating the good availability of water. M.B. Vara and Mushidipalli revenue villages are drier and the land use has been mainly cashew plantations accounting for two thirds of the cashew grown in the Mandal. In addition much of this unirrigated land has mango orchards (Government of Andhra Pradesh, Revenue Department, 2008a).

The farmers were managing their agricultural activities largely without government support by taking loans from private money-lenders to level the land and install wells with pumps. In fact, they had never seen much of the government at all including the lack of schools with several villages being without a single adult literate person. They remained poor, much due to the high interest rates they had to pay from the loans taken to clear the land for agriculture,[8] but had self reliance and a hope to do as well in the future as their non-tribal neighbours in the adjacent villages (who were largely not affected by the land acquisition). The area being non-scheduled had seen many upwardly mobile agricultural communities acquiring land in recent decades. The *pucca* cement houses, the cars and motorcycles as well as the agricultural vehicles present in these villages were in stark contrast to the now land-losing villages where one or two motor-cycles were the sum of all capital goods, and cramped *pucca* houses had only been provided to some as part of government housing programmes or, in the case of the earlier displaced, as rehabilitation.

The next section looks at how fertile land and tribal farmers were made invisible in the process of acquisition, and how displacement was kept to a minimum via bureaucratic procedures seemingly aimed at promoting industrialization rather than from a concern for the welfare of the poor.

Government Land to the Landless Poor and Back to the Government

In the non-scheduled parts of the Andhra Pradesh where land titles, as well as the awareness of the importance of officially recognized title deeds and the existence of rights during land acquisition are relatively widespread, the government had to employ significant skills in identifying land and carrying out the acquisition without causing strong enough protests to derail the entire process. It could do this despite significant civil society mobilization and media coverage since it had deep penetration in the particular area with control of the bureaucracy including information on the extent of land and the rights to rehabilitation, and even more so for its political control with the Congress party in power in all four affected panchayats. JSW was largely invisible in this process but provided support behind the scenes.

A look at the discussion of potential alternative sites in the refinery EIA report (Vimta Labs, 2007) is a reading of nearby locations with large concentrations of assigned land. In Visakhapatnam district, Sabbavaram was the original site for the JSW refinery before it was moved to its present location. Makavaripalem is a site later given to the ANRAK Aluminium SEZ, and Achutapuram has been proposed as an SEZ. In Vizianagaram district land is available in K.D. Peta, earlier acquired for a glass factory which never became reality. The impression given in the EIA is that the suitability of an industrial site depends on the ease of land acquisition rather than more tangible criteria such as infrastructure, availability of labour or raw materials, or indeed whether the project is suitable from environmental or social points of view.

Table 3

Caste Composition of Land-losers Compared to Rest of Mandal

	Tribals	*Dalits*	*BC*	*Others*	*Total*
Caste composition of people losing land to the JSW refinery	257 (57%)	34 (8%)	105 (23%)	54 (12%)	450
Mandal composition (2001)	5,749 (8%)	6,629 (9%)	*	*	74,500
District composition (1991)	9%	15.9%			

Source: Revenue Department planning note for JSW land acquisition, n.d., assumed to be late 2007. The composition is likely to have changed somewhat with later revisions to the land actually acquired.

Information about the actual type of land acquired was not readily available at the time of acquisition however. The EIA report did not mention the fertile land and the mainly tribal villagers (see Table 3) who were making a living at and immediately surrounding the proposed site. Instead it claimed that '(t)he land identified for locating the Alumina refinery of 1,350 acres consist of about 85 per cent government land and 15 per cent private land' (ibid., 2007: C2–3). Since displacement was 'minimal', only affecting 30 families, land acquisition was portrayed as unproblematic.

But the Revenue Department was more precise in its internal instruction to acquire 919 acres of assigned land (or 68% of the total) to the uniform value of ₹ 2,00,000 per acre. Government's 209 acres land was also part of the order, likely to have also been cultivated since there is no vacant land in the area. A significant but unknown part of the assigned land was in the hands of non-poor big farmers, many of whom had already moved away from farming and were now residing in the nearby cities.[9] The remaining approximately 170 acres of private land, which existed in pockets between the assigned land, was acquired directly by the company and no public records mention the owners of this land or the compensation received for it (Government of Andhra Pradesh, Revenue Department, 2007a). Several sources placed this compensation significantly higher than what was paid for the assigned land.[10]

The refinery layout was split in three nearby locations with the main plant site and the two waste ponds separated. This is a peculiar choice since the huge volumes of waste created by the refinery would clearly have been easier to dispose of had there been one contiguous site. One reason for this plant design can be understood when nearby villages, which did not appear on any official land acquisition maps, are included (see Figure 1). The way villages on this map are located along the very borders of the site creates the impression that planning has attempted to cause minimal official displacement by acquiring agricultural land but not housesites.[11] Approximately 600 households were losing agricultural land due to this refinery layout but only 30 lost the housesite which allowed them to officially become displaced according to the Andhra Pradesh rehabilitation policy. While the benefits for a farmer who loses farm land but does not get rehabilitated must be questioned, minimized official displacement was certainly in line with the government's main rehabilitation policy objective to minimize displacement, and certainly decreased the likeliness of mobilization against land acquisition.[12]

A number of amendments were made to the above land acquisition map. At times these changes were made since it was found that ex-servicemen owned it. At other times the land was found to be a

Figure 1

Official Land Acquisition Map Prepared by JSW Aluminium

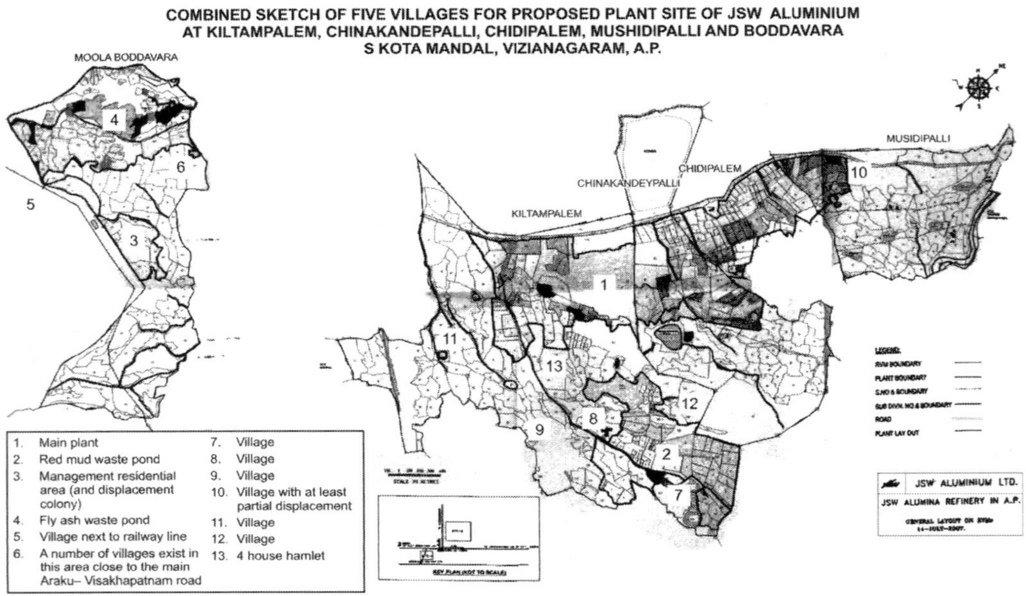

Notes: This map does not incorporate some late changes to land acquisition. Village locations are approximate and non-exhaustie as there is no map which includes all the villages and the land to be acquired with survey numbers among the maps presented in the EIA, the above land acquisition map, revenue village maps or detailed Government of India toposheets.

tank, or adjoining a tank which meant it could not be acquired whether or not this actually meant there was water in the tank.[13] At yet other times official documents simply stated that the land was either part of the refinery site or excluded since it was inside/outside the plant boundary without specifying why this was the case (Government of Andhra Pradesh, Revenue Department, 2008b, 2008d).

Since land acquisition is supposed to be advertised by placing a notice in the panchayat offices, every amendment to the land acquisition risked spreading information which could create awareness of what was being planned. The notices had not been posted for public display as far as villagers were concerned for the initial round of acquisition (interviews in concerned villages), but with media and other pressure on, the bureaucrats decided to attempt to hide changes by amending the earlier government order for the land acquisition when new land acquisition started in early 2008 (Government of Andhra Pradesh, Revenue Department, 2008b). When local journalists nevertheless found out, this did not result in more transparent government behaviour but rather the draft of an official government order a few weeks later to make the changes legitimate (ibid., 2008c).

Certain delays were inevitable however, as land acquisition letters for the new land were only sent a few months later (ibid., 2008e), and remained surprisingly unpaid for the following year, which probably means that the particular pieces of land were never acquired (ibid., 2009b). May be it was not needed in the end. Or maybe JSW decided to go slow on its project having secured most of the land (either due to financing problems for the refinery, or a lack of progress in the establishment of the mines). Some seemingly plausible reasons for land acquisition changes could be found in allegations of corruption. Local newspaper reports stated the real reason for these exclusions was not to exempt the land from acquisition, but to re-label it as private land, for which compensation could be negotiated directly with JSW at a higher price (Rama Raju, n.d.). Similar allegations were made after a probe by the Lok Satta Party which alleged a ₹ 100 million scam due to payments to non-existing farmers (Lok Satta Party, 2009). But changes at times took the concerns of the poorest into consideration. One of the main demands of the refinery opposition group were agreed to when 35 acres of assigned land was excluded from the site since it belonged to tribal people earlier displaced from the Tatipudi reservoir (Government of Andhra Pradesh, Revenue Department, 2008d).

The lack of clear information and frequent changes to the actual land acquired kept many on and around the site guessing whether their land was going to be acquired, and if so what they would receive as compensation. Group discussions held over the above land acquisition map did not impress people despite the seeming clarity of the survey numbers of land due to be acquired. The feeling was that the government could make and change plans at will:

> They [the government] can do anything. What they do today may not be valid for tomorrow. Today's collector will go tomorrow and most of the officials are transferred within a year. The new officers and the government are coming up with new schemes and procedures. (interview with S. Kota Mandal, 26 January 2008)

The confusion over what was planned naturally made it difficult to create a mass movement which could put pressure on the bauxite alliance. But several people in the surveyed village indicated they had actually joined the protest group due to a lack of information since they were expecting their land to be acquired like that of their neighbours and relatives despite being excluded from the first and second round of acquisition notices (see Table 4).

Table 4
Land Loss in S. Kota Mandal Village

	Number of households	*Land to be acquired (acres)*	*Total land (acres)*
Land already acquired	2	2	2
Land to be acquired	10	27.13	32.48
No loss of land	7	–	23.75
Total	19	29.13	58.23

Source: Based on household survey, March 2008.

Based on documents received at a much later stage via right to information, the final count of the displaced was 75 families (or 375 people with the assumption of five people per family). This was more than double what had been indicated in the original planning documents. The displacement was spread across all revenue villages with 23 households displaced in Cheedipalem, 5 in Mushidipalle, 9 in M.B. Vara, 27 in Kiltampalem, and 11 in Chinakandepalli (Government of Andhra Pradesh, Revenue Department, 2007c). The reason for the increased displacement was not detailed in any government document. Was this supposed to happen all along or was it the result of the many land acquisition changes?

Varying Compensation

What remains after both sites have been framed as government land is a discussion on the cash compensation which historically has been shown inadequate for those losing land. The kind of land compensation people could claim depended on the type of land they were cultivating and whether it appeared in the official records. A sort of sliding scale for compensation was created during land acquisition for the refinery from those with clear entitlements put on paper and knowledge of their rights, to those with unclear status or a weaker knowledge of government rules, and finally on to the paperless, landless and uninformed. The direct negotiations between landowners with private land titles and the company are sure to first provide better compensation, and secondly allow less to be siphoned off by various bureaucrats and politicians. Those on government land or cultivating assigned land without holding the titles were in the worst position. The main strategies available for different types of land losers are presented in Figure 2.

Figure 2

Typology of Land Compensation for the JSW Refinery in S. Kota

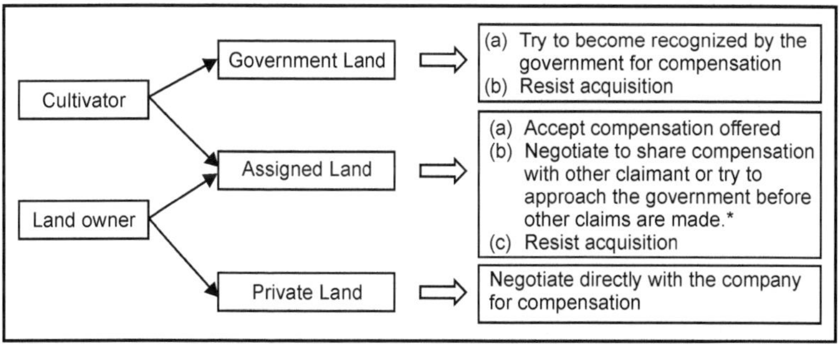

*Other potential strategies for particularly powerful individuals with assigned land is to try to get it excluded from acquisition or to get it included in the private land negotiations for improved compensation.

Best off were the few with private land titles who negotiated directly with the company since they had the right to refuse sale. Rumours were made of significantly higher compensation for private land, up to 10 times as much as for other land, but this has not been possible to confirm (interview with journalist, S. Kota, 19 March 2008). Those cultivating and holding the title to assigned land could be relatively certain of getting compensation, though the final amount paid would depend not only upon whether their papers were in complete order, but also on whether they were aware of their rights to demand compensation according to the 'rehabilitation package' without too much being siphoned off by the local elite.

The original assigned land owner and the actual cultivator had to informally figure out how to share the compensation since the government would only go by what the records stated. This placed the formal owner in a better position than the cultivator who had no legal way of contesting or even often finding the actual *patta*-holder (interview with S. Kota journalist, 27 March 2008). The bargaining power of the individuals was, as for compensation in general, key in settling the share. A common way of dividing the compensation money that was worked out in personal negotiations with the title holder was 50 per cent each. But some better off local (non-tribal) farmers with the ability to access information about the land acquisition were arguing for two-third share of compensation for themselves leaving the title holder with a third (interview with villager, S. Kota Mandal, 25 March 2008).

The cultivator of government land was in a similar position to the assigned land cultivator since the lack of paperwork risked excluding him or her from compensation completely. There was however a clause in the 'rehabilitation package' which allowed those who could prove they had occupied the land for at least five years to claim land compensation (though not a job or other benefits). The feasibility of convincing the government to recognize land use is not known as no cases of government land compensation were encountered at the site.

The promise of economic development from an alumina refinery thus seemed to leave families of illiterate farmers with no other real skills than agriculture to hope for the one promised job in the refinery for future sustenance for the entire (often joint) family. Or may be even this job would not be accepted since there was the possibility to accept cash instead. It was found that only half of those surveyed by Reddy and Mishra (2010) had received a temporary job while waiting for the promised job in the refinery. One fourth of the eligible had accepted ₹ 3,00,000 cash whereas the final fourth was still waiting for jobs. Only 146 people were listed as receiving minimum wages of ₹ 2,200 per month (about £32) from the company in 2009 (Government of Andhra Pradesh, Revenue Department, 2009a; Reddy and Mishra, 2010).

Beyond the payment for the acquired land, the company's efforts to 'develop this backward area' (phone interview with JSW employee, Visakhapatnam, 5 April 2008) were at times quite ambitious though not particularly grounded in the local reality with its aim to transform farmers with no formal education into industrial workers in the course of a year at an industrial training centre. Even more improbable were the plans to develop a call centre at the JSW subsidiary Soft in S. Kota town where farm women via a short training course would move from rural agricultural labourers[14] and housewives to office workers with a salary of at least ₹ 20,000 per month (approximately £260, a very good salary in rural Vizianagaram district) (interview with JSW employee, S. Kota, 5 April 2008).

The cash provided will not be sufficient for anyone to rebuild an agricultural livelihood again as a farmer. And the very limited experience, if any at all, the affected had of other types of jobs do not make a transition to non-agricultural work seem very promising. The people receiving cash compensation can thus not be expected to be able to invest this money productively, nor will migration to a new location be possible. The compensation money might last for a few years but after this the future will look difficult, as has been the experience elsewhere in India in similar situations. Yet it is not very likely that either the larger opposition group or the people directly affected would have accepted an offer for large-scale resettlement given the poor outcomes of such attempts in the past.

Land Acquisition and Panchayat Raj

The reach of the state government, which enabled land acquisition with only a minimum of protest described in this paper, had its roots not only in its control over bureaucratic procedures impossible to grasp for the largely illiterate farmers on the site, but also over political institutions and politicians. The exact nature of this control is difficult to grasp but has to do with money power and to some extent, the control over the bureaucracy and all supposedly independent government institutions. An interview with an agricultural extension worker frequently sent out to do surveys for land acquisition confirmed the behaviour encountered for the S. Kota Panchayat approvals as typical. If local protests are encountered the administrators stay away while party workers and politicians figure out ways to deal with the opposition (interview with local government employee, Visakhapatnam, 14 March 2008). The experience in Andhra Pradesh thus seems to conform to the wider experience in India that 'decentralization has failed to prevent a local (and primarily landed) elite from controlling the local bodies' (Johnson et al., 2003: 2).

Bureaucratic interventions in land acquisition have tended to be in favour of displacement with a minimum of local deliberation. Srinivasulu describes the general administrative involvement in land acquisition for SEZs across Andhra Pradesh as follows:

> The role of local revenue administration ... is crucial in making or rather pressurizing farmers to concede without resistance to the establishment of an SEZ [Special Economic Zone]. Using their connections with the local pyravikaars [local fixers] and the Panchayat raj functionaries, the subaltern bureaucracy of the Revenue Department could successfully spread the message that there was no point in resisting land acquisition as the government has supreme power to acquire 'any land, anywhere, anytime'. (2010: 13)

An important point not elaborated by Srinivasulu is to what extent, if at all, the revenue employees worked on their own initiative or were directed by higher up interests. The experience at the refinery land acquisition was that even though local employees would get rewarded for 'efficient' land acquisition, the real control was with high level politicians who would make phone calls to emphasize current priorities by directing employees of various departments to drop other work and go out to do surveys for projects deemed especially important.

Land for the JSW alumina refinery was spread over five panchayats in S. Kota Mandal and thus required separate decisions for all five. Despite bearing the name of a village council, each of the panchayats consisted of a large number of villages and hamlets, none having more than a few hundred inhabitants and sometimes only a few families. Within each of the panchayats there was only a relatively small amount of land being acquired meaning that many of the panchayat members neither lost land themselves nor lived in the villages affected. The S. Kota area being non-scheduled meant both tribal and non-tribal people were represented among the elected panchayat representatives. Though not being of very large means, the Sarpanchas were found to be significantly better off than most other residents and seemed to be somewhat isolated from pressures from those losing land. Crucially, the Sarpanchas were all Congress party-associated and non-tribal. Panchayats which are supposedly apolitical were found to be heavily dominated by Congress and TDP during fieldwork. Many of the key opposition figures were or had in the past been elected to local positions as TDP supporters.

Approvals according to Panchayat Raj were swiftly created and signed as soon as the refinery move to S. Kota had been decided towards the end of 2006. An administrative order was passed to direct the local government-employed panchayat staff to organize panchayat meetings before end of December 2006 (Government of Andhra Pradesh, Mandal Development Organization, 2006). At these meetings identical resolutions were drafted by all five Congress sarpanches, according to interviews, since they had been developed in consultation with the local Congress Zilla Parishad politician. The only difference between the draft resolutions seen were the details of survey numbers to be acquired (Kiltampalem Gram Panchayat, 2006; Mushidipalli Gram Panchayat, 2006; interviews with sources with insight into S. Kota panchayat operations, S. Kota, 19 March 2008).

The panchayat member of the village surveyed as part of fieldwork, also a tribal, was continuously met in a drunken state during fieldwork and admitted to knowing nothing of these plans. Frequently he would simply put his thumb print to any document he was presented, given that he was illiterate. Whether or not signed and verified copies of the panchayat and Gram Sabha resolutions actually existed remains unknown since it was not possible to obtain these. Certainly no villagers had ever seen the resolutions or discussed them. The resolutions can only be assumed to exist since land acquisition and the environmental approval were able to move ahead. But they were as far as can be ascertained never discussed in any larger forums.

Conclusion

This paper has provided a detailed case study of land acquisition including compensation and local decision-making in order to explain not only how assigned land could be used by a government intent on promoting industrialization, but also provide some understanding of why this has not received more widespread attention and created stronger protest. Key to the usefulness of assigned land for the government was the possibility to via bureaucratic procedures make it into marginal land of little value other than for industrial purposes. Additionally it was inhabited by people so on the margins of society that they could not be expected to protest strongly enough to derail the project even with the support of various civil society actors and groups.

The way land tenure had been framed to exclude many users was found to be the main reason for the poor compensation, but the way planning was being carried out further strengthened this tendency. A higher priority was seemingly given to land acquisition over social justice. The land tenure, compensation and mitigation policies had been framed in such ways that they could be assembled by 'creative' planners, without wider deliberations on the fairness of procedures, in such a way as to leave most people outside of their scope, or only allowing for minimal compensation. Assigned land cultivated by poor, mainly tribal farmers in the refinery area was re-framed into government 'waste' land of little value. This compared very closely to the approach taken for the mining component of the same project where the land was framed as forest land, though not with actual trees on it since this would have created difficulties in getting environmental approvals (Oskarsson, 2010). Also similar to the S. Kota refinery, the layout of the alumina refinery for Vedanta Aluminium in Lanjigarh, Odisha left a number of villages without their fields but just outside of the boundary walls of the plant to face severe pollution once this refinery started to operate (Amnesty International, 2010).

As has been shown the direct compensation policies were tied to formal land ownership. A few lost their house sites and became what the Andhra Pradesh R&R policy considers a 'project displaced family' with the right to rehabilitation, while others received compensation tied to the land holding. The majority of people at the proposed refinery were in the much vaguer category of 'project-affected family' however. These are the many families in the refinery area who supported themselves as agricultural labourers, minor forest produce collectors and livestock herders, or who were simply making a living just outside of the refinery boundaries. The people outside of the boundaries were not counted in any government documents making the analysis difficult of how many and in which ways people might be affected. It seems fair to say that we will never know exactly who they were.

But despite what has been detailed in this paper as a callous official approach to land acquisition, there is no evidence that particular groups of people have been targeted due to ethnic or other criteria. It simply seems like this is the most feasible approach to acquire land without creating protests. But the distributional and justice outcomes of this mode of planning are definitely very worrying since the poorest of the poor, those least likely to be able to cope with a change away from agriculture, were disproportionately affected. At the same time, there were instances where additional compensation was proposed compared to what would have been strictly necessary according to policies. The State Rehabilitation Policy only forms the base and beyond this there are possibilities to demand improvements. This is where the hope seems to rest for a better deal for those in the way of industrialization. While the approach to acquire land for industrial purposes from land earlier given away for poverty alleviation is greatly unfair, it may also show the weakness of the government because it is only by taking away land from the weakest in society that land can at all be acquired. Stronger land tenure and a clearer provision of information about government attempts to target marginal lands and peoples could therefore indicate opportunities for justice.

Notes

1. This is regulated under the Andhra Pradesh Assigned Lands (Prohibition of Transfers) Act, 1977 but nevertheless at least 25 per cent of all assigned land remains in other hands than those originally intended including a 1,000 acre plot found to be in the Chief Minister Rajasekhara Reddy's possession.
2. See, *Land Committee Report* (2006) for the full details of assigned land policies in the state.

3. Bauxite is an ore containing aluminium oxide, alumina and a range of other elements. The ore is refined in two stages to first produce alumina and later the metal aluminium. The main bauxite deposits in India are in central-eastern India in the states of Odisha and Andhra Pradesh. All these deposits are in the Scheduled Areas.
4. The Andhra Pradesh Scheduled Area Land Transfer Regulation 1959 as amended up to 1970. Also known as the 1/70 Act, the 1st Act of 1970.
5. Supreme Court of India, 1997. Judgement in the case of 'Samatha versus the State of Andhra Pradesh and others'.
6. Yet another factor speaking in favour of the move is the water supply for the refinery though also this has proven highly controversial at the new site where the refinery is competing with water for agriculture from the nearby Thatipudi dam.
7. The Godavari and Krishna deltas, not too far from the refinery site, have seen a major economic transformation in recent decades due to increased irrigation (Upadhya, 1988; Damodaran, 2008). Some of this potential could be seen also in the S. Kota area among upwardly mobile communities, but to a lesser extent due to lower water availability.
8. Debt rates in a survey of one village showed each household having significant debts to private moneylenders from ₹ 20,000 to ₹ 100,000 with interest rates from 25–40 per cent. The larger the landholding, the larger the debt tended to be.
9. Land acquisition documents show two relatives of the local main politician, a major landowner in the area, having assigned land titles.
10. Interviews S. Kota, Vizianagaram district, April 2008. The company indicated a slightly increased price for the private land in news articles (Rama Raju, 2009).
11. Another reason is that villages tended to be located close to water storage tanks which cannot be acquired.
12. Land acquisition for the Vedanta refinery at Lanjigarh, Odisha has similarly left farmers landless living just outside of the plant boundaries where they are at the greatest risk of facing serious pollution (Amnesty International, 2010 and 2011).
13. Sometimes minor changes were deliberated at great extent in bureaucratic documents such as what to do with a 0.82 acre water body (approximately 3,000 m^2) within the land allotted to JSW which though abandoned remained a tank in the records. It was decided that the company had to create a separate water body on their land of equal size (Government of Andhra Pradesh, Revenue Department, 2008c).
14. Very few women were found to own land and when they did it was in many cases under the control of the eldest son.

References

Amnesty International (2010). *Don't Mine Us Out of Existence: Bauxite Mine and Refinery Devastate Lives in India*, London: Amnesty International.

——(2011). *Generalisations, Omissions and Assumptions: A Brief Review of the Lanjigarh Refinery and Mine EIAs*, London: Amnesty International.

Balagopal, K. (2007). 'Land Unrest in Andhra Pradesh-I: Ceiling Surpluses and Public Lands', *Economic and Political Weekly*, Vol. 42, No. 38, pp. 3829–33.

Baviskar, A. (1995). *In the Belly of the River: Tribal Conflicts Over Development in the Narmada Valley*, New Delhi: Oxford University Press.

Damodaran, H. (2008). *India's New Capitalists: Caste, Business, and Industry in a Modern Nation*, Ranikhet: Permanent Black.

D'Souza, D. (2002). *The Narmada Dammed: An Inquiry into the Politics of Development*, New Delhi: Penguin Books.

Fernandes, W. (2007). 'Singur and the Displacement Scenario', *Economic and Political Weekly*, Vol. 42, No. 3, pp. 203–06.

Government of Andhra Pradesh (2006). *Land Committee Report*, Hyderabad. http://www.rd.ap.gov.in/ikpland/konerurangaraocommitteeonlandissuesofthepoor.pdf (accessed on 19 September 2007).

Government of Andhra Pradesh, Irrigation and CAD Department (2006). Government Order Ms. 119, Rehabilitation and Resettlement Policy of Government of Andhra Pradesh 2005 Amendment.

——(2005). Resettlement and Rehabilitation Policy 2005: For Project Affected Families.

Government of Andhra Pradesh, Mandal Development Organization (2006). Letter to Convene Gram Panchayat Meetings before the end of December 2006.

Government of Andhra Pradesh, Revenue Department (2007a). Government Order Ms. No. 892.

——(2007b). Resettlement and Rehabilitation Package for JSW Refinery: Annexure II of Government Order Ms. No. 892.

——(2007c). 'List of Households Displaced'.

——(2008a). 2007–2008 Kharif Agricultural Census of S. Kota Mandal.

——(2008b). Additional Documents added to Government Order Ms. No. 892.

——(2008c). Government Order Ms. No. 178.

——(2008d). Memo No. 10810/Assn 1(2)2008–1 dated 13 March 2008.

——(2008e). Land Acquisition Notice 512/2006 dated 19 March 2008.

——(2009a). 'List of Land Losers being Paid Minimum Wages'.

——(2009b). 'Statement of Not Paid Particulars'.

Iyer, R.R. (2007). 'Towards a Just Displacement and Rehabilitation Policy', *Economic and Political Weekly*, Vol. 42, No. 30, pp. 3103–07.

Johnson, C. (2003). *Decentralisation in India: Poverty, Politics and Panchayati Raj*, London: Overseas Development Institute.

Johnson, C., P. Deshingkar and D. Start (2003). Grounding the State: Poverty, Inequality and the Politics of Governance in India's Panchayats, presented at Politics of the Commons: Articulating Development and Strengthening Local Practices.

Kiltampalem Gram Panchayat (2006). Unsigned Kiltampalem Panchayat Resolution Approving Land Acquisition for Jindal.

Lok Satta Party (2009). Lok Satta Demands ACB Inquiry into Jindal Land Scam. http://www.loksatta.org/cms/index.php?option=com_content&view=article&id=292&itemid=60 (accessed on 17 March 2010).

MoU between GoAP and JSW (2005). Memorandum of Understanding between the Government of Andhra Pradesh and Jindal South West Limited, signed on 1 July 2005.

Mushidipalli Gram Panchayat (2006). Unsigned and Undated Mushidipalli Panchayat Resolution Approving Land Acquisition for Jindal.

Nathan, D. (2009). 'Social Security, Compensation and Reconstruction of Livelihoods', *Economic and Political Weekly*, Vol. 44, No. 30, pp. 22–26.

Newell, P. and J. Wheeler (2006). *Rights, Resources and the Politics of Accountability*, London: Zed Books.

Office of the Registrar General, India (2001a). *Census of India 2001 – Data Highlights Andhra Pradesh: The Scheduled Tribes.*

—— (2001b). *Census of India 2001: A-11 State Primary Census Abstract for Individual Scheduled Tribe.*

Oskarsson, P. (2010). *The Law of the Land Contested: Bauxite Mining in Tribal, Central India in an Age of Economic Reform*, Norwich, UK: University of East Anglia.

Rama Raju, S. (nd). Loopholes ... Misinterpretations ... *Eenadu.*

Rama Raju, V. (2009). 'JSW Aluminium Ties Up Funds for Rs 4,000–cr Vizag Plant', *Business Standard.* http://www.business-standard.com/india/news/jsw-aluminium-tiesfunds-for-rs-4000–cr-vizag-plant/346475/ (accessed on 10 September 2009).

Reddy, M.G. and P. Mishra (2010). *Final Report on Livelihoods Change from AP Bauxite Projects*, Hyderabad: Centre for Economic and Social Studies.

Sampat, P. (2008). 'Special Economic Zones in India', *Economic and Political Weekly*, Vol. 43, No. 28, pp. 25–29.

Seethalakshmi, S. (2009). *Special Economic Zones in Andhra Pradesh: Issues, Concerns and Ways Ahead*, Ongole and Hyderabad, India: Society for National Integration through Rural Development (SNIRD) and ActionAid.

Singh, C. (1986). *Common Property and Common Poverty: India's Forests, Forest Dwellers, and the Law*, Delhi: Oxford University Press.

Srinivasulu, K. (2002). 'Caste, Class and Social Articulation in Andhra Pradesh: Mapping Differential Regional Trajectories', Working Paper 179, London: Overseas Development Institute.

—— (2010). *Land Acquisition and Popular Resistance: Politics of Special Economic Zones in Andhra Pradesh.* http://www.indiasezpolitics.org/nopub docs/karli per cent20srinivasulu per cent203:16:10.doc (accessed on 7 August 2010).

Upadhya, C.B. (1988). 'The Farmer-Capitalists of Coastal Andhra Pradesh', *Economic and Political Weekly*, Vol. 23, No. 28, pp. 1433–42.

Vimta Labs (2007). Rapid Environmental Impact Assessment for the Proposed 1.4 Mtpa Alumina Refinery and Co-generation Plant at Srungavarapu Kota, Vizianagaram District, Andhra Pradesh, Hyderabad.

8

Mining and Displacement in South Odisha

Perspectives from a Census Survey

M. GOPINATH REDDY, PRAJNA PARAMITA MISHRA AND NAGARAJU CHIKKALA

Odisha is endowed with varieties of mineral resources and occupies an important position in India's mineral map. Among all the minerals Bauxite is a prominent one. The state accounts for 51 per cent of Indian bauxite reserves followed by Andhra Pradesh (21%). According to the Geological Survey of India (GSI, 1979), this reserves referred as the East Coast Bauxite deposits have brought a spectacular boost to the bauxite resources of the country from 350 million tonnes (1971) to 2,000 million tonnes (1978). The bauxite deposits of Odisha are broadly described under the Southern, Central and Northern groups (Table 1).

Out of the ten deposits, mining leases have been granted to two deposits. Panchapatmali deposit in Koraput district is under the operation of National Aluminium Company (NALCO), a Government of India Undertaking since 1986. Maliparbat deposit in the same district has been granted to Hindustan Aluminium Company (HINDALCO). For Lanjigarh deposit approval for mining lease has been granted in favour of Odisha Mining Corporation (OMC). This project has been tied up with Vedanta Alumina Limited. Similarly for the Kodingamali deposit, OMC has tied up with Aditya Alumina. Utkal Alumina planned to mine Bhaplimali that has been delayed because of people's movement. Larsen and Toubro (L&T) is planning to mine Sijimal. NALCO is trying acquiring mining lease over Pottangi deposit as a part of its expansion. This shows that all the bauxite mines of Odisha are already acquired by different companies or waiting to acquire.

Table 1
Bauxite Deposits in Odisha

Group	*Estimated Reserves (million tonnes)*	*Mine Area (hectares)*
Southern Group		
Ballada	12.41	86
Maliparbat	9.80	109
Pottangi	69.03	265
Total Southern	91.24	460
Central Group		
Panchpatmali	316.98	1,445
Kodingamali	91.4	533
Karnapadikonda	17.2	193
Total Central	425.58	2,171
Northern Group		
Baphlimali	195.73	960
Sijimali	86	1,300
Karlapat	59	973
Lanjigarh	53	564
Total Northern	393.73	3,797
Total Odisha	910.55	6,428

Source: Geological Survey of India (1979).

After getting approval from the government the next step is land acquisition and displacement. Here, we study the displacement scenario on NALCO, the leading public sector enterprise of India. This article has been organized as follows. Section one is an introduction to the study. Section two brings out the past picture of NALCO. Section three deals with the study area. Section four presents results and finally section five concludes the study.

Bauxite Mining in South Odisha: A Look at Past

In the early 1980s it was clear that the bauxite deposits of South Odisha will be exploited with the help of a western transnational and

Andhra Pradesh deposits with the help of a Soviet aided project. NALCO was set up for exploiting the vast bauxite deposits of south Odisha. It was involved with a French Aluminium International (Srinivasan, Vyasulu and Rajagopalan, 1981). There was a public debate on this huge public investment and papers in the leading journal *Economic and Political Weekly* raised number of questions about the ongoing debate (ibid., 1982).

Stanley (1996) gives a clear account of displacement, compensation and rehabilitation in the NALCO Bauxite Mine and Plant at Damanjodi. According to him, 597 households in 26 villages are displaced, out of which 42.55 per cent are tribal (Table 2). Out of the total acquired land of 10,058.76 acres, 69.52 per cent had gone for the construction of plant followed by township.

Table 2

Displacement Scenario of NALCO

Affected villages	26	
Affected families	Tribal	254 (42.55)
	Dalit	56 (9.38)
	Others	287 (48.07)
	Total	597 (100)
Land acquired (acres)		
	Mines	427.30 (4.25)
	Township	2,638.96 (26.24)
	Plant	6,992.50 (69.52)
	Total	10,058.76 (100)
	Government Land	2,805.49
	Agricultural Land	2,834.56

Source: Stanley (1996).

Stanley (1996) has also given a picture of compensation package given by NALCO. Out of the displaced families 74 per cent are rehabilitated and 59 per cent have received job in compensation. Compensation per acre of land is ₹ 2,000 and compensation for tree is ₹ 100. However, there is no compensation for common property resources (CPRs).

Samal (1996) has taken another study in the same year, which covers the NALCO Anugul sector (smelter). There he has mentioned that NALCO rehabilitation and resettlement policy is regarded as one of the best in India. According to Khatua and Stanley (2006),

NALCO paid compensation for *patta* land alone. There was no compensation for CPR or government and village land. However, they are a good source of earning for the landless villagers. All these studies encourage meeting the displaced people and seeing their situations nearly after three decades. With this background the objective of our study is to compare those displaced situations in the pre-mining and post-mining period.

Table 3

Compensation Scenario of NALCO

Families displaced	597
Families rehabilitated	441 (73.87)
Job received	352 (58.96)
Compensation per one acre of land (₹)	2000
Compensation for tree	100
Compensation for CPRs	No

Source: Stanley (1996).

Study Area and Sample Selection

Our study concentrates on Koraput district of Odisha because this district produces more than 98 per cent of bauxite. Bauxite mines in the Panchpatmali hills of Koraput district is taken because it is the largest single deposit in the world. The National Aluminium Company (NALCO) was established in 1981 to produce aluminium from this rich bauxite deposits. It has three operations in Odisha (Stanley, 1996):

(a) Bauxite mining in the Panchpatmali hills of Koraput district with deposits of 112.8 million tonnes;

(b) Alumina refinery complex in Damanjodi, Koraput district, 11 km from the mines. It has an installed capacity of eight lakh tonnes of alumina annually;

(c) Smelter plant at Anugul district. 4.25 lakh tonnes are transported here. The plant has a captive power plant with a capacity of 55.5 MW as against its actual need of 32 MW.

Our study concentrates on the first two areas. It also includes villages near the ash and red mud pond areas. NALCO has divided the surrounding areas into two zones: core zones (area falls within a radius of 5 km either from the plant or the refinery) and buffer zones (area falls within a radius of 6 to 15 km either from the plant or the refinery). This has been decided by NALCO in view of the severity of pollution effects. Villages are selected from each zone. There are 12 villages from three blocks surrounded by the refinery and nearly 40 villages from four Gram Panchayat surrounded by the mines. We visited 11 villages and did a census survey to understand the extent of displacement. We interviewed all household heads of these hamlets and villages. Finally we collected information from 1483 households. A demographic feature of the villages is given in Table 4.

In the mining core zone, Kapsiput is our sample village. It has 142 households out of which 141 households belong to the scheduled tribe category. In the mining buffer zone Khardiguda and Putraghati are two sample villages. Khardiguda has 79 households and all belong to the scheduled tribe. Putraghati has 201 households with mixed population.

Table 4

Demographic Features of Affected Villages

Study Zone	*Village*	*Panchayat*	*Block*	*Households Category*				
				SC	*ST*	*OBC*	*OC*	*Total*
Mining Core	Kapsiput	Bhifaarguda	Lakhimpur	1	141	0	0	142
Mining Buffer	Khardiguda	Littiguda	Koraput	0	79	0	0	79
	Putraghati			26	95	79	1	201
Refinery Core	Analabadi	Matalput	Koraput	68	267	144	128	607
	Ambogam	Littiguda		2	131	0	0	133
Refinery Buffer	Mujanga	Mujanga	Dasaman-thapur	143	93	0	23	259
	Marchimal	Matalput	Koraput	21	0	15	41	77
ARMP Core Zone	Goudaguda	Charangul	Semiliguda	0	0	0	73	73
	Kharaguda	Podampur	Koraput	4	2	14	13	33
	Champapodar	Mujanga	Dasaman-thapur	11	1	9	64	85
ARMP Buffer Zone	Charangaguda	Podampur	Koraput	30	42	0	0	72

In refinery core zone, Analabadi has 607 households. This is a rehabilitation colony consisting of 11 displaced hamlets of the refinery. It also has a mixed population. Second village Ambogam in the refinery core zone consists of 133 households, mostly tribal. This village is almost located in the refinery premises (1.2 km). This village was supposed to be displaced but NALCO delayed the process and later on stopped. These villagers are the victim of all immediate environmental impact. In refinery buffer zone, village Mujanga has 259 households, dominated by scheduled caste and scheduled tribe population. Marchimal is another village in this area with 77 households with a mixed population but no tribal.

In the ash and red mud pond (ARMP) core zone, Goudaguda is a village with 73 households. All the households belong to *Gouda* caste, whose main occupation is taken as livestock rearing. Both Kharaguda and Champapodar in this area are displaced villages. Now they are resettled in one place but they are different villages. Kharaguda has 33 households with a mixed population and Champapadar has 85 households, dominated by other caste. In the ARMP buffer zone Charangaguda is a village with 72 households, dominated by scheduled caste and scheduled tribe population. Most of them have lost land because of the railway track of NALCO. The next section shows the displacement scenario of these affected villages.

Results and Discussions

In the mining core zone, 51 per cent of households have lost their agricultural land. For this none of the households have received compensation. These villagers were practicing *podu* on top of the hills and hill slopes.

Table 5
Displacement and Compensation Scenario

Study Zone	*Total HHs*	*Affected HHs*	*Assets lost*		*Compensation Received*	
			Land	*House*	*Land*	*House*
Mining Core	142	72 (50.70)	72	0	0	NA
Mining Buffer	280	138 (49.29)	138	0	136	NA
Refinery Core	740	383 (51.76)	141	361	129	344
Refinery Buffer	336	34 (10.12)	34	0	28	NA
ARMP Core	191	128 (67.02)	86	103	85	103
ARMP Buffer	72	38(52.78)	38	0	36	NA

Source: Field Survey (2011).

After getting the permission to mine that area, NALCO evicted these villagers from cultivating those patches of land. As these displaced households do not have *patta* for their agricultural lands they have not received any compensation for that. In the mining buffer zone 49 per cent of households have lost their agricultural land. These villagers have lost land because of the rehabilitation colony, Conveyor Belt and another road which connects the mining to the refinery site. Here, almost all the households have received compensation and only two households have not received because of unclear document. The compensation package is ₹ 1,000 to ₹ 1,500 per acre for dry land and ₹ 2,500 to ₹ 5,000 per acre for wet land.

In the refinery core zone 52 per cent of the households are affected by the refinery. Out of the affected households, 37 per cent (141 households) have lost their agricultural land. Out of that 129 households have received compensation and for others it is still pending. The compensation package is same. On the other hand 94 per cent of the affected households (361 households) have lost their home and homestead area. Out of that 344 households have received compensation. For this they have received ₹ 500 to ₹ 5,000 according to classification like hut, semi-*pucca*, *pucca*, etc. These households are also settled in the rehabilitation colony and one job (per house) in NALCO was offered. In the refinery buffer zone only 10 per cent of the total households are affected. They have lost their agricultural land for refinery and a part of red mud pond. Out of 34 households, 28 households have received compensation and for others it is pending.

In the ARMP core zone 67 per cent of the households are affected. Out of all the affected households 67 per cent of the households have lost their agricultural land. All households have received compensation except one. In this area 80 per cent of the households have lost their home and homestead area. Here, compensation package is same. In the ARMP buffer zone 53 per cent of the households are affected. Out of the affected 38 households have lost their agricultural land and 36 households are compensated. The next section compares household main occupation in the pre- and post-displacement scenario.

As a part of compensation packages, NALCO has provided job to those households who have lost their home and homestead area. Therefore, it is interesting to study how the household main occupation has changed in the post displacement scenario. Here, households head may be a different person in the pre- and post-displacement scenario but we have compared the main occupation of the same households.

Table 6

Household Main Occupation: Pre- and Post-Displacement

Main Occupation	*Mining Core Zone*		*Mining Buffer Zone*	
	Pre	*Post*	*Pre*	*Post*
Farmers	118 (100)	75 (63.6)	193 (81.8)	78 (33.1)
Wage Labours	0	0	43 (18.2)	
Others	0	0	0	9 (3.8)
NALCO Contract/ Wage Employee	NA	43 (36.4)	NA	149 (63.1)
Total	118 (100)	118 (100)	236 (100)	236 (100)

Source: Field Survey (2011).

In the mining core zone, all households, main occupation was farming in the pre-displacement period (Table 6). However, in the post-displacement period 36 per cent are engaged in NALCO as contract or wage employee. They are not permanent employee of NALCO. NALCO has given the contract works to contractors. These contractors will recruit the contract and wage labour. They do not have job security and they received weekly payment. The work category divided into four categories are; high skilled works, skilled works, semi-skilled works and unskilled works. according to work category the wage rates are: high skilled worker – ₹ 330 per day, skilled worker – ₹ 280 per day, semi-skilled worker – ₹ 220 per day, unskilled worker – ₹ 190 per day. In the mining buffer zone, farmers dominated the main occupation (82%) in the pre-displacement period followed by wage labourers. However, this percentage has reduced in the post-displacement period and now NALCO contract and wage labourers are the main category.

In the refinery core zone farmers dominated the main occupation in the pre-displacement period (94.5%). However, in the post-displacement period majority are NALCO permanent employees. As many households have lost their homestead area in this zone, they have received the jobs in their compensation package. This is followed by wage labourers and NALCO contract employee. In the refinery buffer zone, in the pre-displacement period both farming and wage labour has a major role. However, in the post-displacement phase wage labour has outweighed farming. As the extent of displacement is very less here so workers employed in NALCO.

Table 7

Household Main Occupation: Pre- and Post-Displacement

Main Occupation	*Refinery Core Zone*		*Refinery Buffer Zone*	
	Pre	*Post*	*Pre*	*Post*
Farmers	665 (94.5)	71 (10.1)	165 (54.8)	100 (33.2)
Wage Labours	27 (3.8)	207 (29.4)	132 (43.9)	172 (57.1)
Others	12 (1.7)	33 (4.7)	4 (1.3)	19 (6.3)
NALCO Contract/ Wage Employee	NA	98 (13.8)	NA	10 (3.3)
NALCO Employee	NA	295 (41.9)	NA	0
Total	704 (100)	704 (100)	301 (100)	301 (100)

Source: Field Survey (2011).

Table 8

Household Main Occupation: Pre- and Post-Displacement

Main Occupation	*ARMP Core Zone*		*ARMP Buffer Zone*	
	Pre	*Post*	*Pre*	*Post*
Farmers	164 (85.9)	16 (8.4)	38 (52.8)	1 (1.4)
Wage Labours	22 (11.5)	90 (47.1)	34 (47.2)	65 (90.3)
Others	5 (2.6)	7 (3.7)	0	3 (4.2)
NALCO Contract/ Wage Employee	NA	9 (4.7)	NA	3(4.2)
NALCO Employee	NA	69 (36.1)	NA	
Total	191 (100)	191 (100)	72 (100)	72 (100)

Source: Field Survey (2011).

In the ARMP core zone also situation is same in the pre-displacement period. The main occupation is dominated by farming. However, in the post scenario it is wage labour and NALCO employee. Here also as the households have lost their homestead land they have permanent employment in NALCO. In the ARMP buffer zone, main occupation was dominated by farmers and wage labourers. However, in the post-displacement period it is dominated by wage labour. Because of water problem and other environmental impact farming is not a profitable occupation now. As the contractors are exploiting the NALCO contract employees these people prefer to work as wage labourer than contract employee.

In the tribal and hilly habitations CPRs play an important role in the subsistence of the livelihoods of the poor and the marginalized. In particular, these regions, unlike in the plain areas, CPRs access and availability to the village communities in terms of basic needs, such as grazing pastures, ponds, streams, forests for minor forest produce play important role for their livelihoods. The access to them is usually free and unrestricted.

Interaction with affected households in these areas revealed that NALCO does not offer any access to their health facilities in terms of issuing health cards and making available medicines and other facilities. The attitude of NALCO, a profit-making public sector undertaking, towards this section of affected people was found totally inadequate and unsatisfactory. Permanent employment opportunities available to them were also very limited in the plant. Whatever employment was offered is only contractual that too through contractors, not directly by the company. It was also told during the survey that once employed person got married, left the house, the others, especially the elderly become totally dependent without any sources of regular income. Land to land compensation was eminently possible during early 1980s, but this option was not followed. It was pity that the affected households became addicted to certain social evils as a result of cash compensation.

Many women from mining surrounding areas are working in mining as cleaners; cement works masonry cleaning and helpers. They are getting employment through the contractors not NALCO. The wage rates are ₹ 90 to ₹ 120. The women are saying that no adequate transport facilities are provided to reach mining site. It was observed that people from surrounding villages are working in refinery, and they engaged in both technical and non-technical sections. People working in technical sections are technicians, fitters, electricians, and non-technical people working as maintenance workers, daily wage workers in boiling section, and other works.

It was found that transport is the major problem from refinery to refinery surrounding villages. It is observed that men are using bicycle or motorcycle for their transport and women trek long distances by walk. It is very difficult because they have to walk 9 to 10 kms on *kutcha* road to reach refinery and it takes more than one hour. They are saying that due to transport problem they are not able to reach home on proper time and have no time to spend with their children at home. They are expecting NALCO to provide transport facility to reach refinery and on time.

Besides the problems enlisted above, there are certain environmental and ecological problems observed in the field. Dust emanating from the conveyor belt carrying bauxite is affecting the agricultural lands and hence their productivity. There is no mechanism to compensate such losses. Natural resources like ponds and streams were adversely damaged due to mining and conveyor belt hence the water sources are totally diminished. It was observed during the survey that some of the problems identified in Goudaguda village. Leakage in caustic soda and septic water pipeline led to septic water flows into the agriculture fields hence fertility is affected and the crop production has been decreased. The canal water is contaminated due to caustic mud and septic water. The village elders said that in 1995 due to contaminated water affected by caustic mud and septic water few livestock were dead. Villagers fought against NALCO and received compensation. Villagers are facing health problems like skin problems, tuberculosis and other health illness.

When it comes to other infrastructural facilities, most of the villages are facing water problems. They depend on well and hand pumps for both drinking and domestic usage. For agriculture they depend on stream, ponds and rainfall. NALCO gets water from the Kerandi river which is 8 km far from the refinery. The pipeline is connected to carry water from the river. Due to water pipeline some of the villages have lost their agriculture lands. It was told during the survey that people's request to access water from the pipeline was denied by NALCO, though there is huge water wastage due to leakages.

Interactions with associations like Peripheral Development Committee, LDP Welfare Association and LAP Association show that due to NALCO many people have lost their agriculture lands and houses but NALCO provided job opportunity to few people only and rest of them are not yet benefited. There was no proper guideline for job recruitment. After job recruitment, NALCO has conducted Minimum Literacy Programme to the displaced people. The programme duration was nine months, at that time some of the displaced people who got jobs have died due to health problems and their spouses have applied for their husband's job but NALCO has not offered any job to them. Still these people have been trying to get their jobs with help of the associations/unions.

In the year 1984–85, NALCO started Peripheral Development Programme. The area which is 10 kms from kefinery and mining consider as a peripheral area. Under this programme, NALCO has promised to provide all the facilities like health, education, roads, drinking water and infrastructure development (school building, etc.) but did not provide any service to the peripheral area. Above that associations presidents said that as for their knowledge the Peripheral Development Funds have been diverted in to other areas. All association members demand that NALCO has to provide jobs to all affected people, and to provide services to notified peripheral area. Local priority should be given for the contract works and contract jobs. Health card access to all the displaced people are needed to be given irrespective of whether they are directly or indirectly affected.

Conclusion

NALCO, a profit making public sector called 'the pride of Odisha' cannot really be characterized as such from the perspective of affected population. The data shows very clearly that the most vulnerable sections, viz., scheduled tribes and scheduled castes who have lost lands, houses and other assets could not be able to get back their livelihood status as a result of cash compensation policy. The fact that land scarcity was not there in 1980s as is felt now, NALCO should have adopted land to land policy. As a result of this approach, we could see from the data that the above sections were reduced from farmers to casual labourers and became helpless. Even the job allocation was confined to one member of the family reducing others to mere dependents. The other infrastructural facilities promised by NALCO were not adequately provided and there are still loose ends in the whole approach. On the whole the resettlement and rehabilitation measures by NALCO are found to be piece-meal and ad hoc. The company with its huge profit base could have done much better to these much marginalized people.

Acknowledgement

This paper is part of a project titled 'Bauxite Mining in Koraput Region of Orissa: A Socio-Economic Impact Analysis', funded by the Jamshedji Tata Trust, Mumbai. The authors acknowledge this support. Field work was carried out with the help of M.S. Swaminathan Research Foundation (MSSRF), Jeypore, and Odisha. We are thankful to Mr S.V. Ramana and his team for this support.

References

Geological Survey of India (1979). 'The East Coast Bauxite Deposits of India', *Bulletins of the Geological Survey of India*, No. 46.

Khatua, S. and W. Stanley (2006). 'Ecological Debt: A Case Study from Orissa, India', in A.K. Peralta (ed.), *Ecological Debt: The Peoples of the South are the Creditors, Cases from Ecuador, Mozambique, Brazil and India*, Geneva: World Council of Churches.

Samal, K.C. (1996). 'NALCO-Induced Transformation: Linkage Effects, Displacement, Rehabilitation and Environmental Pollution', Working Paper No. 28, Odisha: Nabakrushna Choudhury Centre for Development Studies.

Srinivasan, K., V. Vyasulu and S. Rajagopalan (1981). 'The Orissa Aluminium Complex: Points toward a Debate', *Economic and Political Weekly*, Vol. 16, No. 49, pp. 2005–14.

Stanley, W. (1996). 'Machkund, Upper Kolab and NALCO Projects in Koraput District, Orissa', *Economic and Political Weekly*, Vol. 31, No. 24, pp. 1533–38.

Subrahmanyam, K.V. (1982). 'Orissa Aluminium Complex', *Economic and Political Weekly*, Vol. 17, No. 5, pp. 168–72.

Part III

Problems in Policy Implementation and Design

9

Swelling Displacement and Elusive Rehabilitation

Deficits in Policy Interventions

K.B. SAXENA

The model of development pursued by the Indian State since independence has never come up for such sharp scrutiny as, lately, in the context of the magnitude of displacement it has produced and the trauma and impoverishment it has caused to the displaced persons due to the apathy towards their rehabilitation and resettlement. This explains why the iniquities in development and resettlement of persons displaced by it have acquired a degree of centrality in public and policy discourses never witnessed before. In the past, however, resettlement of displaced persons has received greater attention from researchers, activists and civil society organizations than the nature of development which causes compulsory acquisition of private property resulting in displacement and impoverishment. This is because people in the forefront of research and social action have largely been anthropologists, sociologists and social workers whose interest lies in studying the social impact of development and suggesting how its benefits can reach the people concerned. The added reason could also be that the mobilization of displaced persons for seeking proper resettlement does not bring these agencies into confrontation with the state or the dominant sections of society which could be the case if they were to question the nature of development itself which induces displacement. The advocacy on the improvement in resettlement efforts has also greater chance of receiving a positive response at various levels in the government than the efforts for revision of acquisition of laws or review of development policies. Even so, the heightened interest in resettlement of displaced persons currently witnessed is a post-1980 phenomenon triggered by people's resistance to acquisition of their land, increasing scale of displacement from habitat, livelihood and environment, disappointment with the rehabilitation efforts in the past and the World Bank initiative in repairing its image in the context of the widespread critique of its policies which had caused impoverishment of persons affected by projects financed by it. An impressive literature has now emerged on the subject with considerable theoretical inputs being provided by the experts of the World Bank and the scholars from developed and developing countries. But scholars in India have been engaged in this study from before, though with less sophisticated theorization of the issues involved. India has produced an impressive literature on the rehabilitation and resettlement efforts and their impact which is substantial, rich in quality and a 'richer thesaurus' than is available for any other part of the world (Cernia, 1999).

Displacement, until recently, remained a non-issue. This explains why there was neither a law nor a national policy nor even a firm commitment to address the numerous problems created by displacement. While the pressure from the World Bank hastened the formulation of the first ever National Policy on Resettlement and Rehabilitation for Project Affected Families, 2003 (MoRD, 2003), the commitment to give a fair deal to the oustees remained weak since the policy that emerged was far removed from the aspirations of the displaced persons and the parameters outlined by the advocacy organizations engaged in this field. Even this policy was not enforced while the land acquisition for projects continued unabated and, in fact, increased substantially. The resistance of the affected persons across the country in the recent past, however, brought to a halt to the acquisition of land for mega development projects. This forced the central government to revise the policy (2003). The (revised) National Rehabilitation and Resettlement Policy, 2007 has been notified by the Ministry of Rural Development (MoRD, 2007). The Rehabilitation and Resettlement Bill, 2007 to provide statutory support to the Policy has been introduced in the Lok Sabha (Lok Sabha, 2007). Faced with a similar situation in the state and under pressure to provide a humane resettlement to the affected tribal peasantry to smoothen the progress of its high profile projects, the Government of Odisha notified the Odisha Resettlement and Rehabilitation Policy, 2006 (GoO, 2006). The paper would look into both policies to highlight the deficits in these interventions.

National Rehabilitation and Resettlement Policy

The policy for the rehabilitation and resettlement of displaced persons covers all projects where involuntary displacement takes place. One of its objectives is to minimize large scale displacement by avoiding acquisition of irrigated and multi-cropped land. It also commits to provide a standard of living to the displaced persons which are better than the one enjoyed before. Within the project area, the policy extends benefits to not merely the land owners but also to those losing livelihood. It incorporates requirement for social impact assessment of the project and puts in place dedicated administrative arrangements for preparation and implementation of the rehabilitation and resettlement plan in consultation with the affected persons. The admissible set of entitlements for the displaced persons include provision of house sites, allotment of agricultural land, preference in access to employment in the project and training for employability outside, financial grant for construction of house, cattle-shed for agriculturists, workshed for rural artisans and subsistence allowance to all the displaced persons for a specified period. The core amenities and social infrastructure needed for the resettlement colony have also been broadly indicated. An elaborate institutional arrangement for monitoring and grievance redressal has been laid down. The additional measures for the Scheduled Tribes (STs) require preparation of a Tribal Development Plan which involves settlement of pending land rights, restoration of alienated land and a programme for development of alternative fuel, fodder and non-timber forest produce on non-forest lands within a period of five years where the affected tribals are denied access to forests. The tribals have also been promised preference in the allotment of land if the government land is available in the resettlement area and additional financial assistance for the loss of customary rights or usages of forest produce. The displaced tribal families shall, if possible, be settled in the scheduled area in a compact block and if settled out of the district, they would receive 25 per cent higher rehabilitation and resettlement benefits in monetary terms in respect of the specified provisions. They shall also get allotment of land for community and religious gatherings. It has also been mandated that the Gram Sabha or the Panchayat in the Schedule V areas and the councils in the Schedule VI areas would be consulted in accordance with the provisions of the PESA, 1996 and the other relevant laws in all cases of land acquisition before issue of notification under the Land Acquisition Act, 1894. The tribals, who were in possession of forest lands prior to December 2005, would be eligible for the benefits of the policy.

But the policy does not address the major problems which agitate the affected peasantry. The most important of them is that the government should avoid the spectre of displacement and, if that is not feasible, to scale down its level. Unlike the declaration that the acquisition of the irrigated and multi-cropped land would be avoided, the policy makes no such concession for the scheduled areas or the STs in respect of the acquisition of land. It does not even contain an assurance that the acquisition of tribal land would be avoided unless absolutely necessary and minimized, if unavoidable. The promised exercise enshrined in the objectives of the policy to minimize displacement and to explore non-displacing and least displacing alternatives does not specifically contextualize it in respect of land held by the STs. Even as an exhortation of a general nature irrespective of the affected groups, it lacks seriousness, sincerity and commitment. The displaced persons are not associated with this exercise which has been entrusted to the administrator in charge of the rehabilitation and resettlement in consultation with the concerned project agency. This limited objective is also not incorporated in the Land Acquisition (Amendment) Bill, 2007 where it was most needed.

The policy has been made applicable to the projects in future and has ignored the huge number of displaced persons from the earlier projects who have remained un-rehabilitated. Besides, the numerical benchmark specified for its applicability makes it evident that even in respect of the new projects; the policy would not be applicable to all of them. This benchmark though lower in respect of the tribal, hilly, desert areas than in respect of other areas is irrational and arbitrary in the case of both categories and would exclude a large number of the affected persons from even the meagre benefits that the policy offers. The policy also creates doubts about its universal coverage for rehabilitation and resettlement even in the areas of its applicability on account of the definition of 'affected family' incorporated in it. It fails to take note of the phenomenon of 'secondary displacement' and therefore ignores to include persons who suffer such displacement on account of project activities though their land is not acquired. The tribals are among the major victims of this displacement which is neither recognized nor addressed in the policy.

As for the entitlement of benefits, the approach in the policy continues to be property-centric since the loss of livelihood and access to the common property resources (CPRs) is not covered by any compensatory arrangements. There is only a provision for development of fuel, fodder and non-timber resources on non-forest lands where the tribals are denied access to forests. There is no similar commitment to provide common lands in respect of the non-tribal inhabitants. The discrimination in entitlement of individual benefits to the affected persons such as allotment of land and provision of employment between those who lose land and others who lose livelihood is also implicit. On the issue of allotment of land, the policy offers no concrete assurance at all. There is no commitment to provide land for land even for the tribal displaces, let alone others. There is similar lack of assurance for allotment of land whether in the case of irrigation/hydel projects or other projects. The provision of land has been made conditional to the availability of the government land/wasteland in the resettlement area. This condition is most unlikely to be satisfied. The option to acquire private land for such distribution for the vulnerable groups like the STs has been specifically disregarded. The provision of employment to one person from the each affected nuclear family lacks positiveness and credibility. It has been subjected to the availability of vacancies and the eligibility of the displaced job seekers. In the current paradigm of the economy, projects public or private, create meagre employment opportunities and, that too, in the skilled category, by and large. Due to the low literacy levels and lack of skills, the displacees generally and tribals among them in particular, would fail to satisfy the requirements for such jobs even if available. With regard to the infrastructure and amenities, an invidious distinction has been introduced in the range of entitlements admissible between the projects which satisfy the specified numerical benchmark and those which do not do so. As the concerned state government has been authorized to determine the civic amenities and social facilities, the provision would lend itself to arbitrary decisions and conservative assessment of requirements influenced by financial and political considerations.

The gender bias is also reflected in the policy since the definition of 'family' has failed to treat unmarried adult daughter as an independent unit deserving separate rehabilitation. The women-headed households (widows, divorcees and those deserted by their husbands) do not attract attention in the policy. The concerns of women in general have been ignored since neither the baseline survey and census collect information relating to their specific requirements nor the rehabilitation and resettlement scheme incorporates affirmative action to provide for them. The displaced tribals would suffer additionally if intra-family distribution of land has not been entered in land records since even the adult sons would not be entitled to separate units of rehabilitation and resettlement.

The requirement for a Tribal Development Plan in the policy suffers from serious inadequacies. It is characterized by a homogenized and standardized approach and fails to reflect the diversity of the social and ecological situations in the tribal areas. The land management practices differ widely in the tribal areas with varying degree of community control over natural resources. The shifting cultivation areas where the tribals use land on hilltops by rotation are inhabited usually by the 'primitive tribes' (pre-agricultural groups). The land records have not mapped all such areas and individual uses of land particularly on slopes beyond 9° have not been documented since no plough agriculture is possible in that terrain. In the sixth schedule areas, the pattern of land holding is communal with individual use, the land records do not exist and the tribes are opposed to their preparation. There is an extensive variety of rights and interests in access to land resources covered by the customary laws. In addition, the hunter and food gathering tribes are entirely dependent on forest resources with no fixed habitat as they move from area to area in search of food. There are also nomadic tribes, de-notified tribes and pastoral communities with different patterns of habitat and access to land, food resources and fulfilment of other needs. The variety is also reflected in the pattern of land management ranging from settled agriculture to terrace and shifting cultivation. The Tribal Development Plan, therefore, cannot be neatly standardized and prepared in terms of a uniform model which has been made applicable to the non-tribal communities which the policy seems to do. The conceptual and structural frame for rehabilitation and resettlement of the displaced tribals needs to be designed taking into account their ethnic characteristics, specific social structure, ecological situation and the pattern of economy. This is particularly important for the tribes in remote areas, least exposed to the outside world. This complexity in planning has not been recognized, let alone accommodated in the policy.

Besides, on the issues of social disarticulation, devaluation of culture and emotional trauma experienced by the displaced tribals resulting from the sudden break with their kinship networks, exposure to the hostile larger society and intrusion of the incompatible cultural and social norms from the immigrant non-tribals in the area, the policy is totally silent. It does not even take note of the seriousness of the problem let alone address it.

Overall, the policy offers a faltering and fragile commitment in respect of the fundamental concerns of the peasantry with neither a right based entitlement nor unambiguous assurance in respect of land and employment and a guarantee of a congenial and culturally compatible relocation with replacement of the facilities and amenities, if not better, enjoyed by them prior to their displacement.

Odisha Policy, 2006 and the National Policy, 2007: Comparative Assessment

The Odisha government brought out a rehabilitation and resettlement policy in May 2006. Considerable inputs provided by the United Nations Development Programme (UNDP) went into its formulation though not all its suggestions found acceptance. The policy is considered to be an improvement on the National Policy (Mathur, 2008) and has been described as the best policy in India (Mehra, 2007). These observations presumably compare the Odisha Policy with the National Policy, 2003. But the National Policy, 2003 has already been revised and the National Rehabilitation and Resettlement Policy, 2007 has been notified. Therefore, it may be relevant to compare it with the National Policy, 2007. The Odisha Policy scores over the National Policy in respect of the following features.

It applies to persons displaced on account of the acquisition of land carried out through negotiations also and not merely those affected as a result of compulsory acquisition by the government. If the process of negotiation includes land procured/purchased directly by the corporates/private parties, as seems to be the case, since the definition of 'project area' includes land which is acquired/alienated/purchased, it is certainly more equitable, just and humane in its applicability. On the issue of coverage, unlike the National Policy which restricts it to those affected by projects satisfying the specified numerical benchmark of the level of displacement, the Odisha Policy does not place such a barrier and is therefore more liberal.

The norm of eligibility for R&R (rehabilitation and resettlement) benefits in the Odisha Policy updates the list up to 1 January of the year in which the physical displacement is scheduled. This formulation for the coverage of displaced persons is superior to the one adopted in the definition of the 'affected family' in the National Policy.

The definition of 'family' is more inclusive in the Odisha Policy than in the National Policy. It recognizes unmarried daughters and sisters more than 30 years of age, a widow or a woman divorcee as a separate family for the benefit of rehabilitation and is, thus, gender neutral. Additionally, it empowers physically and mentally challenged persons and minor orphans by conferring the status of a separate family. The National Policy continues to show bias against these social groups.

The Odisha Policy includes, as one of its objectives, the need for ensuring environmental sustainability through the resettlement/rehabilitation process which the National Policy omits to incorporate. The Odisha Policy has also shown requisite foresight in mandating a comprehensive communication plan for awareness creation with the involvement of civil society at the cost of the project. No such provision has been made in the National Policy. The Odisha Policy has also provided for dovetailing of normal development programmes with the resettlement and rehabilitation package to be made available to the displaced community on a priority basis. This is intended to be in addition to the benefits which a displacee is entitled to under the Policy. The National Policy does not make any mention of it.

The Odisha Policy clearly stipulates that no physical displacement shall be effected before the completion of resettlement work while the National Policy is less equivocal on this issue. It merely requires 'adequate progress' in the rehabilitation and resettlement to be ensured before physical shifting of the affected persons and, therefore, shows lesser sensitivity to the inconvenience faced by the displaced persons.

'Multiple displacements' does not even attract the attention of the National Policy. The Odisha Policy recognizes the harassment involved to the affected persons who have gone through the experience before and, therefore, provides for, at least, additional 50 per cent compensation over and above the normal compensation to mitigate it. The Odisha Policy also requires steps to be taken by the rehabilitation and resettlement agency to acclimatize the resettled people in the new habitat including development of cordial relationship with the host community in the resettlement site. Though measures required for this purpose have not been spelt out, the concern itself for the social trauma involved in adjustment to the new physical and social environment has not been reflected in the National Policy.

On the issue of rehabilitation assistance, the Odisha Policy marginally scores over the National Policy in some respects. It classifies projects into five types: (a) industrial; (b) mining; (c) water resources/national parks; (d) urban and linear projects; and (e) any other projects. It makes provision for employment only in type (a) and (b) projects while in type (c) projects, it replaces provision for employment with assistance for agricultural land. Type (d) projects have no provision for either land or employment while type (e) projects are silent on the package of benefits which would be notified later. Linear projects are also required to provide employment to one member of the family where total displacement is caused. The provision for employment, however, is restricted to one member of the pre-displacement family. But, like the National Policy, there is no assurance in respect of this benefit in the Odisha Policy. The policy only talks of giving preference in the matter of employment in the project. A facilitating condition has, however, been added that the eligibility age would be relaxable by five years and the project authorities would be required to notify their employment capacity in advance. In terms of concrete benefits, this provision is as valueless for the displacee to get a job as in the National Policy. The only difference is that one time cash compensation ranging from five to one lakh where employment cannot be provided has been added in the Odisha Policy. The sliding scale of compensation here is linked to the relationship of the nominated member with the displaced family, with a minor son receiving the maximum amount, while a widow or a woman divorcée getting the lowest amount. The discrimination made inter-se between members of the family is both irrational and indefensible besides being a potential source of conflict within the family. On the issue of vocational training and skill development, the National Policy makes a provision for scholarships which the Odisha Policy does not do.

A mandatory provision has been made for allotment of 2.5 acres of irrigated agricultural land or five acres of non-irrigated agricultural land to each ST displaced family in type (c) projects while the displaced families of all other social categories would be provided with two acres of irrigated or four acres of non-irrigated agricultural land. But this assurance suffers from lack of will to effectuate it even in respect of STs since a cash equivalent of ₹ one lakh per acre for irrigated and ₹ 50,000 per acre for non-irrigated land including the cost of reclamation or at the rate as decided by the government in the case of non-availability of land has been added. Type (d) projects neither provide for employment nor land. The National Policy also provides for rehabilitation grant to the affected families who have not been given land or employment. Both policies opt for cash option as the most convenient mode of wriggling out of the assurance to provide land or employment.

On the provision of homestead land and house building assistance, the Odisha Policy is more liberal than the National Policy. It provides for at least 1/10th of an acre for this purpose along with a house building grant of ₹ 1,50,000 for projects in rural areas and 1/25th of an acre with a house building grant of ₹ 1,50,000 in urban areas. The National Policy is conservative in respect of both the size of land and the cash grant for construction of house admissible.

It is in respect of benefits to the landless and the homesteadless encroachers that the Odisha Policy shows greater sensitivity than is to be found in the National Policy. The landless encroachers will get ex-gratia equivalent compensation admissible under the Land Acquisition Act for a similar category of land provided the encroachment is of 10 years duration continuously and 'unobjectionable'. The entitlement, however, would be restricted to one standard acre of encroachment. The homesteadless persons would similarly get cash compensation against encroached homestead of 1/10th of an acre in rural and 1/25th of acre in urban areas subject to the above conditions. This would be in addition to the cost of structure. Where encroachment is 'objectionable', only the cost of structure would be compensated.

The National Policy contains some provisions which are either superior to the Odisha Policy or are omitted in the latter. This includes the mandatory Social Impact Assessment, gamut of physical amenities and social infrastructure to be provided at the resettlement site, detailed enumeration of rehabilitation benefits, norms of compensation assessment, unutilized acquired land, procedure for preparation of a rehabilitation plan, updating of land records, arrangement for grievance redressal and monitoring. The National Policy has also placed a distinct focus on Tribal Development Plan with restoration of alienated tribal land, settling land rights, provision for forest to replace the forest lost and additional financial assistance. The National Policy is, therefore, a more comprehensive version of the Odisha Policy. But on the basic issues, there is little by way of a major difference. Neither of the two policies assures replacement of land for land lost not even to STs or a durable, sustainable and dignified employment. Both policies ignore rights of people in CPRs for compensatory entitlements. Both policies have failed to take note of the tenfold risk which the displacees face and to provide for a risk-wise mitigating counter-risks action. The end result is that the beneficiary of either policy would continue to face acute vulnerability to 'spiral of impoverishments'.

Gaps in the National Policy

From the foregoing, it is evident that there are inadequacies in the two policies which need to be bridged if the current level of agitation and social unrest on account of displacement is to be reduced. The major gaps in the National Policy, which is the latest and a more comprehensive document on the subject, are indicated below. These would also apply to the Odisha Policy, where appropriate.

'Eminent Domain'

People dependent upon land need protection from sudden, unavoidable and inevitable acquisition of land causing disruption to their lives. The absolute nature of the power of state through the use of 'eminent domain' for compulsory acquisition of land should be abandoned. Gram Sabha of the village should be mandatorily consulted whether in areas covered by PESA or outside for their consent to the acquisition. The acquisition of land, where absolutely necessary for 'public purpose', should be undertaken after consultation with the Gram Sabha and on terms which they collectively settle with the acquisition authority. These terms would reflect the social cost of land. This is the only democratic and humane method for acquisition of land. The referendum carried out by the Maharashtra government in Raigad for acquisition of land for SEZ shows the way in this regard.

'Public Purpose'

The scope of 'public purpose' should be drastically narrowed down to projects covered by the Directive Principles of State Policy and where project provides to the affected persons direct, tangible and demonstrable benefits.

Exploring Non-displacing Alternatives

The most pressing concern of persons affected or likely to be affected by displacement is to get respite from it. Taking this into account, the policy has laid down as one of its objectives [para 2.1 (a)] the need to minimize displacement and to promote, as far as possible, non-displacing or least displacing alternatives. This commitment should not be hedged by caveats like 'as far as possible'. The efforts should focus on taking this exercise very seriously so as to instill confidence in the affected persons about the sincerity of the efforts involved in it. This part of the policy should be reframed and reworded taking the following into account.

- The policy should declare that the government would explore non-displacing alternatives to acquire land and where this has not been found to be possible after making requisite efforts, shall promote the least displacing alternatives to minimize displacement.
- The mode of undertaking this exercise should not be left to the administrator in consultation with the requiring body as required [para 5.5 (1)] in the policy. It should be carried out in a

transparent manner and through a participatory mode. The persons likely to be affected should be appropriately and adequately facilitated to actively participate in this exercise.

- This exercise should not be entrusted to the administrator but to an independent body outside the government. The composition of this body should inspire confidence of the affected persons who should have a right to represent their case before it through a person of their choice. The requiring body would also have the right to represent its case.
- Public hearing in the affected area should be carried out transparently for this purpose.
- The independent body entrusted with this task should note the facts and arguments made by the parties concerned and should record reasons for coming to its conclusion.
- Prior information about the project and its land requirement relevant to such participation should be made available to the families likely to be affected in a language that they understand and a manner that conveys to them effectively in order that the participation is informed and exclusion is eliminated from this exercise.
- This objective should be appropriately inserted in the Land Acquisition (Amendment) Bill, 2007 so that the extent of land to be acquired is determined on the basis of this exercise.

The objectives of the policy in addition to the provision for non-displacing and least displacing options should also incorporate explicit commitment to avoid acquisition of land belonging to the STs in view of the statutory protection available to them against alienation of their land. The policy [para 2.1 (c)] does not incorporate this commitment and only vaguely talks about protecting the rights of the weaker sections especially members of the SCs and the STs. Where, acquisition of tribal land becomes unavoidable for setting up public utility services, a provision may be made for acquisition of their land on lease rather than by outright transfer along with an arrangement of payment of regular lease rent in addition to the lease premium and its periodical revision. The lease rent should be sufficient to assure subsistence to the affected family. This would be in addition to the benefits of rehabilitation and resettlement under the policy.

Applicability: Area and Project Size

No norm should be prescribed for restricting the applicability of the Policy. The numerical benchmark laid down in the National Policy for Rehabilitation and Resettlement, 2007 and the corresponding bill to projects where 400 or more families en mass in plain areas or 200 or more families en mass in tribal and hilly areas DDP blocks or scheduled areas for eligibility to claim the benefit should be scrapped. The policy should be applicable to all projects irrespective of the number of the displaced persons it involves. This would remove selectivity, irrationality and bias in its application and inequality in treatment of the displaced persons. The provision would, at least, assure that whatever has been promised in the policy document would be extended to all displaced persons without discrimination and that the government is shrinking its responsibility in this regard.

Definition: 'Occupiers'

The definition of the word 'occupiers' should include all those who are in possession of any land and are engaged in its cultivation/other uses but have not been able to obtain valid rights on it prior to the issue of notification under Section 4(1) of the Land Acquisition Act. This should apply only to such occupiers who are otherwise eligible for regularization of their possession and getting ownership rights in terms of the existing law, policy, guidelines or instructions of the state government.

Definition: 'Family'

The definition of family should do away with the requirement of a continuous stay for a prescribed period to qualify for benefits under the policy. The residence on the date of notification for acquisition of land should suffice for this purpose. Besides, displacement from livelihood can take place even if a person does not reside in the village. This may happen in the case of agricultural labourers, artisans or such other persons. Therefore, loss of livelihood should form the focal point of the definition of 'family'. Appropriate adjustment in the entitlement of benefits can be made in the case of a person falling in this category. Such a person may not be resettled in the new location but may be provided cash compensation for loss of his/her livelihood.

The definition of family must remove gender bias and should explicitly recognize unmarried daughter, sister (of specified age), widow, divorcee, desertee (women) as a separate family for the purpose of rehabilitation. Similarly, disabled persons and orphans should also receive the same treatment.

Social Impact Assessment

Environmental Impact Assessment and social impact assessment should be mandatory in all cases irrespective of the size of the project or the nature of purpose for which land is acquired. This exercise should be carried out through a participatory mode. The structure and processes of participation should be laid down. The exemption provided to the Ministry of Defence from social impact assessment in respect of the acquisition of land by them should be removed because such acquisitions do have serious social and environmental externalities. No institutional safeguards can emerge without such assessments having been made. In the case of extreme urgency, these assessments can be carried out expeditiously. The social impact assessment should specifically focus on the impact of the project on people, their economic conditions, social status, cultural values, identity and access to resources and benefits and not merely on infrastructure and institutions.

Updating of Land Records

The provision in respect of updating of land records should be undertaken prior to the issue of notification under Section 4(1) of the Land Acquisition Act, 1894 in order that all matters pending resolution which affect rights and interests of the individuals and groups involved are sorted out and their status duly recorded. It makes no sense to undertake updating of land records after the preliminary notification has been issued as it would not enable such claimants to get recognition of their rights and to file claims for compensation. The process of updating of land records should specifically regularize eligible cases of occupation of government/public land, mutation of intra-family distribution of land, allotment of government land, transfer of land, sale and purchase transactions, classification of land, change in land use, status of possession, etc. In case of tenancies, specifically, efforts should be made to record all tenancies, formal and informal, irrespective of the contestations involved. While formal tenancy rights would get finally resolved in the competent court, the policy should accommodate all such tenants in the ambit of rehabilitation and resettlement without waiting for the outcome of the adjudication process.

Approach to Rehabilitation Compensation

The scheme of compensation should be restructured on the following lines.

- The scheme of compensation should provide for all types of losses – land, livelihood, access to community property resources and externalities such as social disruptions, mental trauma, loss of networks, etc. Appropriate value should be assigned to each such loss/externality. This exercise should be transparently worked out by a body of experts.
- Compensation for loss of land should include all types of access to it, whether formal or informal, recorded or unrecorded. It should specifically cover tenants, sharecroppers, forest dwellers, artisans, fishermen, agricultural labourers, etc. Those accessing common property resources should also be included in this ambit. Appropriate values for such losses should be transparently worked out by a body of experts for computing the amount of compensation.
- Compensation for loss of land should be assessed taking into account its 'replacement value' in the close proximity of the area of settlement rather than the 'market value'.
- The rehabilitation and resettlement authority should function as the custodian for the compensation amount in the case of the Scheduled Tribes and such other weaker sections lacking in capacity to handle cash, in order to build up durable productive asset for them suited to their existing skill base, choice, experience and to which they consent.
- The determination of compensation, taking the above norms in view, should be settled by an independent body so as to inspire confidence in the displaced persons.
- Necessary protective measures should be taken to prevent compensation amount being squeezed by corrupt bureaucracy or intermediaries or/and spent in unproductive expenditure. The responsibilities for its productive investment shall lie with the specified authority.

Mitigation of Risks

The paradigm of a Rehabilitation and Resettlement Policy must explicitly incorporate the internationally recognized 10-fold impoverishment risks which a displacee invariably faces. These are landlessness, joblessness, homelessness, marginalization, increased morbidity and mortality, food insecurity, loss of access to CPRs, social disarticulation (Cernia, 1997), loss of schooling (Mahapatra, 1999), loss of access to public services ahead of displacement (Mathur, 1998). The rehabilitation and resettlement plan should provide risk mitigating strategy in respect of each one of these 10 risks. Landlessness should be neutralized by allotment of land. Joblessness should be tackled through provision of employment. Homelessness should be eliminated by provision of housing. Marginalization should be addressed by measures which restore the community and its support system. Morbidity and mortality should be overcome by provision of adequate health services right from the day the displacees are shifted to the new site. Food insecurity should be dealt with by provision of subsidized food grains, availability of public distribution system (PDS), improving the purchasing power of the affected persons, extension of ICDS to children, mid-day meal to school going children, free grains (Annapoorna) to the elderly and destitute and the disabled. Loss of access to CPRs including water bodies should be compensated by alternative provision of land for grazing, fuelwood, medicinal plants, etc. Social disarticulation should be countered by strengthening the community networks, removing hostility and irritation with the host community, creating institutional mechanism for social assertion, etc. Loss of schooling should be made up by providing functional school at the site so as not to disrupt the education of children. Access to public services should continue at the existing site till the time people are fully shifted and alternative services are available at the new site. The specific measures required for each risk mitigation strategy are discussed below.

Landlessness

The entitlement to land mitigates this risk. With regard to the provision of land to tackle landlessness, there should be no vagueness about this entitlement. In the first place, transparent and informed choice should be given to all displaced persons about the mode of rehabilitation they would prefer to have. Those who are most comfortable with land-based rehabilitation, as for example, the members of the STs, must be mandatorily allotted land. This provision could be made through the following ways:

- Identifying government/panchayat or public land in the vicinity and allotting it to the beneficiaries after developing it adequately and making it cultivable at the cost of the project.
- Identifying degraded land and restoring its productive capacity through necessary development inputs at project's cost and thereafter allotting to the displaced persons.
- Purchasing land from the market with the compensation money given to the displacees and meeting the deficit, if any. Before purchasing the land, it must be ensured that there are no disputes over it. The land should be allotted, possession over it should be delivered and the entry to this effect should be made in the land records.
- Acquiring additional land and make it cultivable by providing necessary development inputs.

One or more of these modes should be adapted to, meet the commitment, at least, in respect of the STs and, if feasible, the SCs.

The primitive tribal groups, who are still at a pre-agricultural stage, must be allotted forest land and, if no forest land is available, certain areas of the acquired land must be converted into forest for their benefit so that there is no violent break with their existing pattern of life.

Joblessness

The joblessness should be tackled upfront by provision of employment and durable income generating opportunities to each family affected by displacement whether landed or landless. This could be done through the following measures:

- All jobs up to the semi-skilled categories in the project should be assessed in advance and exclusively earmarked for the displaced persons against which, at least, one person from the each affected nuclear family could be adjusted.
- Ahead of displacement, a detailed exercise should be undertaken about the qualifications and experience needed for such

jobs and how such requirements could be met by preparing nominated displacee candidates. Among the displaced persons, at least one from each family could be identified who would be suitable for doing such a job, if necessary, after appropriate training and skill development. This training and skill development may be arranged whether within the project or outside and thereafter the candidates may be absorbed against the posts. No pre-conditions about certification of technical capability in terms of a degree should be insisted upon in such cases as they have acquired adequate training and work experience suitable for the concerned jobs. No outsider should be appointed against these jobs in order that the project is persuaded to make the displaced persons employable.

- It should be the sole responsibility of the project to provide durable and dignified employment to at least one person of each family whether within the project or outside. This objective should be pursued by undertaking training, skill development and apprenticeship of a standard which enables them to get this work and of a vocation for which there is adequate market demand. If necessary, multi-skilling should be resorted to so that redundancy can be avoided. It should be the responsibility of the project to ensure their placement for this purpose.
- Until the identified nominee of the displaced family obtains such durable employment, the family should receive wages of two unskilled labourers from the project. This is being suggested because in the family of self-employed farmers and agricultural labourers, etc., both husband and wife usually work and contribute to the family income. One person's wage would be inadequate for family subsistence. This alone would minimize acute economic impoverishment. The period of payment of this subsistence allowance should be utilized for adequate skill development of the husband and wife at project cost in order to create their employability.
- Independent experts should certify the level, standard of training and its relevance to the job market and work experience in order to eliminate the possibility of sub-standard training.

This drill should be followed in respect of those displaced families who fail to get either land for cultivation or regular employment of the project. No distinction should be made in this respect between those who owned land or were landless prior to acquisition. Those who are not keen to get the entitled employment may be given attractive cash compensation.

Those who are not keen to get land in place of land lost or employment in the job market could be asked to choose from a range of alternatives which would create sustainable and dignified self employment which can assure reasonable income. They should be facilitated in this regard with necessary inputs of credit, training and market facilitation along with cash grant as capital. This alternative should not be tried for displaced persons from the STs and other weaker sections who have no skills other than agriculture, are not exposed adequately to the market economy and have no risk taking capabilities. Self-employment should not be an option for them except where they were already engaged in non-agricultural jobs with reasonable and sustained income. But the displaced persons from the upper castes and the middle castes who were already socialized in alternative vocations could be given these options.

Homelessness

This risk should be mitigated by provision of a decent, environmental, healthy dwelling with each adult son or a daughter or a widow/divorcee (women) as a separate unit. No distinction should be made between the sizes of the house occupied prior to the acquisition of land as it would discriminate against the poorer households particularly the SCs/STs. An area of 10 cents corresponding to what the Odisha Policy provides should be allowed for this purpose so that landless families can use the small backyard area for income generating activities and future expansion of facilities. The requirement for the urban areas should also follow the Odisha norm. The family should be given an option either to have a constructed dwelling as per a standardized model prepared in consultation with beneficiaries for this purpose or the cost of construction which is adequate. Separate arrangements for sanitation, livestock should form part of the dwelling plan/construction estimates. The layout of the colony should provide drainage arrangement and a gathering place for the community.

Marginalization

The following measures may be taken to address this phenomenon:

- The pre-displacement 'community' existing among the displaced persons should be restored or recreated. This could be done by reorganizing the traditional community structure as a valid agency for negotiations, articulation and engagement different from the statutory panchayats.
- Forests and CPRs lost in the process of displacement should be restored/recreated. A common fund should be set up for its development. Management of these resources should be taken over by the community around which the traditional structures of participation and decision-making could be rejuvenated.
- In respect of heterogeneous villages, option should be given to various ethnic groups to decide whether they would like to be joined with other groups as in the pre-displacement village or resettled separately. Many ethnic groups who have experienced domination/hegemony would like to utilize resettlement as an occasion to disengage from the old oppressive relationship. They should be consciously helped to do so which would facilitate building community spirit and self-confidence.
- Where heterogeneous groups prefer to live in the old composite village, new community structures would need to be created to build solidarity around common activities such as common property management, fairs and festivals, cultural activities, group specific activities (women/youth,) religious activities, etc. Common school system should be promoted. The new resettlement site should be notified as a village so that three-tier panchayat system operates and development activities are extended. Separate resources should be devoted to community activities which facilitate bonding (Mahapatra, 1999).

Food Insecurity

Food insecurity can be tackled if following steps are taken:

- Extension of public distribution system by opening a fair price shop to be managed by a person selected by the community consensually.

- In the tribal areas, 'grain banks' may be set up to be managed by the community with transparent rules and participatory decision-making.
- Intensified rural employment programme should be taken up under the National Rural Employment Guarantee Scheme (NREGS) to provide necessary purchasing power.
- Social security by way of pension to the elderly and the other eligible persons, free rations to destitute and elderly persons (Annapurna) should be extended.

Increased Morbidity and Mortality

The risk of increased morbidity and mortality should be mitigated by provision of functioning health facilities at the site of resettlement. The range of facilities should take into account not only the common illnesses afflicting the area of resettlement but the likelihood of new one resulting from the trauma of displacement such as mental illness. The functional health facilities include requisite service providers (doctors, specialists and para-medics), diagnostic aids and equipments, drugs, mobility, modest number of indoor beds and an effective referral service for emergency cases. Where necessary, visits of specialists to the colony may be arranged on specified days to attend to patients not treatable at the Primary Health Centre (PHC). The existing standardized structure of a PHC should be strengthened for this purpose. A counselling unit managed by a non-government organization (NGO) should be attached to this health facility.

With arrangement for food, security and generation of purchasing power, the risk of under/malnutrition can be reasonably met.

Social Disarticulation

- Social disarticulation is a serious consequence of displacement and requires sensitive handling over a period of time. This could be tackled by counselling, confidence building, adjustment with new surroundings, re-building support groups and conflict resolution within the displaced community and with the outside community. For this purpose, NGOs, social activists, anthropologists/sociologists, university departments of social work, etc. could be associated. The time frame for this work and the terms of association of these agencies should form part of the rehabilitation and resettlement policy.

Loss of Access to Common Property Resources

The loss of access to CPRs should be met by mandatory provision of common land and water bodies attached to the resettlement site with well defined rights of users and a structure of participatory management. Initial development of these common resources should be accomplished by the rehabilitation and resettlement agency. Subsequent maintenance should be entrusted to a democratically constituted structure of the resettled community sufficiently representative of the weaker sections – SCs, STs and women. A separate fund should be created for this purpose which this community structure should manage.

Loss of Schooling

The loss of schooling should be made up by the following arrangements:

- A primary/middle school which is functional from the day the physical shifting of the displaced persons takes place.
- The rehabilitation agency should arrange for admission of students in nearby schools who are in higher classes. If there is no such school within a reasonable distance, the existing school should be upgraded.
- Hostel arrangement should be arranged for students studying higher classes in schools where distance cannot be traversed on foot or cycle. The provision of a cycle for such students should form part of the rehabilitation plan.
- Arrangement of facilities should take into account the needs of both boys and girls.
- To avoid hassles in admission to schools in the resettlement area, special directives from the competent authority should be issued.
- The date of shifting should ensure that it does not lead to the loss of academic year, missing of examination and admission into an appropriate class in the new school.

Loss of Access to Public Services

This can be avoided with the following decisions:

- All public services should continue to function at the existing location until the displaced persons have physically shifted to an alternate site.
- The public services available at the site of old settlement should be available at the new site before physical shifting is arranged.
- The affected persons should be consulted well in advance about the withdrawal of services and their wishes should be taken into account in deciding on this matter.

Social and Physical Infrastructure

The provision of social and physical infrastructure laid down in the policy should be provided in all resettlement colonies irrespective of their size and should not be left to the state governments to determine. To the extent certain facilities exist in the already existing villages adjacent to the resettlement site, appropriate adjustment can be made to avoid duplication. But it must be ensured that the existing facilities are appropriately strengthened in such situations taking into account the addition of users due to the location of the resettlement colony.

Integration with Development Planning

This objective needs to be concretized by the following structural arrangement for its implementation:

- This objective needs to be concretized by structural arrangement for its operations. A dedicated organization should be created to integrate rehabilitation concerns into development planning on a long-term basis. This would require that the body should continue to engage with the displaced persons for a long period after they are shifted to their new resettlement site. For this purpose, a long-term regional plan should be drawn up which appropriately integrates them into the emerging opportunities for upgradation of their standard of living. This should also take into account the secondary displacement caused by the project after the project activities have started. Their concerns should also be brought into the ambit of development planning. This would provide the displaced persons a continuing structure of support to deal with their multifarious problems long after they are shifted to the resettlement site.

Rehabilitation and Resettlement Plan

There should be a provision for awareness creation well in advance of the initiation of the rehabilitation process. In fact, the work relating to awareness should start before the land acquisition so that the affected persons can make informed decisions at every stage from land acquisition to resettlement. A dedicated functionary may be assigned this task. The civil society groups may be associated with this work. The modalities for this work may be laid down.

Tribal Development Plan

The Tribal Development Plan should not have a uniform and standardized approach. It should be left to the local agencies to design such a plan taking into account the wide diversity of social and ecological situations and land management practices in the tribal areas. The Tribal Development Plan must officially recognize traditional community quite different from the village panchayats as a stakeholder. PESA, 1996 does this precisely by empowering Gram Sabha for various protection and development activities. It should be enabled to record land use pattern and management in shifting cultivation areas in order to map out land under use of the individual families. The Tribal Development Plan should recreate variety of rights and interests in access to land resources covered under respective customary laws. Such a plan for groups like primitive tribes, hunters, food gatherers and nomadic tribes would obviously be different from the plan which is prepared for the tribals engaged in settled agriculture. The plan should specifically address the problems of social disarticulation, devaluation of culture by arrogant non-tribal groups, emotional trauma caused by sudden break with their traditional pattern of life and kinship network and stresses faced on account of pressures to adjust a new and hostile environment.

Gender and Disability Bias: Separate Development Plans

The definition of the 'affected family' should remove the distinction between major sons and major daughters in respect of its composition. Adult, unmarried daughters, women headed households (widows, divorcees) should be counted as a separate unit for the purpose of entitlements in the policy.

The policy should also treat physically and mentally challenged persons and minor orphans (having lost both his/her parents) as a separate family for this purpose.

This would remove the gender and disability bias from the definition. The policy should address gender concerns specifically through a development plan for women which focuses on (a) access to land, (b) provision of CPRs, (c) employment, (d) drinking water and sanitation facilities, (e) health concerns, and (f) security. Similarly, development plans should be prepared for differently-abled persons taking into account their specific needs. For this to happen, the policy should have a provision to collect relevant information concerning these groups in its census and surveys.

Periphery Development

Development projects besides causing direct displacement on account of acquisition of land also unleash indirect displacement in areas adjoining the acquired land due to pressures generated by the project activities on the existing settlers. The provision regarding periphery development has not taken this contingency into account. This dimension of development should, therefore, be specifically included. A periphery development plan focusing on this aspect, among others, should be prepared which incorporates preventive as well as developmental measures. A designated authority charged with the responsibility for periphery development should be specified. The structure and processes for planning and implementation of periphery development may also be laid down.

Acquisition for Urgency

In case of land acquired under urgency, the policy should provide for the return of the land if the contingency forcing such acquisition has ceased to exist. There should be no blanket provision for permanent acquisition in all cases of urgent acquisition. The existing provisions regarding urgent acquisition are too wide ranging and create possibilities for their misuse. The provision for 'urgent' acquisition can be easily resorted to it for normal acquisition to tide over peoples' resistance to the project. The scope for use of these provisions should be narrowed down. Appropriate checks should be introduced so that acquisition under urgency is used only in the case of natural calamities or such other unforeseen situations.

Process of Consultation

The provision for mandatory consultation with the Gram Sabha for acquisition of land as required in PESA should be facilitated by the land acquisition authority. The process of facilitation would involve furnishing necessary and sufficient information to the displaced persons in a manner that is easily intelligible to them and in a language that they understand. A dedicated functionary should be earmarked for this purpose to ensure that the information reaches people in time and their doubts, apprehensions in this regard are cleared. The policy should specifically mention that any attempt to obtain 'manufactured consent' of gram sabha by intimidation, threat, use of force or fraud would be constitute a punishable criminal offence.

Unutilized Land

The provisions regarding unutilized land should expressly lay down that after reversion of such land to the appropriate government, it would be distributed among the erstwhile land losers in proportion to the quantum of land lost by them. In the unlikely event of the erstwhile land losers or their legal heirs not traceable despite efforts, this land should be distributed among the landless displaced persons of the village/area. This distribution of land whether to land losers or to landless persons should not require any payment to be made by the beneficiaries. If the government wishes to utilize this land for improving the infrastructure and services in the resettlement colony, the cash equivalent of this land calculated at the current market price may be distributed among the erstwhile land losers in proportion of the land lost by them. The project agency should be charged with this amount as a penalty for inflating its land requirement resulting in its unutilization.

The central government should fix norms for requirement of land for projects of different categories and capacities.

Transfer of Acquired Land

The transfer of land from one purpose to another should carry financial cost to the government by way of a liability to pay additional compensation to the erstwhile land losers. This cost should be determined on the basis of the current market value of the unutilized acquired land at the time of its utilization for a different 'public purpose'. The amount should be distributed among the erstwhile land losers in proportion to the land lost by them.

Participation

All structures created for monitoring should have participation of the affected persons with due representation of SCs/STs/women besides NGOs/social activists engaged in working for the displaced persons. Therefore, where such structures have not provided for participation, this may be done.

Past and Future Projects

Considering that 75 per cent of persons displaced from the earlier projects remain unrehabilitated, the policy should, without reservation, extend rehabilitation to them even at this late stage. The policy should not be restricted to projects taken up after its notification. This would remove the sense of despair and neglect in persons left out and help to assure those likely to be displaced in future that the government stands by them. The task of identification of persons from past projects who remain unrehabilitated should be left to the National Commission/State Commission, as the case may be, proposed in the policy. The Commission would determine its norms for such identification through a process of wider consultation with civil society groups representing the interests of the displaced persons.

Private and Public Acquisition

The policy should apply to all acquisition of land whether done under the land acquisition laws or procured privately by the companies through negotiations. The agencies acquiring/purchasing land privately should be fully bound to observe the norms laid down in the policy.

Norms of Rehabilitation

There should be no differentiation in the nature and content of rehabilitation and resettlement irrespective of whether a project is large or small. In respect of past projects, the range of benefits to be admissible should be guided by the actual conditions on the ground both in respect of common benefits such as the physical amenities and social infrastructure as well as individual entitlements. The deficit in entitlements taking into account the norms laid down in the policy should be identified and met. This task should be left to the

National/State Commissions to accomplish. Expert assistance should be mobilized to work that out. This aspect would obviously get sorted out while preparing the rehabilitation and resettlement plan as per the procedure prescribed in the policy.

Conclusion

The perspective of resettlement presented here highlights the complexities of addressing multiple impoverishment risks which displaces experience. The challenges faced in the process require strong determination, sustained commitment, dedication, resources and capacity over a period of time. The magnitude of the task is mind boggling considering the huge backlog of unattended cases and the rapidly increasing number that is in the pipeline. But, the quality of efforts required are even more demanding since a genuine beginning in terms of comprehensive risk mitigation has not even been conceived let alone accomplished in the resettlement attempted so far. While seriously pursuing these dimensions would test the political commitment of the government and the skills, capacity and patience in governance, the more nagging issues associated with the paradigm of development which causes this level of displacement would not disappear. Social disruption on a scale that has taken place and is increasingly unfolding is simply unacceptable. The conflicts which this development gives rise to have to be resolved to the satisfaction of those who bear the brunt of its adverse effects.

References

Cernia, Michael M. (1999). 'Forward: The Power of Synthesis', in L.K. Mahapatra, *Resettlement, Impoverishment and Reconstruction in India*, New Delhi: Vikas Publishing House.

——(1997). 'The Risks and Reconstruction Model for Resettling Displaced Population', *World Development*, Vol. 25, No. 10.

Government of Odisha (GoO) (2006). Odisha Resettlement and Rehabilitation Policy, 2006, Bhubaneswar: Revenue Department.

Lok Sabha (2007). The Rehabilitation and Resettlement Bill, 2007, Bill No. 98 of 2007.

Mahapatra, L.K. (1999). *Resettlement, Impoverishment and Reconstruction in India*, New Delhi: Vikas Publishing House.

Mathur, H.M. (1998). 'The Improvement Risk Model and its Use as a Planning Tool', in Mathur and David Marsden (eds), *Development Projects and Impoverishment Risks*, New Delhi: Oxford University Press.

—— (2008). 'Involving Resettlement Policy of Orissa, India: A New Deal for the Displaced in a Globalizing World', *Social Change*, Vol. 38, No. 4.

Mehra, Puja (2007). 'SEZ Controversy: Course Correction', *India Today*, Vol. XXXLI, No. 5, 30 January–5 February.

Ministry of Rural Development (MoRD) (2003). National Policy on Resettlement and Rehabilitation for Project Affected Families, New Delhi: Department of Land Resources.

—— (2007). The National Rehabilitation and Resettlement Policy, 2007, New Delhi: Government of India.

10

Whither National Rehabilitation and Resettlement Policy for the Displaced?

GANESHA SOMAYAJI AND JOANNA P. COELHO

'Despite best efforts India has not been able to come out with a proper rehabilitation policy including the fact that more than 75 per cent are yet to be rehabilitated. One of the major reasons is the failure of governance – the latter is apparent when governance failed to understand the nuances of displacement, failed to address the issues comprehensively, and also governance failed to understand the cultural specificities of social categories.'

– Muzaffar Assadi, 2012

'... It is when administrative categories begin to be treated as sociological categories and vice versa, that we face serious problems of description and analysis.'

– Veena Das, 1996

'A Bill to ensure a humane, participatory, informed consultative and transparent process for land acquisition for industrialisation, development of essential infrastructural facilities and urbanisation with the least disturbance to the owners of the land and other affected families and provide just and fair compensation to the affected families ...'

– Preamble to the Land Acquisition, Rehabilitation and Resettlement Bill, 2011

Successive governments ever since independence have promulgated a number of policies to ensure the welfare of various categories of people who have needed state's involvement for respectable living. While improving the life conditions of millions of people these policies and programmes have not been successful in fully achieving their stated objectives. Committed to the ideology of welfare and also to cater to the vote-bank politics, the successive governments of the Indian nation-state have been enacting these policies. Many of these policies were necessitated by the colonial legacy on the one hand and India's joining the mainstream modernization process on the other. Both these are irreversible historical processes. Our attempts at debating, criticizing, and revising welfare policies need to take into account these historical legacies and contemporary national and world forces and influences. The policy relating to resettlement and rehabilitation (R&R policy) of displaced people is one such policy.

I am of the opinion that the task of suggesting revisions and the actual carrying out of the revisions in the R&R policy through democratic processes and its implementation is long pending requirement. Especially the policy relating to land acquisition is outdated, draconian and anti-people. In this paper, I am not engaging in an appraisal of the Acts passed by and Bills notified by the successive governments from time to time in India towards land acquisition for the purpose of development. Nor am I examining the resultant administrative arrangements for rehabilitating and resettling the displaced. Already many respected social scientists and activists have been engaged in pursuing such an examination. Though such an engagement is academically challenging and administratively useful, it does not fit into my objective in this paper. From the vantage point of sociology of displacement, to begin with, I recognize the need for constructing displacement as an inclusive category that encompasses various types of de-territorialization, involuntary movement, as well as the 'alienage' that characterizes refugees. I will then bring in the distinction between displacement as a sociological category and R&R policy as an administrative category. Later, the paper argues that the administrative attempts at resettlement and rehabilitation through policies and programmes need to address the plural sociological contexts of displacement. The paper concludes with the need to re-look at the R&R Policy design taking into account the sufferings of different categories of the dislocated. Administrative solutions to the complex ground level sociological concerns need policy formation from pluralistic socio-culturally sensitive perspective.

Introducing the Contours of the Sub-discipline

The phenomenon of displacement is as old as human civilization. When humans migrated from one place to the other, when one group colonized the other and when one group invaded the original habitat of a population and pushed it to the interiors, displacement did take place in various geographical areas during different historical times. However, with the emergence of modernity the quantum of displacement due to human plans and the resultant concerns of painful ruptures of symbiotic relations between humans and their ecology have been unprecedented in human history. The worldwide process of colonization during early modernity, civil wars and formation of nation-states, wars and ethnic violence, violent political revolutions have been some causes of displacement of populations. Though displacements due to these factors were confined to specific regions of the world during specific times, they have generated unique concerns to the affected people.

During the formative years of the discipline sociology, while choosing the specific concerns for study, sociologists were guided by the methodology of positivism. The aim was to establish a general and objective science of society which could not include in its scope the concerns of displacement along with scores of other issues found in human societies. The scope of the discipline was not as broad as it is now and the scale and funding of sociological knowledge production too was limited. Today's sociological research is guided by methodological pluralism. The scope of sociology is acquiring new proportions, and from the disciplinary orientation we are moving towards the trans-disciplinary. All these happenings have facilitated the formation of the new sub-discipline conceived in this edited volume. However, what is most striking is the dislocation due to development which informs the thread of this volume. I am of the opinion that the sub-discipline of the sociology of displacement has the potential to grow beyond this contour.

It is only recently, as a result of the worldwide spread of the project development due to globalization of the ideology of capitalism that displacement has become a common and generally observable social concern. The concern has acquired the proportion of formidable social ecological problem and has unleashed sufferings of many types across the countries of the South. In many parts of the South, the problems have become matters of life and death as documented by the contributors to an edited volume by Johnston (2011). Especially, development-induced environmental devastation and improper disposal of the nuclear waste have threatened the very existence of some indigenous peoples on this planet.

To the category of the people dislocated due to developmental activities of various types we can also include such categories of people as the dislocated due to violent ethnic conflicts, political revolutions, and the refugees. Thus, sociologically, the 'displaced' becomes an inclusive category. Arguing for an inclusive conceptual category of dislocation, Das (1996: 1509) gives an example of the concept 'environmental refugees': A number of scholars have recently suggested that the term "environmental refugees" may be used to refer not only to those who have been displaced due to development projects but also to all categories of persons who have been so affected by drastic and irreversible environmental change that they cannot sustain their ways of life in their original habitats.' In Das's (ibid.: 1510) opinion if in a single inclusive category we consider all those who have had to migrate compulsorily from their original habitation due to various reasons, it is possible to view the problem of 'structural coupling' of the events forcing people to migrate in their respective societies. Das' views relating to the concept dislocation are associated with her attempt at defining the anthropological field for those who are concerned with dislocation and resettlement. For practical research and activist purposes constructing the category of displaced is not problematic for those who work with the conceptual trio: 'development, displacement, and rehabilitation'. To think in the direction of new possibilities for the R&R policy in future we have to go beyond this conceptual trio.

Defining displacement as an inclusive conceptual category needs to construct the ideal types of dislocations and then make clear which type of dislocation we intend to address. In other words, we have to associate the type of dislocation we address as one of the many types of dislocations. For the purpose of this volume the definition of the displaced is associated with the project development and the draconian Land Acquisition Act. I fully agree with the editors of this volume and other contributors in emphasising the issue of development-induced displacement as a major issue for building the sociology of displacement in India. Here, I propose that we can conceive of displacement as an inclusive category representing dislocation of various types, for the sociological issues and the pathological forms of social suffering are comparable in all dislocations. The first ramification of such a conceptualization for sociology of displacement is widening of its contours. Along with development-induced displacement sociology of displacement can address various other displacements. The next step is the formation of a transdisciplinary subject by name 'displacement studies'. Though neither of these is in the scope of my present paper, I will use this idea to analyse the possibilities of formulating and implementing an inclusive R&R policy to cater to different types of displacement. To do this analysis I have to first bring in a distinction between the categories of displacement and rehabilitation. At the level of policy implementation the Indian government has to explore the possibilities of one omnibus policy and multiple governmental agencies to implement it.

Displacement as Sociological Issue and Rehabilitation as Administrative Policy

Both displacement and rehabilitation are social processes taking place at two different and interrelated levels. The nature of the forces underlying these processes is different with respect to the social, geographical, cultural and temporal dimensions of the space where they take shape. The former is a geo-social process which involves involuntary dislocation of the population from their traditional habitat. As a sociological issue, displacement needs to be constructed as a category to include all occurrences of involuntary population movements from original habitats. While constructing the category 'displaced', the reasons for de-territorialization can be identified in the form of a prefix, for example, development-induced displacement, war-induced displacement, revolution-induced displacement, ethnic-violence-induced displacement, and terrorism-induced displacement to name a few.

We may bring in a distinction between internally displaced and internationally displaced people. The types of displaced mentioned earlier within the national border do not encounter the problems of citizenship and national identity. On the other hand, refugees are internationally displaced who encounter the problem of alienage. Due to various historical reasons India has accepted refugees from the nation-states in the neighbourhood and their number is increasing. Strictly speaking, sociology of displacement should consider issues pertaining to their life too within its scope.

The displaced are the victims and are therefore vulnerable. They require the support of the state machinery to restart their livelihood in alien environments. The rehabilitation policies enacted by the respective governments are administrative mechanisms to facilitate the displaced to start a decent living in a new environment. The displaced have to build new societies and new cultural atmospheres in new locations. The R&R policy provides guidelines and support in this process. Though R&R policy is now synonymous with rehabilitation of the development-induced displaced, ideally it should look into the administrative aspects of the internationally displaced also. However, there is a separate sub-discipline by name Refugee Studies and the Ministries of External Affairs and Home implement the policies relating to their lives. I am of the opinion that to manage the administrative aspects of all the internally displaced peoples we should work towards evolving one inclusive R&R policy.

Whither R&R Policy Design?

The R&R policy, an administrative instrument to rehabilitate the displaced, need to be sensitive to the social background and cultural moorings of the displaced. The first task is to build a detailed knowledge base of different types of displaced and their differential needs. Even when we take the case of the victims of the development-induced displacement the study of the heterogeneity of the displaced populations especially their social and cultural specificities have to be first understood. First and foremost the policy as a mechanism of good governance need to be people oriented. Unfortunately, it is not the case. Fernandes (2004: 1191), a staunch critic of displacement due to development, opines on the rehabilitation policy: 'The policy draft appears to be more concerned with protecting the interests of big business rather than the livelihood security of the displaced'. Most of the displaced communities face livelihood insecurities. Livelihood security is more than the economic deterioration. With displacement the natural rhythm of life is disturbed, the meanings associated with the geography are shattered, and the displaced are impoverished.

Assadi identifies and draws our attention to the issues of governance in India. Some such issues of governance are listed as follows: (a) The governance has not been able to focus on such issues as community ownership of land by the villagers and tribals. (b) Ineffective governance has further marginalized the already marginalized. This is apparent whenever the displaced have been rehabilitated in far off places, wherein the needed economic opportunities do not exist. (c) Absence of political commitments of the governance also defeated the rehabilitations. The bureaucratic delays do not allow the packages announced in the policy to the households of the displaced. (d) The power relations in the governance have placed the displaced in disadvantageous position. Given their relative weak positioning in the governance hierarchy the displaced have not been able to demand effectively their rehabilitation. Whenever they demanded their rights, displaced have been treated as those challenging those who are in power. This has increased the friction between the state and the displaced. Only when a policy is enacted with a built in mechanism for its people friendly implementation, the policy will achieve its objective.

Rethinking Displacement and Rehabilitation

While displacement has been fallout of the civilizing process since millennia, it has assumed an unprecedented scale with the arrival of modernity and institutionalization of the ideologies of modernization and development. The efforts at addressing the casualties of project development have remained unsuccessful, and the numbers of those who have benefited from the various rehabilitation and resettlement policies and projects remain abysmally low. In this paper, I have argued that there is a need to re-examine the R&R policy that is presently being discussed in India. The policy takes displacement as a given, as a necessary corollary to the implementation of the ideologies of progress and development. Being displaced is such a deeply traumatic experience having serious psychological, sociological and economic ramifications that it cannot be lightly reduced to being a necessary corollary of development. Such a stance will limit the orientation and scope of the policy. Serageldin (1999: 110) has argued that the policies of rehabilitation and resettlement that have been implemented this far, have followed the 'property compensation approach' wherein the focus has been on the land and other assets that have been usurped on account of the projects. He opines that the approach should be on a 'people-centred development focus'. Such an approach focuses on the displaced people. It asks whether they are re-integrated into the mainstream of the development process. Displacement needs to be looked at from a pluralistic socio-culturally sensitive perspective. Such a perspective calls for a broadening of the category displacement. Such an understanding which takes into account the heterogeneity of the experiences of displacement will ensure a more people oriented and therefore humane R&R policy.

References

Assadi, Muzaffar (2012). *Interface between Displacement, Rehabilitation and Governance in India: A Critique.* http://www.napsipag.org/pdf/muzaffar.pdf (accessed on 7 August 2012).

Das, Veena (1996). 'Dislocation and Rehabilitation: Defining a Field', *Economic and Political Weekly*, Vol. 31, No. 24, 15 June, pp. 1509–14.

Fernandes, Walter (2004). 'Rehabilitation Policy for the Displaced', *Economic and Political Weekly*, Vol. 39, No. 12, 20–26 March, pp. 1191–93.

Johnston, Barbara Rose (Ed.) (2011). *Life and Death Matters: Human Rights, Environment, and Social Justice*, 2nd edition, Walnut Creek, California: Left Coast Press.

Serageldin, Ismail (1999). 'Valedictory Address', in B.K. Sinha and Pushpendra (eds), *Displacement and Rehabilitation in India: Future Perspectives*, Proceedings of a National Workshop conducted during 1–3 June, Mussoorie: Lal Bahadur Shastri National Academy of Administration, pp. 108–22.

11

Displacement and Resettlement in China

A Case Study of Three Gorges Dam

SATYA PRAKASH DASH

The Three Gorges Dam (TGD) project was approved by the 5th Plenary Session of the 7th National People's Congress (NPC) in April 1992 and formally launched in 1994 on the Yangtze river. The conception of the dam was visualized since the time of Sun Yat-sen, the provisional President of China in 1912. The dam, as scheduled, has been completed on time in 2009, and is 'the largest dam ever built in terms of both of its hydropower generating capacity and the number of people in need of resettlement; over 1.2 million people uprooted' (Heming et al., 2001: 201). However, unofficial figures believe the number to be resettled would be between 1.4 to 2 million people (Dai, 1998). 'In China, an estimated 10.2 million people were uprooted by the construction of dams and reservoirs between the 1950s and the late 1980s. This figure has now been updated to over 17 million to allow for the natural growth of the population, including those affected by the two largest ongoing hydro projects – the TGP and Xiaolangdi on the Yellow River' (Tan et al., 2005: 712). According to the Reservoir Development Bureau of the Ministry of Water Resources of China (1999), more than 83,000 reservoirs and dams were constructed in China between 1949 and 1998. The population displaced and to be displaced from these projects amounts to around 12.5 million (ibid., 2003: 6). The directly affected populations, whose homes will be inundated by the TGD reservoir, number more than 846,000 (CWRC,

1993). The total number to be displaced by 2009 will be somewhere between 1.13 million (REG, 1988) and 1.9 million (Dai, 1998). Rural persons and women constitute 50 per cent of this total. TGD will affect the lives, habitat or economy of at least 20 million people above the dam and another 300 million downstream (Jackson and Sleigh, 2000: 223). Apart from the population displacement and resettlement, the TGD is also a concern for the destruction of the environment and ecological hazards, and the submergence of the valuable historical relics. In spite of these threats, the TGD had its own advantages that includes, flood control, river transportation and electricity generation. The Chinese records show that there were more than 200 major floods from 185 BC to 1911 AD; three catastrophic floods of 1931, 1935 and 1954 killed a total of more than 320,000 people (ibid., 2000: 225). River transportation will connect the east coast to the industrial Chongqing. Electricity production was another major concern as China is dependent on coal for electrical energy, and with industries expanding at an average annual rate of 22 per cent (SSB, China, 1996: 204 and 403); hydropower can be an effective alternative source.

As is the case in the resettlement management of many countries, China also has a poor record in resettlement management due the numerous dams constructed since 1949. 'By 1996, there were 118 large and medium hydropower dams across China's seven major rivers and its tributaries, built at great and unmeasured social cost with an estimated total of 10.2 million displaced people. The TGD displacement will exceed the combined total of the three largest Chinese dams: Danjiangkou in Hubei province (380,000), Sanmenxia in Henan province (320,000) and Xin'anjiang in Zhejiang province' (280,000) (Jackson and Sleigh, 2000: 226; Fearnside, 1994). During the period of the 1950s and 1960s, more dams were built than ever before in China's history and about 7.8 million people were moved to make way for these water control works (World Bank, 1997). Even though people have to be displaced for such mega developmental national projects, it is the responsibility of the government and the project implementing agencies to effectively resettle and rehabilitate the affected people, but it was not implemented in a humane manner what the past experience suggests and 'no serious effort was made to respond to local concerns over matters of compensation, community break-up, economic recovery, or social adjustment in the new communities' (Jing, 1997: 74). With a positive growth in the economy due to the economic reforms (open door policy) of China since 1978, the displaced people will face lot of problems on their own if they are not properly resettled and rehabilitated, and this assumes greater proportions in the mega-city of Chongqing municipality that is to settle majority of the displaced.

Prior to the 1980s, the Chinese resettlement programme was in a very bad shape with the resettled persons becoming the worst victims of the water projects. These people constituted the rural farmers and they never had a say in matters of displacement and resettlement. The compensation paid to them was meagre to meet the new life situation and challenges in the changed circumstances after being resettled, and this contributed to their impoverishment. In fact, China's leading poverty relief agency acknowledged in a 1989 publication that more than seven million, or roughly 70 per cent, of the country's existing 10.2 million reservoir resettlers were living in 'extreme poverty' (*jidu pinkun*), suffering from acute shortages of food, clothes and decent shelter (Leading Group of Economic Development of Poor Areas, 1989: 25).

In 1981, China formulated the reservoir resettlement law and created the 'reservoir maintenance fund' from the proceeds of the hydro-electric projects for the welfare of the resettled people. The hydro-electric corporations were required to give .001 yuan for every 1 kw of electricity generated for managing the fund. In 1982, the law of Land Acquisition in State Capital Construction hiked the compensation rates, protected the displaced from land title, income and assets, and also made provisions for consultation with the people to be displaced. These were added to the land administration law in 1986. Supplementing to this, the Ministry of Water Resources and Electric power also made provisions for the development of resettled persons.

It is to be noted that the World Bank has not financed the TGD however, it is funding other large dams in China and also in other countries. The cost of this huge project is met by China itself from different sources. Primarily, the funding was from three sources. 'Since 1992, a Three Gorges Dam Construction Fund has collected a nationwide levy of 0.015 yuan/kW of electricity sold annually and has collected 30 billion yuan for the first 11 years. The second source was from Gezhouba Hydro-Dam situated 40 kms downstream from the Three Gorges, where the rate of electricity was raised. Last source was from domestic loans from the China Construction Bank and partly from bonds and shares in Three Gorges Project and the

Gezhouba Co. Ltd.' (Jackson and Sleigh, 2000: 229). The cost of resettlement is expected to over 100 billion yuan (US $11.76 billion) by 2003. This will include the compensation for the lost homes and agricultural land, construction of new roads and bridges, water, power and other infrastructural developments, and allied cost to the receiving villages where the displaced are to be settled. Along with this, the inflationary pressures are also to be included in the resettlement budget, leading to its reduction subsequently and utilization in the construction of the dam.

The Chinese government is concerned about the impact and resettlement management of such a huge population movement on the economy and society. With a wide array of experience on involuntary resettlement, the Chinese government has gradually matured to design a developmental resettlement policy, which is summed up in the slogan 'being moved out, being stable and becoming wealthy gradually'. This policy emphasizes both the restoration of the resettlers' livelihoods during the transition period after displacement and improvement in the later stages' (Tan et al., 2005: 713). The goal of this procedure is to guarantee the creation of a viable economic base to provide resettlers with tangible benefits such as industrial jobs, low-interest bank loans, and training classes for farmers to grow cash crops or acquire other skills to participate in China's emerging market economy (ROHBSP, 1998). Chinese officials describe the new policy as 'blood-creating assistance' (*zaoxue fuzhi*), contrasting it to 'blood-giving assistance' (*shuxue fuzhi*) in the past that relied merely on monetary compensation and poverty alleviation to solve resettlement problems (Xiujing, 1997). The Chinese government, in order to make the policy of developmental resettlement popular, also made provisions for (a) hiring the rural resettlers to work at construction sites; (b) allocate low interest loans for growing cash crops and establishing rural industries; (c) fund large-scale reclamation of wasteland as a major means of continuing agricultural production; (d) helping the rural resettlers to find factory and urban jobs; (e) use earnings from the hydro-station to establish a fund for capital construction at the resettlement sites; and (f) giving the rural resettlers priority in using electricity after the hydro-station is in operation.

Resettlement Policy

The resettlement policy for the TGD has been stated in the Changjiang Three Gorges Project Resettlement Regulations (SCC,

1993, 2001). The resettlement policy was framed in 1993 but again in 2001 it was modified to meet the requirements at the field level. The Chinese government, in order to have a fool-proof resettlement management, had a trial resettlement for the TGD displacees in 1985 and implementing it somewhat successfully, adopted the approach of 'near resettlement', whereby the displaced people were resettled and rehabilitated to their original position, as far as practicable.

Table 1

Displaced Population in TGD areas

Administrative Unit (number of affected Counties)	*Total Population*	*No. of Displaced Persons (% to total population)*
Chongqing City (3)	3,270,000	13500 (<1%)
Fuling Prefecture (3)	2,240,000	126700 (6%)
Qianjiang Prefecture (1)	470,000	8400 (2%)
Wanxian Prefecture (8)	7,290,000	571000 (8%)
Hubei Province (4)	1,730,000	126900 (7%)
All 19 Counties	15,000,000	846478 (6%)*

*Baseline population in 1994, by 2003 the total population in the affected counties will grow to 19 million and the displaced population will reach at least 1.13 million.

Source: Jackson and Sleigh, 2000: 227.

The original resettlement policy for the TGD had the support of Li Peng, the former Premier of China. This policy clearly stated that the government would control all aspects of resettlement, including moving people to new places, providing agricultural land, houses and jobs in the urban area. Later in 1999, the then Prime Minister Zhu Rongi, who was the head of the Three Gorges Construction Committee's Resettlement Bureau, formulated a revised policy for expeditious and effective resettlement of the displaced persons. In general, academics and scientists have welcomed Zhu's directives, believing that the central government has recognized that the old plan was not working and is now trying to improve the situation (Three Gorges Probe, 1999). With this objective, the State Council approved the revised resettlement policy on 15 February 2001 and it came into effect on 1 March 2001, thereby replacing the original policy of 1993.

Under the new policy, the government would encourage the displaced people to move to areas of their choice, either rural or urban, but for this the displaced would have to get the permission from the host area. For providing financial assistance to the resettled persons, they were to get a part of the funds that would have been given to the host community for infrastructure and allied costs, over and above the compensation received for their property and livelihood.

As per the original resettlement policy of 1988 the displaced persons were to be resettled at the uphill sites within the immediate reservoir area, but this was modified to encourage the rural displaced persons to move to more distant resettlement sites. This is contained in the national policy on distant resettlement implemented from 26 January 2000 (TGPCC, 2000). Most of the reservoir area has steep slopes unfit for farming and the central government recognized that this would lead to environmental problem. Secondly, the relocating and re-establishing the industrial enterprises in the reservoir area was later changed to 'restructuring, merging, and closing down small and unprofitable enterprises' (Tan et al., 2003: 6). Thirdly, the original policy had provision to rehabilitate 40 per cent of the rural displaced persons in secondary and tertiary industry (REG, 1988). However, this was not feasible over a period of time, as the industrial units were of out-dated technology with low marketing strategy and were not able to meet the competitive market situation. A total of 1012 industrial and mining enterprises among the 1599 enterprises affected by the project in the reservoir area have been identified as being unprofitable and are to be shut down, and of those, 1008 enterprises are in the Chongqing reservoir section (CMG, 1999). The rural resettlers coping with the new non-agricultural jobs and competing with urban employees became a problem 'owing to low education, lack of skills and lack of relevant social networks' (Tan et al., 2003: 9). Fourthly, the original policy stated that displaced persons who have violated the one-child family planning policy would be eligible for compensation if such persons have paid the penalty and children must have been born prior to 1992. However, later in October 2001, the TGP Construction Commission ordered that displaced families with lesser than four children would be eligible for compensation under the distant resettlement scheme, whereby such families would be resettled at a distant province. Fifthly, the revised policy emphasized upon environmental protection, ecological agriculture, closure of polluting industries and penalty for defaulters. It banned clearing of virgin forests for resettlement due to the risk of soil erosion and also cease of terracing on slopes exceeding 25E. Sixthly, agriculture that was earlier the basis for resettlement was no more considered as a pre-requisite. This was due to insufficient availability of agricultural land and people's preference to settle in urban area.

Again, the revised policy gave priority to the finance allocated for resettlement management and stated that it should be used for the resettlement purpose only. This was done specifically to avoid financial misappropriation and corruption. It lists six points on which the resettlement funding should be spent: compensation for rural resettlement; moving and reconstruction of towns and cities; compensation for moving and reconstruction of industrial enterprises, reconstruction of infrastructure projects; environmental protection; and other resettlement projects that are initiated under the TGPCC (Three Gorges Project Co-ordinating Committee) (Heggelund, 2006: 194). It also contained penalty provisions for the people refusing to be displaced, adopting dilly-dallying tactics, returning to their original place after getting compensation or trying to get compensation again. Hence, the revised policy made it mandatory for the people to displace even if they are reluctant.

Types of Resettlement Schemes

Yan Tan, Graeme Hugo, and Lesley Potter (2003) have stated various types of resettlement schemes adopted for the TGD. These are, (a) 'near resettlement' scheme (*jiudi houkao*), by which rural displaced persons are moved uphill from the reservoir within their county of residence; (b) 'government organized distant resettlement' (GODR); (c) 'self-employed resettlement' (*zi mou*); (d) 'living with relatives and friends' (*touqin kaoyou*) in an urban area; (e) 'voluntarily-scattered distant resettlement (VSDR) (*zizhu waiqian*); (f) 'transferring rural migrants to secondary and tertiary industries' (*er san chanyei anzhi*); (g) 'productive resettlement population' (*shengchan anzhi renkou*) refers to persons who will lose their farmland or other production resources and need to be provided with land or means of production to restore agricultural production or job opportunities; and (h) 'affiliated migrant family members' (*suiqian renkou*) are eligible to receive only some of the compensation and funds, and it includes the direct kin or the children of the displaced persons.

In the GODR scheme, the resettled persons enjoyed three years' tax exemption for agricultural products, house reconstruction funding and taxation reduction during the transition period of resettlement (ACTB, 1999). It was conducted in two phases, first by trial resettlement taking a few numbers of displaced persons followed by sending the total number of displaced persons. Selection of the resettlement sites under GODR addressed five criteria, viz.; (a) physical environment, transport and infrastructure, (b) abundant farmland, (c) higher economic development level, (d) strong leadership at the village and villagers' group level, and (e) sound folklore and traditions (Tan et al., 2003: 15). However, fulfilment of all the criteria was not an easy possibility, and hence many of the resettled families under this scheme had to face problems at the later stage. There were also a limited number of locations under this scheme that restricted the choice of the displaced persons. Issues relating to land, infrastructure, social security and potential benefits, and conflicts between the host and guest people were unavoidable (ibid.: 16).

In the GODR scheme, representatives from each of the displaced households were sent to the distant located resettlement sites in other provinces. The representatives, after physical verification of the land, are required to sign a contract either to purchase or build a house in the recipient area. The resettlement authorities of the sending and receiving counties are required to sign an agreement for transferring the household registration and to provide land to the resettled person. After getting the land, the houses are constructed and usually three systems are adopted for house construction. The first one is 'entrusting construction' (*weituo jianfang*) by which the resettled person entrusts the house construction to a builder after negotiating the price. The second system is 'collective construction' (*jiti lian jian*), where a group of resettled persons themselves construct the house for each other in order to make it cost effective. The third system is 'independent construction' (*zi jian*), where the resettled persons independently construct the houses. After the houses are constructed, the entire households are shifted and the agricultural lands are redistributed.

The redistribution of land are conducted in such a way that every resettled person gets land not lesser than the average land holding of the host population. As per the revised State Land Administration Law of 1998, all rural land is collectively owned by the community and a family has the right to utilize the agricultural land without any land-holding right and transferability. The approaches involved in the redistribution of land are as follows (ibid.: 17):

- Breaking down the original land allotment system in a village and redistributing land to each host and the displaced household in terms of the current total population including the displaced;
- Slightly readjusting the original land relationship of the host residents by allocating a part of land collected from the host peasants to the displaced;
- Using a part of retained land which is kept for emergency use by the community in a host village as contract land for displaced; and
- Adjusting farmland from the state-owned farms to the displaced.

Resettlement Management

According to official report, 23,800 ha of farmland and 4,100 ha of orange orchards will be lost to the reservoir (REG, 1988). A survey of 470 displaced families of the TGD project was conducted in 1997–98 by Li (2000). One of the major findings of the survey was that for the displaced in the Three Gorges reservoir region, the area of the farmland after their relocation tends to be smaller and of worse quality than they had before: about 66 per cent of respondents regard their farmland after relocation as 'worse off' or 'much worse', while 12 per cent report their situation as 'same' and 21 per cent said that they were 'better off' (ibid.: 224). In the case of the distant resettlement, the resettled had the problems of adjusting to the new environment, cultural practices, language and more importantly to the change in the mode of production and cultivating new crops. The cultivation systems, methods, techniques and farming tools are quite different (Tan et al., 2003: 18). The TGD area, being a mountainous area, the people cultivated corn, wheat, sweet potato, citrus fruits like oranges. But in the distant resettlement in the eastern coastal provinces, mainly rice, cotton, rape seed, is cultivated and the cultivation processes are very different. For example, a study of the displaced suitability for production after relocation revealed that some 78 per cent of distant resettled persons from Zigui County were not used to growing grain and 81 per cent of them were not accustomed to growing cotton and vegetables (Jin, 1998). The people of Zigui County predominantly cultivated fruits, particularly oranges. Interviews with relocates showed many displaced persons felt they had suffered a lot more than economic loss through the destruction of their orange groves and their removal to a distant location; they were unable to contemplate life without oranges, which represented not just a major source of income but also a way of life full of cultural, symbolic value (Li et al., 2001: 206).

Similarly, in 1995, 80 displaced families from the TGD project were sent to the distant Hainan Island. Here, they were engaged in rubber plantation by the officials and it was planned to permanently resettle them in Hainan Island. However, the resettled families were disgusted with the working conditions and living environment due to low wages and the hot and humid climatic conditions. In less than two months, all the families moved back to their home villages. In another instance, 200 displaced persons were sent to the distant Inner Mongolia from Fengjie County, Chongqing Municipality, but had to return back within a month. In the case of TGD project, moving relocates to entirely different parts of the country has proved a failure (ibid.). Both the instances of Hainan Island and Inner Mongolia were provided by Wang Chengjun, an official of the Relocation Bureau of Wanxian, on 28 May 1998 (ibid.: 209).

The people resettled under the scattered distant resettled scheme had their own problems. They were not given any transportation facility to carry their belongings and had to pay an additional amount. They were not permitted for any type of subsidy for living expenses during the transition period and no tax exemption from agricultural tax. These people also had to pay 3,000 yuan for transfer of household registration but no agricultural land or jobs were provided to them. These people moved from Xiangxi, Zigui County to Shengnongjza Forest district, Hubei province. The scattered resettled people also had the problem of not having any type of social relations with the host population.

Jing (1997: 83) writes that the resettlement budget of 18 billion yuan is not adequate to give compensation to the displaced people. This amount is not only limited to compensation but also includes excavations of major archaeological sites that will be flooded. Again, as per the new developmental resettlement, the local governments are directed to keep and manage the compensation funds for agricultural and industrial investments and infrastructural development. The rural resettlers will receive compensation for moving to the resettlement sites and the cost incurred for dismantling their houses.

The land given to resettled persons was very often of poor quality and inadequate in comparison to the pre-displacement phase. In spite of this, the resettled persons accepted it in order to obtain the required three certificates, viz., (a) house building certificate, (b) residency registration transmission certificate, and (c) certificate of contract land allocated in receiving locations. These three certificates are required for those resettled through VSDR scheme, implemented in 1997–99, so as to obtain permission to resettle their households and to receive compensation and funding from the local resettlement authorities in the sending counties.

Lack of adequate land for redistribution led to loss of agricultural production and food insecurity. 'In the Three Gorges area, the current lack of farmland already poses a threat to local food production. With the inundation of fertile, it is expected that the problem will be aggravated' (Heggelund, 2006: 187).

Employment

The developmental resettlement policy of China has categorically stated that the agricultural community will have to change their occupation and will be provided with jobs in the industries. The resettled people were given jobs in industrial units, mainly in government owned industries. These people themselves also opted for industrial jobs as this would facilitate them to move from rural to urban areas, added with the advantage of getting a job. This may also be due to the fact that agricultural land was not adequately available to be redistributed to the resettled persons. With this objective, during the period of experimental resettlement from 1985 to 1993, '28 industries were set up, but they were small and only employed 2,400 rural resettlers' (Natiao, 1994: 16), and 'lacked a competitive edge on the market because they are poorly run and have a very low level of management and technology' (Ping, 1992: 32). The displaced from rural to urban found that they often soon lost their new urban jobs, though they did experience an improvement in infrastructure and social service (Li et al., 2001: 203). In Yichang County alone, some 2,000 displaced workers had been laid off by April 1998, accounting for 60 per cent of the total displaced workers re-employed in county-owned, town-owned, and private-owned enterprises (Li, 2000). It may be mentioned here that the rural resettled persons had low level of education and so they were not suitable for the technical industrial jobs. The prospects for the rural population to move into urban areas and engage in non-farm jobs are expected to be poor due to current overstaffing and unemployment in urban industrial sectors (ibid.).

Compensation

The Land Administration Law of 1999 contained provisions for compensation. The basis of compensation is land, resettlement funds and assets and green crops on the land. 'The compensation amount for the first item is 6–10 times the derived land productivity (DLP), which is the average annual production per hectare in the preceding three years. The amount for the resettlement funds is four to six times the DLP, subject to a maximum of 15 times the DLP. The combined amount of these two is set at a maximum of 30 times the DLP ... Consequently, the gross compensation for arable land was 2,701 yuan/mu, which is only 3.5 times the DLP, and the average compensation for flooded orange orchard was 5,763 yuan/mu, a mere 2.3 times' (Tan et al., 2003: 20). The compensation allotted to the displaced persons was much lower than what they expected. In China, land compensation is given on the basis of infrastructural development in the concerned land, and the reservoir area was a less developed area with many poor people, in spite of the economic opening up initiated since the late 1970s. House construction in the reservoir area was banned since 4 April 1992, and any such building owner was not entitled to get compensation. The house structure itself was assessed in a faulty manner, assessing only the structure above the ground and leaving the foundation of the building. The standard set for the rural displaced is much lower than that for the urban dwellers, at differences of 51 yuan/square metre for main buildings and 24 yuan/square metre for out buildings (RBKC, 1997). Given the average per capita of 3500–4000 yuan for housing compensation in the Chongqing reservoir section to construct a new house, example in Deyang city, Sichuan, for a four-member displaced family, a gap of some 20,000 yuan has to be filled through other means, often borrowing money from relatives or friends (Tan et al., 2003: 20–21). Again, the displaced persons had reservations towards the disproportion in compensation they received and resettlement funds allotted to the receiving community/village for infrastructure development and other provisions. The displaceds' misconceptions of the compensation scheme are mainly caused by the various adjustments made to the resettlement schemes, lack of standardized operations in implementing the compensation policy and unrealized expectations of the displaced to shake off poverty through the displacement. (ibid.: 22)

Rural–Urban Discrepancy

The TGD resettlement differentiated between the rural and urban displaced persons. Whereas, higher compensation was paid to the displaced from the urban area, for house building purpose, in comparison to the rural displaced, in case of infrastructure development also, urban area were allotted more funds than rural area. A comparison to this effect is presented below:

Category	*City*	*County*	*Town*	*Rural*
House building	3,953	3,400	3,000	1,197
Infrastructure	4,547	4,100	2,000	903
Total	8,500	7,500	5,000	2,100

Source: REG (1988), figures in yuan per person.

The urban displaced also did not have to move very far from their original habitations, as the new towns and the cities were made close to their existing cities and towns. In the case of rural displaced, they were resettled at distant locations. However, the rural displaced persons, as per their preference, were adjusted, as far as possible, in towns and city areas.

Host–Guest Relationship

The relationship between the host and the guest was not always cordial and there was tension between these two groups of population. The tension arose due to the redistribution of agricultural land that is already inadequate. It is for this reason that many host communities were usually unwilling to receive the resettled population. Supplementing to this is the policy provision that accorded preferential treatment to the resettled community over tax collections and other living subsidies, for the initial few years of resettlement. Chinese villagers put significant emphasis on being one clan (*shi*), bearing the same surname: the relocates are thus regarded as strangers, a situation which could last for one to two generations, making the resettlement in new areas even more difficult (Heggelund, 2006: 189).

Opposition and Protest

Participation of the people in the decision-making process was at the lowest level in the TGD project resettlement management.

'Moreover, arrests and humiliation of protesting relocates occurred frequently. This relates to the broader consequences of displacement including human rights, which the IRR (Impoverishment Risks and Reconstruction) model does not encompass' (ibid.: 190). Resettling the displaced in the steep and infertile slopes above the reservoir brought strong resentment among these people. The displaced people of Gaoyang village, Yunyang County, protested against this and on their own collected one yuan from each person and organized a protest movement. They secretly went to Beijing to meet some officials and to ventilate their grievances. However, they were unable to succeed in their endeavour. These people were concerned about the sustenance of their livelihood in the slopes.

The displaced people of Gaoyang township, Yunyang County were resettled in Dafeng city, Jiangsu Province, about 1,000 kms from their homes. The resettled persons were dissatisfied with the facilities provided to them. They complained of being paid lesser compensation than what the government promised to give them. According to a newspaper report, government documents promise the peasants in Yunyang County a sum of 20,000 yuan, but local officials offered 10,800 yuan (*South China Morning Post*, 1999). Added to this, they later came to know that funds allotted for resettlement have been diverted for other purposes by the authorities. This created resentment among the people who were yet to move out of Gaoyang township, and they requested the government of Yunyang County to consider the problems. Instead of doing anything positive, the County government accused the people appealing as 'disturbing the Three Gorges resettlement'. The people then decided to send some representatives to Beijing and meet the central authorities and appraise them about their grievances. Three representatives were arrested by police in Beijing for appealing to the central authorities for help (*Probe International*, 2001; *South China Morning Post*, 1999).

Jing (1997: 68) gives two instances where people protested against the compensation. In one case, government officials had to be protected by the police from the fury of resettled people over discrepancy and unequal compensation. In the second instance, 300 resettled villagers tried to block a motorcade of leaders who were on a trip to inspect the relocation programme. The protesting villagers had to be dispersed by the police. Jing also cites the arrest of 179 people of the rural Kaixian County, Wanxian Prefecture, Sichuan

Province in May 1992. A report by the Wanxian Public Security Department claimed that these people belonged to a so-called 'Democratic Youth Party', an allegedly dissident group accused of 'counter revolutionary activities aimed at sabotaging the policy of opening and reform and at disrupting the smooth progress of the TGD project' (*Human Rights Watch*, 1995: 10). From this particular County, at least 70,000 people were to be relocated and resettled.

Conclusion

Despite China's improved resettlement performance, the Three Gorges resettlement process has encountered a number of problems, many of which are related to the environment, the resource situation and the insufficient farming potential in the area (Heggelund, 2006: 180). The displacement and resettlement programme has been devised by the central government and the provincial and county resettlement bureaus merely implemented and supervised the programme. The people had no say in the entire process and had to obey the directions of the government. Since the resettlement was carried by government officials there were many constraints on the part of the people affected by the TGD project. Redressal mechanism was not at all present in the entire process for which the people suffered a lot without voicing anything against the diktats of the government. Occasionally, the national and provincial resettlement authorities organize 'on-the-spot meetings' (*xianchang bangonghui*) to identify, examine and solve problems, and draw lessons from the experiences of existing resettlement operations, but few resettlers are invited to participate in such official meetings to voice their questions and problems (Tan et al., 2005: 722). Yan Tan, Graeme Hugo and Lesley Potter (2005: 718) have stated:

> Lack of participation in the selection of resettlement locations has increased resettlers' dependence on the government and resulted in many problems relating to house building, land allocation and their reluctance to move ... Some common expectations of the resettlers included the opportunity to receive more compensation – and so improve their lives – by seizing this unprecedented opportunity of relocation, to change their hukou (household registration) status from rural to urban residence as an improvement of their social and economic status and to rely upon the government to restore their livelihood and reconstruct production after displacement.

The World Bank (1996 and 1998) commended the work of China in the resettlement management of the TGD project. It was very positive on the aspect of decentralization decision-making, whereby the provincial and local authorities were given autonomy to manage the resettlement of the displaced. As contained in the IRR model, China adopted the trial resettlement in 1985 so as to ascertain the ground realities. Training facilities were given to the resettled persons as per their preference, industrial or agricultural occupations. Again, in 1996 the National Development and Reform Commission provided for a 'Later Stage Support Fund' that will collect revenue from the hydro-power units and would utilize it for the development of the resettled population.

Professor Wang Chunguang of the Institute of Sociology, Chinese Academy of Social Sciences said that the land for the Three Gorges project was acquired by the local government and the compensation amount was also given to the people by the local government. The compensation amount was sanctioned by the central government and given to the local government. This compensation amount was a matter of controversy among the local people and the local government. The local villagers alleged that they were not given the right amount of compensation sanctioned by the central government. Again the correct amount of compensation was not known to everybody as it was not made public. Some people at their level tried to get the information of the actual rate of compensation amount. After getting the information and realizing that they have been paid a lesser amount, they started to mobilize the people so as to oppose the local government. In this context, the people have demonstrated before the local government buildings by sitting in *dharana*, but it was all in vain. Some local villagers have also travelled to Beijing to report their grievance and opposition with the Three Gorges Project Construction Commission Office. This also did not yield any positive results for them. Local villagers have also protested before the Commission's Office in Beijing on different issues at different times, but it was all in vain.

He said that the local villagers were allotted land by the government in the new places where they moved. This land was purchased by the government by paying money to the people who possessed the land, and this was given to the displaced people who moved to the new resettlement areas. Some houses in the resettlement areas were constructed by the government and were sold to the displaced people, where as many displaced people opted to construct their own houses. This house was made out of the compensation amount.

On the problem of the social assimilation and integration, Professor Wang was of the view that among the displaced people and the original inhabitants living in the new villages or areas of resettlement was another problem faced by the new people settling there. They did not have very cordial relationships among the host-guest populations in many instances.

Professor Wang was very much concerned about finding work opportunities for the young population moving out of their original villages and settling in the new places and identified it as a major obstacle for the resettled population. The younger group of population had to move to the urban centres and other remote areas for employment and work opportunities, leaving behind the elder parents alone and in distress. This group of the elder citizens had no one to look after and care them. They had to do all the household work by themselves, which was not possible by them at this stage of their life. In a research study conducted by him, he said that, 'the elder group of people said this with all pain and anguish and this was a problem that had to be endured by themselves as there was no other alternative option of work opportunities in the new resettled areas for the younger generation. The government also did not devise any type of Old Age Home Care Institutions in the resettled areas. The problem of the gerontology was one of the major problems in the new resettled villages.

According to Professor Wang, the role of the media was also very limited in reporting the condition of the displaced people and more importantly in highlighting their pitiable condition. This was due to the fact that the entire media is controlled by the government, and hence the media did not go against the government programmes. Here by media it is referred to the electronic media. With regard to the newspapers also the same thing applies but the difference is that in the villages very few people read newspapers, as buying a paper is not possible on the part of the poor villagers, and secondly, the newspapers did not contain anything of their interest.

In an interview with Professor Guoqing, Director of National Research Centre for Resettlement, HoHai University, Nanjing, said that 'before the economic reforms of 1979, there was the collective economic system whereby the agricultural land was collectively farmed and the output was shared. After the economic reforms, the village community owned the land collectively but individual control over land was given. Since the land was individually controlled, it contributed to increased efficiency on the part of the farmer controlling the agricultural land and this in turn increased the agricultural output ultimately resulting in higher incomes'.

He said that 'from 1949 to 1979, China constructed around 4000 large dams and 10 million 81,000 small and medium dams. For this about 10 million people had to be displaced but the resettlement programme was not implemented properly. The central government realized that many projects committed mistakes for which the displaced people had to face problems. Keeping this in view, in mid 1980s, the State Council made a large survey and reviewed the situation so as to ascertain the problems that need to be addressed. After getting the consolidated information, the State Council in 1984, directed the Ministry of Water Resources to do the needful. The Ministry of Water Resources then set up the Resettlement Office that would specifically deal with issue of resettlement and rehabilitation. The office looked after the past misdeeds and devised ways and means to lessen the problems of the people in the future. In 1998, a government policy to this effect came into force and similar offices were established at different government levels, province, county, etc. This indicated that resettlement is the responsibility of the government and it should take effective steps to solve people's problems with regard to displacement and resettlement management. At the provincial level, the Planning Design and Research Institute was established in each of the provinces of China for hydropower projects. These institutes were entrusted with all the water resources issues like, irrigation, power generation, resettlement, etc'.

In Chinese social and political system, the village is an important stakeholder. The villagers elect a Village Committee with its leader. This Village Committee takes the responsibility for administration of the community in the village and takes decisions on their behalf. The Village Committee and the leader coordinate and negotiate with the government and the local people on various issues, including displacement. The Committee takes the responsibility of the resettlement and rehabilitation within the community and with partnership with the local government, connects the local villagers with the local government. The Committee is responsible to distribute agricultural and household land, construction of public infrastructure and public facilities. The compensation for the community agricultural land is paid to the Village Committee and it decides how to utilize it. Hence, the Village Committee is an important body and it assumes higher proportions in sensitive matters.

He referred the Land Administration Law of China that has provisions for regulations on land acquisition and compensation. These were: (a) implementation regulation, (b) basic farm land protection regulation, (c) large and medium scale water resources and hydropower project land acquisition compensation and resettlement regulation, and (d) Three Gorges construction resettlement regulation. The first two are for different land acquisition projects and the last two are specifically for water projects with the last one particularly for the TGD resettlement. The Chinese system allots compensation for land acquisition under four parts, viz., (a) compensation for land, (b) resettlement subsidy, (c) compensation for crops in agricultural land, and (d) emotional/psychological attachment compensation. The main objective for paying compensation is to restore income and livelihood and to generate new employment opportunities.

He said that the government resettlement office coordinates with the Village Committee for redistribution of community agricultural land to the resettled persons. This institutional arrangement is more important and is different from Indian context.

According to him, individual compensation is based on the replacement cost for houses and other things. However, now this practice has been changed. As per the new regulation, actual cost of construction of new house is given. The minimum is fixed at 24 square metres per individual in a family and per square metre the cost is given at the rate of 530 RMB for construction. This new regulation was not applicable to the TGD project.

With regard to the management of the construction and resettlement, he said that the government takes the responsibility. For the TGD project there is the Three Gorges Project Construction Committee, with representatives from different ministries and the army. It was headed by the Prime Minister and at present the Vice-Premier is the head. The Committee has two bodies. The first is the Three Gorges Project Company that is responsible for construction and management and the second body is the

Administration and Resettlement Bureau. Resettlement Bureau is also set up at the provincial and county levels.

Describing the operationalization of compensation and resettlement process, he said that it involves a survey. The physical losses have to be surveyed and the result has to be confirmed by the individual household. Survey is conducted by the county, township and village group leaders and assisted by the Planning Design Institute. The head of each of the family has to countersign the survey. This is a sort of agreement between the people and the resettlement officials. After the survey is complete, two tables are drawn that reflects the Physical Loss Card and the Finance Card that includes the compensation to be distributed. This process systemizes the compensation to be allotted. There is also a Grievance Bureau, which is a channel to communicate the grievance of the people to the government. However, it is not a decision-making body and if the grievances are not addressed then the people can go to the courts for legal recourse.

He narrated instances of family conflict with regard to the individual compensation. In China, one is registered under the Household Registration System (*huckou*) and it is treated as a single household. The family gets the compensation amount and it is the family that decides how the compensation is to be utilized. First, it is negotiated within the family, and if this negotiation fails, then the family can either approach the Village Committee or they can take legal measures. In Nanjing, a family of about 100 members went to the court to settle the compensation dispute. However, family conflicts were not a recurrent feature and were very limited.

According to Professor SHI Guoqing, 'one-third of the total displaced is living in poor conditions. Prior to 1980s, there were much more number of persons, but now due to the economic reforms and management, their number has reduced. At the same time, we also cannot say that there is no impoverishment because now we are living more in a market system and hence a sustainable recovery to each household cannot be guaranteed. It is no doubt that things have improved from the past. Important to note that usually host people are richer than the resettled persons for which reason there is relative poverty'.

Professor Chen Kin of the Institute of Youth's Study, Chinese Academy of Social Sciences, was of the view that the common notion in China, Japan, Korea, and in the East Asia, in general, is that the nation's interest is more important than individual interest. Hence, if the country wants to implement a project, then the people have to sacrifice for the nation's interest. He said that China has a totalitarian democratic system, where democracy and dictatorship is mired together in promoting a huge project like the TGD. This in other words is 'democratic centralism'. It controls social risks and economic efficiency and at the same time balances democracy and centralism. He opined that the civil society and the media in China are weak in comparison to the state and hence lack the capacity to oppose, or at least be critical, of the state's policies.

Jun Jing in the thematic review to 'Displacement, Resettlement, Rehabilitation, Reparation and Development-China Report' to the World Commission on Dam states that 'all studies of reservoir resettlement in China conclude that access to farmland, preferably in the vicinity of the hometowns of the targeted rural people, is the key to successful resettlement, especially in building large-scale dams and reservoir in densely populated areas. However, the reality is that little extra land is available in these areas and hence the creation of industrial or service jobs must be guaranteed. Otherwise, resettlement will fail. Furthermore, a relatively new problem in some of China's resettlement programmes is official corruption'. According to the National Audit Office in early 1999, officials had embezzled 232 million yuan from funds earmarked for resettlement in the Three Gorges area (Becker, 1999).

References

All Chinese Taxation Bureau (ACTB) (1999). Circular about 'Relevant Taxation for Rural Migrants Displaced by Distant Resettlement Schemes in the Three Gorges Reservoir Area', Government Document No. 845.

Becker, Jasper (1999). 'Dam Cadres "steal $217m"', *South China Morning Post*, 14 February, p. 1.

Changjiang Water and Resources Commission (CWRC) (1993). *Changjiang sanxia gongcheng shuiku yanmo shiwu zhibiao diaocha baogao*, Survey Report on the Physical Flooding Indices for the Initial Design of the Three Gorges Project, Wuhan: CWRC.

Chongqing Municipal Government (CMG) (1999). Official Document No. 193, Chongqing, China.

Dai, Q. (1998). *The River Dragon has Come!: The Three Gorges Dam and the Fate of China's Yangtze River and its People*, translated by Ming Yi, Armonk, New York: M.E. Sharpe.

Fearnside, P.M. (1994). 'The Canadian Feasibility Study of the TGD Proposed for China's Yangtze River', *Impact Assessment*, Vol. 12, No. 1.

Heggelund, Gorild (2006). 'Resettlement Programmes and Environmental Capacity in the Three Gorges Dam Project', *Development and Change*, Vol. 37, No. 1.

Jackson, Sukhan and Adrian Sleigh (2000). 'Resettlement for China's TGD: Socio-economic Impact and Institutional Tensions', *Communist and Post-Communist Studies*, Vol. 33, No. 2.

Jin, Z.F. (1998). 'An Approach to Migrants' Suitability for Production in the TGP Area', Unpublished MA Dissertation, Huazhong University of Science and Technology, Wuhan.

Jing, Jun (1997). 'Rural Resettlement: Past Lessons for the Three Gorges Project', *The China Journal*, No. 38.

Leading Group of Economic Development of Poor Areas (LGEDPA) (1989). *Outlines of Economic Development in China's Poor Areas*, Beijing: Agriculture Press, p. 25. Quoted by Jun Jing in *Displacement, Resettlement, Rehabilitation, Reparation and Development: China Report*, Contributing Paper to World Commission on Dam.

Li, H.M. (2000). 'Population Displacement and Resettlement in the Three Gorges Reservoir Area of the Yangtze River', Unpublished PhD Dissertation, School of Geography, UK: University of Leeds.

Li, Heming, P. Waley and P. Rees (2001). 'Reservoir Resettlement in China: Past Experience and the Three Gorges Dam', *The Geographical Journal*, Vol. 167, No. 3.

Natiao, Wu (1994). 'Population Relocation for the TGP', *Beijing Review*, 10–16 October.

Ping, Li (1992). 'Trial Resettlement of Residents', *Beijing Review*, 6–12 April.

Resettlement Bureau of Kaixian County (RBKC) (1997). 'Compensation Standard for Flooded Housing of Kaixian County', Unpublished Official Document, Kaixian County, China.

Reservoir Development Bureau of the Ministry of Water Resources of China (1999). 'Probe Chinese Characterized Reservoir Resettlement Ways', *Water Resources of China*, Vol. 2, No. 23.

Resettlement Expert Group of the TGP (REG) (1988). *Sanxia Gongcheng Yimin Xiangmu Kexinxing Yanjiu Baogao*, Feasibility Report on Resettlement Scheme of the Three Gorges Project, Beijing: Water Conservation Press.

Resettlement Office of the Hydraulics Bureau of Shandong Province (ROHBSP) (1998). 'On Effective Management and Utilization of

Resettlement Funds for the Promotion of Economic Development in Reservoir Regions' (Guanlihao yonghao shuikou yimin zhouzhuan jin), Memorandums of Hydraulics, Poverty Relief, and Development of Reservoir Areas (shuili fupin yu kuqu kaifa dongtai), Issue No. 1, pp. 37–43.

State Council of China (SCC) (1993). 'Changjiang Sanxia Gongcheng Jianshe Yiming Tiaoli' (Resettlement Regulations for the Three Gorges Project), *Sichuan Daily*, 28 August.

—— (2001). 'Changjiang Sanxia Gongcheng Jianshe Yiming Tiaoli' (Resettlement Regulations for the Three Gorges Project), *People Daily*, 26 February.

State Statistical Bureau of China (SSB) (1996). *China Energy Annual Review*, Beijing: China Statistical Publishing House.

Tan, Yan, Graeme Hugo and Lesley Potter (2005). 'Rural Women, Displacement and the Three Gorges Project', *Development and Change*, Vol. 36, No. 4.

—— (2003). 'Government Organized Distant Resettlement and the Three Gorges Project, China', *Asia-Pacific Population Journal*, Vol. 18, No. 3.

Three Gorges Probe (1999). No. 9906, 8 October.

TGP Construction Commission of the State Council (2000). 'Resettlement Fund Administration in Rural Residents' Distant Resettlement Out of the Chongqing Reservoir Section', Official Document No. 3, Beijing.

World Bank (1996). *Resettlement and Development: The Bankwide Review of Projects Involving Involuntary Resettlement 1986–1993*, Washington, DC: Environment Department.

—— (1997). *Zhongguo feiziyuan yimin* (Involuntary Resettlement in China), Report 11641–CHA, Nanjing: HoHai University.

—— (1998). *Recent Experience with Involuntary Resettlement: China-Shuikou*, Washington, DC: Operations Evaluation Department.

Xiujing, Meng (1997). 'Tentative Ideas on the Methods of Handling the Leftover Problems of Reservoir Resettlement' (qiantan chuli yimin wenti de zuofa yu tihui), Memorandums of Hydraulics, Poverty Relief, and Development of Reservoir Areas (shuili fupin yu kuqu kaifa dongtai), Issue No. 3.

Index